Sir John Lister-Kaye is one of Britain's best-known naturalists and conservationists. He is the author of ten books on wildlife and the environment and has lectured all over the world. He has served prominently in the RSPB, the Nature Conservancy Council, Scottish ̇ral Heritage and the Scottish Wildlife Trust. In 2002 he was ̇ed an OBE for services to nature conservation. In 2016 he was ̇ ̇ded the Royal Scottish Geographical Society's Geddes Medal for ̇ ̇vices to the environment. He lives with his wife and family among ̇ ̇e mountains of the Scottish Highlands, where he runs the world- ̇mous Aigas Field Centre. His book *Gods of the Morning* won the ̇augural Richard Jefferies Prize.

The Dun Cow Rib is the perfect read: funny, moving and packed with evocative recollections of a '50s childhood . . . His accounts of adventures as a (mostly) free-range child exploring the wonders of the natural world are simply delightful'

'I should love to pay a visit to and shake this fine author by the hand'

'A wise and affectionate celebration of Britain's natural landscape'

'No one writes more movingly, or with such transporting poetic skill about encounters with wild creatures'

'Excellent'

'Lister-Kaye sometimes writes like the lon ̇
Famous Five'

D0494800

Also by John Lister-Kaye

The White Island (1972)
The Seeing Eye (1979)
Seal Cull (1979)
Ill Fares the Land (1994)
One for Sorrow (1994)
Song of the Rolling Earth (2003)
Nature's Child (2004)
At the Water's Edge (2010)
Gods of the Morning (2015)

THE
DUN COW RIB

A VERY NATURAL CHILDHOOD

JOHN LISTER-KAYE

CANONGATE

This paperback edition published in Great Britain in 2018 by Canongate Books and in the USA and Canada in 2019

First published in Great Britain in 2017 by Canongate Books Ltd, 14 High Street, Edinburgh EH1 1TE

Distributed in the USA by Publishers Group West and in Canada by Publishers Group Canada

canongate.co.uk

1

British Library Cataloguing-in-Publication Data
A catalogue record for this book is available on request from the British Library

ISBN 978 1 78689 147 1

Typeset in Dante MT by Palimpsest Book Production Ltd, Falkirk, Stirlingshire

Printed and bound in Great Britain by Clays Ltd, St Ives plc.

For my mother
τροφεῖα

'A boy's will is the wind's will,
And the thoughts of youth are long, long thoughts.'

My Lost Youth, Henry Wadsworth Longfellow
(1807–82)

'If I can stop one heart from breaking,
I shall not live in vain.'

Part One: Life, VI, Emily Dickinson (1830–86)

Contents

Foreword

The Deep Heart's Core

Years ago I built a hut overlooking a pond – a small loch or 'lochan' in Highland parlance – where, like Thoreau at Walden, I go to write or just bare myself to the effervescent mysteries of nature and life. It's called the Illicit Still, named by my children because for years I kept a bottle of whisky locked away from their prying teenage eyes. It has a lumberjack's oil drum stove, some rough and ready bunks, an old sofa, a table and chairs – just about everything serious contemplation requires. It has become a treasured centre of separateness, a place to muse, an escape.

Sheets of wind and light cruising the surface of the loch are there to distract me, and flights of mallard come streaming past to land squabbling in the marsh. On looping wings a heron often shoulders in to stalk leggily through the shallows, or house martins and swallows skim through like fighter jets, hawking flies across the cloud-brimming surface.

Occasionally a stream of bubbles grabs my eye and the quizzical mask of an otter peers from among the water lilies; or, ballerina *en pointe*, a roe doe tiptoes down to drink, and, every once in a while, an osprey crash-dives right in front of the hut. I jump up, concentration shattered like a brick through a window, to watch it lift off again with a brown trout writhing in its long, black talons – death and glory intertwined, the death of necessity and the glory of life eternal. My neck cranes to catch the last silhouetted image as it levers out of sight above the trees. I catch my breath. It's a drama I have witnessed hundreds of times, but I still emerge swaying, dazzled, blanked, my work suddenly lost and meaningless. Such stark, irrepressible images have been etching themselves into my soul for more years than I care to remember.

I was there recently, supposed to be roughing out an article on Scottish wildcats. A lazy June afternoon of bright, backlit cumulus and sun shafts burning through the vitreous brilliance of spring leaf, dressing the birches and willows as precious gifts. Our spring has kept us on tenterhooks this year, it arrived, fled and came again, twice hijacked by a relentless northeasterly from somewhere above Russia. In May I lit the log stove in sunshine as sharp as chilled vodka. And it was there, in this vibrant corner of our little Highland world, emerging from the cold sun shimmer on the loch, that a familiar notion came rollicking in as it has done many times before. Yet this time it was strangely different, punching in with power and pizzazz, the way that a sun-burst spotlights something that you'd really never noticed before and forces you to look again.

It wasn't exactly a surprise. It was a notion that had been there long enough, decades in fact, loitering, like something I'd been meaning to do for ages but kept forgetting. So I never pursued it. But the seed was set; as the years passed, slowly and silently it grew, becoming something altogether rounder and fatter than just a fanciful notion – yes, pressing and personal – more like a hunger, that signal shift from an ache to a pain, but much more urgent, refusing to go away, until I could ignore it no longer.

For forty years now, I have run a field studies centre from my home at Aigas, in Strathglass, one of northern Scotland's wildest glens. Folk come from all over the world to learn about the ancient natural and cultural history of the Highlands and Islands. Our environmental education work for local schools serves thousands of youngsters every year, helping them to value and enjoy nature as well as grasp the essential ecological processes for human survival. It has never palled. I still get a buzz from the lectures reeled out by our dedicated young staff, or from our visitors raving about the acrobatics of the pine martens they watched from a hide last night. Seeing youngsters pond dipping for newts and dragonfly larvae in the shallows always makes me smile. It spins me back – back to the story of my own, not-so-lost-and-forgotten childhood all those decades ago.

It was Gavin Maxwell – one of Britain's most celebrated non-fiction writers of the '60s – who brought me, still in my twenties, to the Highlands of Scotland, a land so very different from the rest of Britain. In 1969 I headed north to work with him on a rocky lighthouse island in the straits between the Isle of Skye and the mainland – it could not have been a more extreme shift from my own English pastoral background and my unhappy job on the heavily polluted coastline of industrial South Wales.

The Highlands was a shock, a shock of joy and freedom, the heady thrill of escape, the tang of fresher air, new rock beneath my feet and the surging wave of the spirit. It was a rebirth, a release wholly intoxicating. I felt alive again for the first time since childhood. But such elation would be disastrously short-lived. When Gavin suddenly and unexpectedly died that September it seemed that my entire world had crashed in ruins around me. I was out of a job and a home. But the drug that is the magic of the Highlands had curved deep like the osprey's talons, and was not about to let go. So I elected to stay and try to make a go of being a naturalist and a writer, to put down roots and find a home here – a tough call, but one I have never regretted.

On a crisp January day a few years later I discovered Aigas, an unloved, abandoned and faintly ridiculous Victorian mansion, all battlements, cannon spouts and spiky candle-snuffered turrets, arrestingly sited on a hillside overlooking the River Beauly – and condemned, within a month of being torn down, totally demolished. The roof leaked where thieves had ripped out the leadwork, windows were broken and plaster ceilings had come crashing down. When I first entered the house, snow had piled in through collapsed skylights and blanketed the hall floor. A car was parked outside, the front door wide open. I followed yeti-footprints through the snow and up the main staircase, on up a spiral stair and out onto the roof with no idea of whom or what I might find. A man in huge boots was standing there with a clipboard, assessing the scrap value of the building before demolition. 'Who are you?' he challenged. 'I'm a prospective buyer,' I said. The words just tumbled out. But it was a half-truth, and not the first time such a thought had entered my head. I had long nurtured the idea of starting a field studies centre somewhere. This time it had the ring of truth.

A sleepless night. The Victorian building wasn't even a hundred years old. I loved its wild woods and fields; the tangle of its long-forsaken gardens and its shimmering loch tucked into a fold in the hills all seemed to be calling out to me. Its position overlooking the glen was magnificent and, besides, I'd seen swifts' nests in the tower and a roe deer had frolicked away into the rhododendrons as I departed down the drive.

I had no idea what it would cost to restore the house and grounds or how to set about it, and if anyone had given me even the sniff of a clue, I would have walked away and never given it another thought. But they didn't. Hotheaded youth can be a handy set of blinkers when you don't really want to grasp reality. You can gloss over problems that would frighten the heck out of wiser folk. And yet, oddly, its very desolation invoked piquancy, an added romantic allure. I loved it. Not the dottily turreted house, but the whole Aigas *place*. It had somehow entered my blood – a Shangri-La, a personal Lake Isle of Innisfree – and I heard it 'in the deep heart's core'.

So a few days later I bought it. Impulsively and without a second thought I borrowed the money and bought it for a home and a place where I could create a field studies centre for the Highlands – an unheard-of notion back then, and one people laughed at with mockery in their voices. To me it presented what many said was an impossible challenge, and to such I have always risen like a greedy trout to a fly.

So, yes, forty years now, family all fledged and flown, and somehow we have survived. More folk than I can count or remember have come to slough off the stresses of hectic lives, to learn about the bloody tribalism of the Highland clans, to witness our splendid wildlife and unwind among the mountains and glens of our glorious upland scenery. I have never tired of it, never regretted that youthful impulse despite the scorn and the multifarious trials heaped upon us down the years.

To have been a working naturalist; to have striven to fill the unforgiving minute, and to have shared the joy of these mountains, lochs and glens with so many other people has been its own reward. I have never doubted that it was the right move, the right place to be, but after so many years you begin to wonder just how on earth it all happened. When did it all start? Long before I'd even heard of Gavin

Maxwell. Where did this predilection for wild nature come from? Was it genetic – nature or nurture? Who handed me the chalice? And whence the faith that spurred the 'sixty seconds' worth of distance run'? From whom, precisely, more than fifty years ago, did the precious mantle of conviction come? Suddenly I needed answers, to tie them down, get them straight in my head. That was it. That was the irrepressible notion – more than a notion, it felt like a summons, a gauntlet hurled at my feet by the colliding forces of time and joy – that finally gripped me at the Illicit Still and refused to let go.

John Lister-Kaye,
House of Aigas
April 2017

Wildcats and wilderness

The Scottish wildcat isn't just any old cat, it's special – no, way more than special. It's unique, and unique in so many different ways, bad and good. It's Britain's most endangered mammal – that's bad, capital BAD. And it's wild, *wild*, WILD, with its own marque of spitting, feline wildness – that's far beyond good, it's brilliant.

From the sort of glimpse you might be lucky enough to get in your headlights, a wildcat can look a bit like an over-size farm tabby, but that's where the resemblance ends and the conflict lies. It's the black that defines both the wildcat's fur and its sombre northern climate, an aggressive camou-flage that breaks up its outline into bands of shadow exactly as a tiger's stripes do, but without the perpetual sunlight shafting through jungle. Its bushy club tail with a dense black tip has four to six clear black rings; its fur is of dulled zinc with vertical sooty stripes – stripes that also run up and outwards from its burning, emerald eyes. It hunts at dawn and dusk, retiring bandit-like to its lair to lie low throughout the day. A stealthily prowling, silent, green-eyed arch-predator of the dark and dripping Highland woods, it is reputedly untamable, a top carnivore. Ferocious. A snarling, hissing, spitting demon of a cat with murder etched into its soul.

The trouble is that we humans have been introducing domestic cats into wildcat habitat for centuries. Wildcat toms cannot resist domestic pussy, and vice versa. The evolutionary lineage of both is too close and the hybrid progeny of such unseen nocturnal pairings are fertile. Invisibly their genes blend and nowadays many hybrids stalk the Highland woods. By their own promiscuity our precious wildcats are genetically polluting themselves into extinction, a situation only humans can resolve.

In 2012 we at the field studies centre joined forces with Scottish Wildcat Action to implement their optimistic-sounding 'Conservation Action Plan' to try to save the last few remaining wildcats in the Highlands (*Felis silvestris grampia* – cat of the Grampian woods), part of which would be captive breeding for release into carefully monitored, prime quality habitat. That was the bit that interested us: the breeding and release of sexually mature kittens to bolster whatever remains of the wildcat population still out there. If there is any. We don't know – nobody does. We hope there might be a few left in the remoter mountain reaches of our local glens.

The Scottish wildcat is the very essence of wildness and wild places, and, hope or no hope, it's ours. It badly needs a marketing manager. Throughout recent history our wildcats have been present the length and breadth of Scotland, a top predator in some of the most rugged and wild landscapes in the UK, perfect for a super-cat. If your average domestic tabby is a Ford, our wildcat is a Ferrari. They call it the Highland tiger: bigger, stronger, meaner, sleeker, stealthier . . . and, like poor old Shere Khan, the tiger in the *Jungle Book*, it's in serious trouble because of us and the way we've always treated land as a resource without much thought for wildlife: there for exploiting and to hell with the consequences. It's our fault – our ignorance, our stupidity, our negligence, our selfishness, our greed. That's bad, very bad. We could do much better if we put our minds to it – if *only* we would put our minds to it. We could, you know: humans don't have to behave like mindless vandals. We have the wit and the ways; it's the *will* that snarls us up. We could stop the rot and reverse the destructive trend for most wild-life if only we could focus minds. The wildcat is precious. We must not lose it.

It seems to have taken forever to get some official conser-vation action, but it has happened at last. We pray it's not too late. The whole bureaucratic machinery of government recently lumbered into action. The National Lottery stumped up. Money shouts and has claws. Suddenly there were press releases, websites, blogs, tweets, posts – all that social media guff buzzed around the world before you could say kitty. We held meetings, published plans to neuter or remove feral domestic cats and hybrids, created research and monitoring jobs, consulted everyone except God and the cats themselves. We were beginning to feel a bit smug – dangerously smug. After two years and twenty meetings we hadn't saved a single wildcat. So I took myself off to Spain to learn about their highly successful captive breeding and release project for the Iberian lynx – just what we were trying to achieve with the wildcats at home.

I met up with the Spanish biologists near Seville. We all spoke the same language of nature conservation, if not in quite the same tongue. Spanish wildcats are slightly smaller than ours, the same species without the *grampia*. From the illustrations and photos, theirs – *gato montes* – have a paler pelage to reflect the higher levels of sunlight and make the black stripes look blacker, but they are otherwise identical.

They've suffered the same old problems: loss of habitat to industrial agriculture and forestry, persecution by game-keepers and hunters, hybridisation with domestic and feral cats, and road kill . . . all the familiar insults we've thrown at ours. We think we're down to the last few hundred animals in the Highlands, and it's pretty doubtful whether any of those are pure wildcats. The Spanish don't seem to have much of a clue about their *gato*, but they're doing great things for their lynx.

So I headed for Coto Doñana National Park, 1,300 square miles of coastal dunes and salt marsh, *Las Marismas*, and semi-natural pine forest stretching from just south of Seville down to the Portuguese border, the Gulf of Cadiz foaming at its fringes and one of the last refuges of Europe's most endangered cat, the deliciously spotted Iberian lynx. I longed to see one in the wild; a slim chance, but one I wanted to try. I would not see a lynx, but I was to discover much more about myself.

I knew a bit about Doñana. Memories came lancing through. I'd been there once before – back in . . . was it '65 or '66? – when my parents had stayed at the grandiose former hunting lodge Palacio Doñana, a large, ornate, whitewashed mansion, back then a stylish hostel for intrepid visitors. My father had rushed back to London on business and left my mother there for a few days. She'd loved it and urged me to join her. There were good reasons for always wanting to please my mother.

A tantalisingly brief visit all those years ago, just one night – supper and a schooner of dark amontillado together in the Palacio, her silvery laugh, a gentle totter out into the glove-soft moonlight – all her fragile health could cope with. The heady perfume of night-scented jasmine, *dama de noche*, wrapping us round, then back to the fireside in the echoing, whitewashed salon, olive logs crackling like pistol fire till bedtime. In the morning we were off again, driving away. A toe dipped in, just that and no more. I had always hoped to make it back one day. Now, almost fifty years later, I was there again.

I turned off the main road and bumped down a sandy track. To my left the tidal marshes and rippling reed-beds stretched away toward the Guadalquivir river. Then, a mile or two later, wholly unexpectedly, and without any announcement, the imposing edifice of the Palacio loomed up in front of me like a mirage, tucked into the edge of the forest, its compound enclosed by a perimeter wall of startling white. 'Oh my God! I've been here.' I called out, forgetting that there was nobody to hear me. 'That's it! That's where my parents stayed yonks ago.'

It had been a grand hunting lodge like many that were built in the Highlands of Scotland at the height of the Victorian sporting era, although this was considerably older. The Duchess of Alba had entertained Francisco Goya there in the eighteenth century and it had harboured many other dignitaries, including General Franco, to hunt deer and wild boar. So had Lord Alanbrooke, the British Field Marshal and Second World War Chief of Allied Staff who'd had a stormy relationship with Winston Churchill but still managed to be powerfully influential over the Allied victory.

When Alanbrooke rented the Palacio in 1958, he and his wife had hosted a natural history expedition led by the founding triumvirate of what would later become the World Wildlife Fund: Guy Mountfort, Julian Huxley and Max Nicholson, three towering grandees of the embryonic nature conservation movement. With characteristic brimming enthusiasm, my mother had bought me a copy of Mountfort's splendid book, *Portrait of a Wilderness – The Story of the Coto Doñana Expeditions*, and I had spent many hours poring over the black and white photographs. I still treasure it today, her fluid handwriting in the flyleaf, 'I hope you can join expeditions like this one day.'

Memory billowed in – jaw flexing and a lump forming in my throat. Yes, it was here, on the edge of these marshes. That was the building; I'd stayed here in the '60s, spent a night with her here. Then, just then, trapped by that implausible cocktail of circumstance and emotions, my abstract notion came flooding back in.

I suddenly saw that it had taken me most of a lifetime properly to understand that from early childhood every encounter with nature, each little glimpse of truth and comprehension of the natural world, had braided together to make me what I am. From some formative vital spark I had been hoarding images of birds and mammals, of reptiles and insects, of plants and soils and landscape and of their very essence, the wildness that defines them all, until at some consciously unordained past moment they had silently taken me over and modelled me into the creature I have become. Over the decades of working with nature everything had coalesced into a deeply personal *raison d'être* – yes, I suppose I mean a vocation. It was an extraordinary sense of destiny, mildly unsettling, and demanding questions I could not at that moment answer. But why? How did it happen? Was it one principal influence, or several flowing together like mountain streams? When, exactly, did it start? And just who or what could have been responsible?

In those few minutes my world had shifted. That notion – that misty, blurry, hovering thing I had been ducking for years – was suddenly as crisply defined as a bright mountain peak when the clouds part. My brain was fizzing. I needed to reconnect with that last haunting image of my mother.

Was it her unflagging love and encouragement that had been the determining force? The rare chance of being together in that wild and beautiful place, the squeezed hand, the gift of a book? Is that what had been happening all along? Had her fortitude and zest for life been the moving force throughout my childhood? Or was it the unintended consequence of her ghastly, life-shortening illness that had somehow funnelled me into what I am? My head was spinning. Memories and images crowded in, colliding, swamping each other and leaving me light-headed, floating in an emotional limbo. Did she spark a flame that night in the Palacio? Did it spin me off into a dizzying parallel universe, from which I would never fully return? I needed to capture that moment again and follow its lead.

*　　*　　*

There are thought to be no wildcats left in Doñana, but there is a stable population of around fifty Iberian lynx (*Lynx pardinus*), a mesmerisingly beautiful, medium-sized spotted cat with ear tufts and a bob tail, closely related to the longer-legged Eurasian lynx (*Lynx lynx*), the one that used to roam Scotland 750 to 1,000 years ago and that many would now like to see reintroduced. The park authority works closely with a lynx captive breeding complex on its western boundary, a shining conservation success: by the time I visited, sixty-nine radio-tagged lynx had been released into good habitat since the project started eleven years ago. Those lynx are out there and breeding. That's exactly where we would like to be with the Scottish wildcat.

The welcome by Dr Antonio Rivas bowled me off my feet, his enthusiasm mirrored and endorsed by his entire team. Two days later I came away elated, rejoicing that nature conservation held such splendid people at its noble heart. I was exhilarated but tired, very tired. I turned in early.

In my hotel room I re-read my notes, added a few more and climbed into bed. I sat tapping into my laptop. Suddenly my eyes weren't focusing, lids leaden, sleep rolling in like a fog. I jerked awake, once, twice, three times . . . just catching the laptop before it slid to the floor. I gave in. In free fall – altogether out of it.

Much later, at an unlogged moment in the small hours, I surfaced sufficiently to dream vividly. I was back in the Palacio, aged nineteen, with my mother. Not just vividly, I was there. It was as real as a dream could possibly be. I caught her perfume on the sultry air, heard her voice and felt her arm in mine.

The notion I had harboured for ages was that a very long time ago some accident of fate had made me want to be a naturalist – no, not want, *NEED* to be a naturalist, a person wholly engaged with nature, philosophically, emotionally, practically and professionally. Now, after a long career in nature conservation, I needed to look back and tie down influences, analyse roots and causes, and above all work out just who and what had spun the wheel, handed me the potion, spiralled me into being what I am and have been for more than fifty years.

My mother was no naturalist. She had no scientific training at all, very little knowledge beyond what she had read, and even less opportunity to spend time in the wilds anywhere. My parents came to Spain every year for her health – British winters were always bad for her. They had built a home here, an eyrie high above the ancient Roman and Moorish fishing village of Fuingerola, long before it became a tawdry tourist resort. That one brief expedition to Coto Doñana was an exception, but one she loved.

The book she gave me, Guy Mountfort's natural history classic with its wild boar, fallow deer, lynxes, flamingos and imperial eagles, had sparked a new sense of purpose. I don't believe that the idea of her son becoming a naturalist had ever entered her head – the profession barely existed in the 1960s. No, I'm sure she only saw it as an uplifting hobby, a worthwhile pastime; but that was it, that was the moment the idea of participating in such an expedition and perhaps one day even mounting one myself had fired me with a restless, vaulting ambition.

In that time-eliding dream she was beside me, eyes flashing, smiling, laughing, encouraging – 'Why don't you stay here for a few days and try to see some of the wildlife?' In a burst of memory as bright and shining as leaves after summer rain, I saw her chatting to the locals, old women swathed in black sitting in the afternoon sun outside their whitewashed cottages, and the little children playing in the dusty street. There she was; in self-taught fluent Spanish she was embracing the local people she so loved – '¿Son estas sus nietos?' – and I watched her throw back her head with a little flick of her hair as she always did when laughter bubbled out of her like a mountain spring, and that slightly startled look, wide-eyes flashing, as though her own mirth had caught her unawares.

She had died suddenly and shockingly in her fifties, catching us all off guard – my father, my sister, me, her own twin sister, everyone who knew and loved her. None of us were prepared for it, although for God's sake we'd had enough warning. Years of it. She'd been an invalid since my birth, battling with a degenerative heart condition, a struggle against hopeless odds with never the remotest chance of winning, yet never giving up. We knew it but we hadn't seen it. We hadn't seen it coming because we ruddy well didn't want to and because she'd fooled us – brilliantly fooled us – for years and years. Even when all the chips were down she still managed to trick us into thinking she was OK, that somehow she'd pull through, that she'd always be there for us. She'd led us through a lifelong masterclass of endlessly loving, benign deception – a life of perpetual, courageous, stoical, dogged, resolute, unflinching – yes, bloody astounding – concealment because never once through all her trials did she ever complain about her ghastly, crippling condition, never once gave up hope or gave in to the slightest flicker of self-pity. We all knew she was seriously ill, but we blindly and stupidly refused to believe it. It's called denial.

Suddenly it was night. She leant on my arm as she walked slowly and unsteadily, only a few yards, all she could manage, away from the dim lights of the Palacio, out into the warm, thick darkness. Her aluminium stick clicked with each step and her breath came short and sharp. Stars winked and glistened high above us and a weakling moon hung like a segment of white peach among rags of back-lit cloud. We stood and listened to the night sounds of *Las Marismas*: nature's wild orchestra in its finest fling. Far off geese haggled excitedly out on the distant water, the soft fluting of flamingos rising and falling, broken by shrill arpeggios of waders from the shallow lagoons in front of us. 'I love this.' Words whispered with an instinctive reverence for wildness. I knew exactly what she meant.

My dream was as vivid as a dream can ever be. I was with her in body, mind and spirit. Right there. I could see the moon-gleam on her greying curls and I could hear the way she rested her front teeth invisibly on her lip and drew air through them with a thin, barely audible whistle when she was thinking. I could feel the warmth of her arm as that old familiar perfume wafted out to bind me to her as it had done ever since I was a small child climbing into her bed.

Our conversation was brief – no need for elaboration –

words primed with resonance of the moment, the place, the mood. A collusion of loaded silence and love piling in like grace. I felt my spirit lifting off and soaring to the stars. It was as though something I had been searching for all my life was suddenly there beside me. We laughed together, as one.

I don't know how long it lasted – difficult to tell with dreams – but I sensed that it was long enough to slough off the thirty-four years since her death, long enough to whirl back through the Spanish darkness to those transcendental moments of unity I had never thought I could know again. In all the intervening years I had never come so close, never so distinctively re-lived her presence with such intensity, never guessed that it was possible. I woke up wondering where I was.

The room was hot and airless. I rose and went to the casement, flinging it wide. A breeze off the marshes as soft as thistledown caressed my face. There, only a few yards away, was the moonlight flickering across the black lagoon, the gossip of distant geese, the woodwind of flamingos floating into satin air, the redshanks' piccolo piping and the insistent whistles of wigeon drakes. Then it came. From somewhere deep inside me, from some visceral cavern I didn't know existed, catching me completely unawares, an unstoppable upwelling of emotion rose volcanically within me, choking, convulsing, overpowering. Tears flooded down my face.

I recognised it instantly, as instinctively as you know the sound of your own voice. Grief – Latin: *gravare*, heavy; Old French: *grever*, to burden – that weight, that overwhelming burden of desolation I thought I'd conquered thirty years before had never gone away at all. It was still there, hidden, padlocked, forgotten, lurking deep in the darkest canyons of my hippocampus, silently waiting for this moment.

*   *   *

I returned to rainy Scotland buoyed up and inspired by the Spanish project and determined to pursue my mother's influence further. I had learned so much, not just about captive breeding. Twelve years ahead of us, they had made and resolved many of the mistakes with lynxes we were now making with our wildcats. For hygiene, we were diligently removing cat faeces every day.

'No,' Antonio had said, 'leave them in for at least a week or two. They contain pheromones, important territorial signals.'

'Oh,' I answered blankly, wondering why the hell I hadn't thought of that.

*   *   *

For thousands of years since the last ice cap retreated, these deeply glaciated glens, carved through unyielding metamorphic schist, have stubbornly resisted the severest ravages of mankind. Drawing strength from the rock beneath, nature has always fought back. It is how so much of the Highlands' precious wildlife has been able to cling on. Ours is a land of golden eagles tilting on glider wings and the metallic screams of peregrines echoing from the walls of the river gorge. I never cease to catch my breath when I see the Bourneville blur of pine martens filching food from the bird tables. My heart beats faster at the sudden flash of a salmon shimmering up the rapids, and every autumn dawn I awaken to the hills echoing with the roaring of rutting red deer stags. Although we very rarely see them, somehow, against all the odds, a few Scottish wildcats might have managed to hang in there too.

One of the many joys of living among the mountains is arriving home after forays further afield. On a clear day, turning west just after Inverness, the Highland capital, the great grey rampart of the nearly 4,000-foot Affric mountains looms out of the distance, solid and reassuring. I never tire of that rugged molar horizon, a welcome home that wafts my spirit skyward like the red kites we so frequently see wheeling and soaring over the rich dark soil of the Black Isle fields. Without those mountains my life might have been entirely different.

A squealing, wiggling welcome from my two Jack Russells, Nip and Tuck, a spousely hug with hot tea and a slice of my wife Lucy's banana cake settled me straight back into cosy domesticity. Oh, it was GOOD to be home. But for me home has always been so much more than the cushioned refuge of the complacent. I have lived at Aigas so long that the land has claimed me, shaped me to match its wildness and its contrary needs, so that whenever I've been away I need to relocate and tune up again like a harp that has had to travel. So as soon as I tactfully could, I slipped out into the fresh cool of the evening and walked briskly uphill to the secret forest location of our wildcat project. I needed to stand and look at them with the brighter, wider eyes of the Spanish experience.

We haven't given our cats names. They are identified by gender and their pens: ♂ in Pen 1, ♀ in Pen 2, ♂ kitten in Pen 4 . . . and so on. There's no good reason why we shouldn't name them, but, respecting their innate wildness – as far from fluffy moggies as wolves from a poodle – we have avoided humanising them as much as possible. They have all been DNA tested and are high quality, over 89 per cent wildcat – probably as good as we are going to be able to find in the remaining wild population. By careful selective breeding we can further diminish the hybrid genes, sharing high quality kittens with other captive breeders to broaden the gene pool and reduce the risk of inbreeding.

The pens are big and built on the woodland edge, with grassy spaces between natural cover of broom, brambles and thickets of wild raspberries; the damp patches have sprouted clumps of grasses, rushes, docks and nettles – as natural a wildcat habitat as we can achieve. Sunlight flickers through the trees, gnats dance, bees drone, the breezes shimmy through. Unthinking, wild birds – chaffinches, dunnocks, wrens and robins – dip and bob just out of reach, keeping the cats alert and, unlucky for some, foraging mice and voles make the mistake of blundering in.

As the still evening air settled around me I stood at the gate to Pen 2. The male, a big rangy tom with attitude, jumped silently down from a high perch. Panther shoulders rolling in sinister ripples beneath the fur, he stalked slowly but purposefully across to stare me out. Ten feet from the wire, he sat on his haunches and glared. He glowed with all the assurance of a million years of evolution. He was magnificent. I resented the wire and wanted to be in the pen with him. When I moved to unlock the gate he hissed, lips curled and long fangs gleamed. His ears flattened and he crouched; his whole mask bristled with rancour. The emerald eyes flared, long white whiskers arrayed in a bright fan. This cat has a history of disliking men and makes his feelings clear. The black club end to his ringed tail twitched. And that stare – you get the feeling that he is in charge of the world.

We keep human presence to a minimum. Every day one of the rangers enters the pens to feed and to clean away the detritus – bones, feathers, the scaly legs of quail or pheasants, rabbit fur. Every two weeks their bedding is changed for fresh, sweet-smelling straw. The rangers had often told me that the tom in Pen 2 was threatening, possibly even dangerous. 'Oh yeah,' I'd shrugged, smiling smugly to myself. 'Dangerous? Nah, don't believe it.'

I unchained the gate and entered the safety chamber, carefully closing it behind me. He hissed again, louder, his anger rising to something akin to fury, ending the hiss with a sharp 'Spat!' A duty ranger would always have food – quail or rabbit, or fluffy, yellow day-old chicks (a by-product of the ghastly intensive poultry trade) we buy frozen – to throw to a hungry cat that came close. It's a routine, expected when we enter the pen: they pounce, snatch up the prey and whisk away into cover, up onto a high perch or into a den. I had none – hadn't thought it important; besides, my head was full of Iberian lynxes and new ideas. I wasn't thinking right, dull stupidity eclipsing brighter reason. I opened the second gate into the pen. He was five feet away, no sign of backing off. 'Hullo,' I spoke softly, shaking my head. 'Sorry, Tomcat, nothing for you tonight.' I showed my empty hands.

It happened so fast, so dazzlingly lightning fast, that I had no time even to flinch. He sprang. He lashed out with both front paws, razor claws fully extended, slashing down my trousers and onto my boots. Then he was gone. Fire without smoke. In one blur of black-striped fury he had launched, slashed, turned and vanished under a clump of broom. The corduroy at my left knee was torn open and blood began to well up from a blade-thin slice in my kneecap. Long white streaks in the green rubber of my boots marked where the claws of both paws had ripped downwards, streaks eight inches long. But for the boots he would have slashed my left leg to the bone.

I had felt nothing. It happened so fast and with such accuracy that the tomcat had not bodily hit me, not followed through with brute force, rather it was delivered at a perfectly calculated distance, the down-swiping claws at full stretch, pulling away the instant they hit home. That cat knew exactly how to use its claws as weapons of contempt, just as a thug with a knife might slash to disfigure you.

I looked down at my knee as the blood roped and plied itself through the torn weave of my trousers. I cursed, a curse as much at my own disregard of the warnings and my crass appearance in the pen without food as at the tomcat himself. I limped out. Only twenty-four hours earlier I had told the Spanish biologists that even though our cats were captive bred they were still wild animals and totally unpredictable. Some of us only ever learn things the hard way.

I walked back to the house feeling more than a little foolish. 'Serves you right,' my mother would have said – did say many times over – when through impatience or stubbornness, or just mindless folly, I had hurt myself. 'What d' you expect?' she'd ask, gesturing frustration at my stupidity when yet again I had run to her tearful and bloodied after falling out of a tree or grazing my knees.

Once, aged about five, rushing to catch a red admiral butterfly with my hands, I tripped and crashed into a stone wall. I broke a front tooth, splitting my top lip so that blood flowed freely down my chin and onto my shirt. She wiped away my tears. 'Now every time you look in the mirror and see that tooth, it will remind you to be more *careful*.' She hung on the word, hung on to me, love issuing from every pore. But it never did. If it ever existed, the caution gene had been strangled at birth, totally absent from my armoury. I now see that back then, without ever knowing it, I had led both my parents a merry song and dance. My mother, who was never equipped to cope with a rambunctious, hyperactive child always in trouble, must have struggled – must have wondered what she had done to deserve me.

2

Death of a dog

It was a dog and it was dead, unquestionably dead. On its side with one ear and half its head missing. A dog blotched with its own dried blood lying dead in a ditch under a thorn hedge. A dog flat on its side as if it had been thrown there, or collapsed over sideways from a savage blow. Its mouth was slightly agape. A long canine fang curved down from a lip drawn in a last snarl, a snarl that should have been of rage or pain, or perhaps just disbelief, a snarl shattered by oblivion. Blood and saliva shone on a slightly protruding tongue hiding the lower teeth as though the dog had died with a heavy exhalation, thrusting the tongue outwards, never to be withdrawn. A glazed eye stared opaquely, unnerv-ingly, a stare of shock and despair and emptiness. Something terrible had happened here and that eye had been its silent witness.

To a seven-year-old boy who knew dogs and loved a dog, a dog not unlike this powerful, stocky, brown and white bull-terrier-ish mongrel, a boy who knew the bond of trust, the hot muzzle, the velvet ears, the barley-meal breath, who had romped and rolled and held dogs close, it was a catastrophe. The world had lost a dog in wild and terrifying circumstances I could not begin to imagine. My heart convulsed inside my chest and tried to break out through my mouth. I wanted to touch it, to stroke its smooth fur, but I held back. I wanted to cry out, to cry for comprehension of the brute forces that had done this thing, to cry for help and for someone to share with me the intolerable burden of this abruptly shattered life. But no tears came. So I ran.

I ran the quarter mile across the damp Longbottom meadows and ditches above School Lane; I ran a frantic course, crashing through briars and marshy places, slicing the corners off fields, hurling myself over fences in the most direct route home I could take. I wanted home and to find a grown-up to whom I could pour out this breathless tale of dog destruction.

I ran round the bottom of the old pond, stagnant with duckweed, past the moorhen's nest of soggy rushes on a fallen tree. I hurdled over elm branches wind-ripped from high above, on through the orchard's long grass as high as my waist. I burst through the tangy veil of scent from tall balsam poplars and poured myself over the oak-railed fence into the paddock, hands and trousers smeared and stippled with grey-green algae. Hens scattered in front of me as I dodged through the nettle clumps to the big-boarded gates with the rusty latch. I heaved it wide. Leaping the open drain, I raced through the cobbled stable yard, past the servants' lavatories and on to the back door of the house.

Scratched and muddied I burst into the flagstoned scullery, where low stoneware sinks and scrubbed draining boards stood efficiently bare and empty. Nobody there. On into the big kitchen, with its cream Aga range and huge table of bleached pine topped with flaking American cloth. Nobody there either. I yelled for Nellie. No answer. I ran through to the hall, heaving open the heavy green baize door on its stiff spring, down the single stone step and out into the cool, respectful silence of the black and white chequered floor and the deep, ponderous ticking of the hall clock called the Bowler in imitation of its booming chime, which echoed all round the house. Empty. I called out for my sister, my father, for anyone, pealing my seven-year-old voice up the elegantly curving stairs to the landing above and echoing sideways down the corridor to the schoolroom library with its shelves of fusty books. No reply.

The furled iron ring of the front door latch was heavy and took both hands and gritted teeth to turn. It clanked up and the huge iron-studded oak door swung inward with a startling burst of sun. I ran out onto the crunching yellow gravel, leaving the door wide. Across the paved terrace and past the French windows to the drawing room and on to the ancient yew tree ringed round with its white painted seat, the tree in whose dark and scaly caverns a tawny owl always roosted, the tree that seemed to brood and cast its long shadow across the smoking-room lawn.

I leapt down the stone steps and over the neatly mown square, past the bronze sundial on its age-lichened stone pedestal and on towards our grandfather's outer sanctum, his holy of horticultural holies, where we children were strictly forbidden to go – the long, ordered glasshouses, four of them in parallel rows, with their dirty panes and worm-drive roof vents that squealed and juddered open and shut when the handles were cranked. I raced past the green corrugated rain butts in which mosquito larvae wiggled and mice mysteriously drowned, and on into the first long glass-house with a vine espaliered against the once whitewashed brick wall and the slatted benches running full length under the glass, benches crowded with dozens of terracotta flower-pots of many different sizes. And there, at the very far end, hazy through the giddy intoxication of geraniums, he stood.

There he was about his passionate horticultural summer

affairs in a collarless pin-stripe shirt and a tweed hound's-tooth check waistcoat with its gold watch chain, his horn-rimmed half-moon spectacles on his nose above a bristly little silver-grey moustache, and his bald head shining. There were his slender six feet six and a half inches, slightly stooped, long sleeves rolled up and his huge hands holding a pair of parrot-beaked secateurs and a woven trug bulging with dead heads and clippings. There he was with his pipe in his teeth, staring down at me over his glasses with eyebrows raised in pretended astonishment. 'It's dead,' I blurted out. 'And there's blood everywhere.' And then I cried.

My grandfather tossed the secateurs into the trug, placed it carefully on the bench and bent to pick me up. He swept me effortlessly up, up, up and away from the swirling images of blood and death, away from the clutching ache of panic, up and still further up until I too was six feet six and a half inches above the frightening world my exploration had led me into. He held me firmly in his arms and carried me out of the long, airless, stultifying geranium house so unspeakably burdened with sweet and heady scent, out into the sunshine freshness and the birdsong, and back toward the heavy carved oak bench on the edge of the smoking-room lawn.

He sat down and held me on his knees. 'Now you must dry your eyes and tell me what is dead.' His voice was gentle and all-embracing and as deep as a wine cask and as old and wise as Solomon. He drew an acre of silk handkerchief from his trouser pocket and dabbed my tear-salted cheeks. It was soft and springy and smelled of pipe tobacco and bay rum, at that moment the most reassuring incense I could possibly have wished to inhale.

It was the scent of unassailable authority; of great age and timelessness and security and the source of all well-being and the fount of all knowledge and all hope and all sanctity. It was the aroma that lingered in the long upstairs corridors that led to his bedroom – more forbidden territory we would not have dared encroach – and in the smoking-room lavatory we were not allowed to use but where we had peeped in and seen his silver-backed hairbrushes and a tortoiseshell comb laid out on a marble washstand beneath the gilt mirror. It was the lofty perfume of the olden days, of knights and kings and archbishops, the paternalistic aroma of history and Empire, and, in a peculiar way I could not have begun to describe or explain, it was the scent of love.

'It's a dog.' The words choked themselves out. 'And it's dead.' And the tears erupted again, welling into the crumpled silk; the image too stark and the trauma too vivid to be contained in so young a head.

'I think you'd better show me this dog.'

I held his huge hand as we strode up the mossy slabs of the laurel-lined Broadwalk, shady beneath the cloistered intimacy of huge elms and beeches, slabs that had been heaved into tectonic undulations by the ramifications of roots beneath. I had to take three steps to his one long pace, so I jogged along beside him, still jabbering out the awfulness of my find. We climbed the post and rail fences and out into the fields.

White-faced Hereford bullocks frisked away from us as we cut across their moist pasture of buttercups and clover and lanky thistles. We strode up the field hedges of dense hawthorn and may, where blackbirds and thrushes burst out with a shimmer of sun-silvered wings and clucking alarms, undulated away from us and dived back in again far up ahead. A magpie jetted out beside us and flew off cackling like a witch. We drew close and my heart began to pound. I ran forward. We jumped a ditch: a mighty leap for me and one stride for him as he muttered, 'Where on earth are you taking me, boy?'

And there it was. There it was dead and snarling with a buzz of bluebottles about its nose and crawling over the bloody void where the ear and a slice of skull should have been.

'Hmmphhh,' my grandfather grunted from somewhere deep inside his waistcoated chest as he took the pipe from his teeth and pulled his lips forward and together in a pursed grimace of knowing disapproval. Then he nodded solemnly, 'I know that dog. It's been shot at very close range.' And we turned away and began the long walk back to the house, the silence punctuated only by the regular sharp intake of breath from the side of his mouth.

* * *

It was mid-afternoon. My mother was away in hospital. My father, I learned, had driven my sister in the old black Rover the narrow twenty miles of the Roman Fosse Way – as straight as a blade – and a few winding Warwickshire-Oxfordshire back lanes into the quiet Cotswold market town of Banbury on some domestic errand. By the age of seven I had achieved a reputation for never being an asset on any shopping trip.

So that day I had been abandoned to my own devices; even by then I had established blissful contentment at being left to explore on my own, under the vague and undefined super-vision of Nellie – 'Now don't you go getting lost, young Jack, or I'll be for it' – to catch red admiral butterflies on rotting plums or search for birds' nests, things of which adults vaguely approved but had little desire to supervise. As usual I had wandered off that day into the woods and fields of the Manor Farm.

'They'll all be back for tea,' my grandfather told me, pulling out his gold pocket watch and tapping its glass as if it needed waking up before telling him the time. 'In another hour or so. You mark my words.'

He smiled down at me as he lit his pipe with a Swan Vestas, smoke pluming dragon-like from his nostrils, and then he was gone, leaving me earnestly marking his words, striding away from me, the high priest returning to his altar, back to his beloved geraniums and delphiniums and pyrotechnically bursting camellias that almost no one ever saw. He was gone again, gone for the moment, gone in measurable distances of yards and feet and inches, gone in physical presence with his tobacco trail wisping out behind him like an echo, gone in thought and preoccupation as his passion for flowers hauled him away, but to me he had not gone at all. Like the dog's blood, the events of that day had congealed immutably within my seven-year-old head. My grandfather had become as present and live and tangible and knowable and, yes, as mine, as God to a lonely spinster.

At the ritual of five o'clock afternoon tea at the kitchen table, Nellie sliced the large white loaf in her own alarming style. She would hold the loaf on end, cut face uppermost, and saw horizontally across the top with the blade flashing back and forth toward her own ample bosom. The result was thick, ragged slices for making toast on the ancient Aga hotplate in a folding wire mesh frame. (There was a bread slicer for what she called 'proper dining-room bread'.) This hot toast, with its imprint of mesh-singed check, she smeared with salty butter the colour of daffodils from the farm dairy, heaped dripping onto a platter and placed strategically in the middle of the table where two large jars, one of honey and the other of her own strawberry jam, lay invitingly open.

It was an invariable routine and a near-compulsory gathering of such family as were about, possibly for the first time since breakfast. 'I've baked a cake,' Nellie would announce, delivering to the table a warmly volcanic fruit cake rising to a sultana-fissured crater at its summit. Her toast and cake drew us in like moths to a candle. Only on Sundays was the tea ritual extended to the hushed formality of the Jacobean panelled dining room, and that was an adult affair where from the sideboard they poured their tea into Dresden bone-china cups from a silver teapot and the bread was neatly sliced on the slicer. Children stayed in the kitchen with Nellie, and that suited me fine.

Kitchen tea came from a large china pot, glossy brown, dressed in a knitted and fitted blue and yellow cosy, and was poured through a strainer into big blue-ringed teacups of simple household ware. With a long-drawn sigh my grandfather always collapsed his great length into a big, high-backed oak carver at the far end of the table; my father and my uncle sat on either side, while my sister and I perched nearest the Aga under Nellie's watchful eye. 'Now, no tipping back!' she would hiss at me in an audible whisper, flipping her tea towel against my shoulder in mock anger. 'Or you'll be in right trouble and no honey for a week.' And when my sister and I giggled feebly at this rebuke she would add, 'And just you remember your manners at table.'

I can remember dozens of such sleepy summer afternoons and kitchen teas, dozens of days of toast and honey and jam and crumbling fruit cake, of Nellie's teasing and the grown-ups locked in yawningly leaden conversation about the abhorrent politics of the day, but only one when, together like old buddies, my grandfather and I held the family in thrall, when the saga of the dead dog gripped them so; only one when I was at the centre of his world and my world and the whole wide world and everything revolved around him and me and my awful discovery.

'The boy's found a dead dog in a ditch at Longbottom,' he announced as soon as he had lowered himself into the chair. 'He took me out there. It's that wretch Howson's dog – Tramp, I think he called it – a big terrier of a kind. Shot at point-blank range. Half its head is missing.' He loaded strawberry jam onto his toast.

Nellie looked pale and turned away to the Aga to busy herself with more toast. 'Whatever were you doing out at Longbottom?' my father enquired directly.

My grandfather rescued me. 'He was just birds' nesting. It's a good spot. There are magpies in those thorn hedges.'

'Why d' y' think he shot his dog?' my father quizzed, changing tack.

'That man has a terrible temper on him. He'd shoot anything. It disobeyed him, I shouldn't wonder, and he blasted it. Damned shame. It was a decent looking dog and good at the rabbits.'

★   ★   ★

I now see that it was inevitable that those explorations, those dreamy solo sorties into the woods and fields where a child's unfettered imagination could run riot, meeting and treating every encounter with the surging excitement of real discovery, would become an addiction from which I would never fully recover. Every day I longed to escape. I would rush through breakfast, gobbling down Nellie's thick porridge as fast as I could. 'Please may I get down?'

'Yes, you may. Now don't you go getting into trouble, young Jack, or you'll be . . .' But I would be out of the door and away before she could finish the sentence. Usually I didn't know where I was going. There was never a defined purpose, it was just out and away and come what may.

Perhaps that's why I had loved *The Lion, the Witch and the Wardrobe* so much. It was that sense of passing from one world into another, where the known, the measured and the ordered could be cast off like a cloak, and the unknown, alluring yet slightly frightening, became as irresistible as a drug to an addict, while at the same time knowing that safe passage back through the wardrobe was always an option. It was where my imagination spiralled skyward, where make-believe ruled and I could pretend to be anything or anybody I chose, and where nothing else mattered.

My favoured route was up the Broadwalk, a long, paved path that led away from the ordered formality of the gardens to a long avenue of huge old elms and oaks surrounded by brambles and nettles and the tangle of ever-encroaching wildness. If this extremity of the grounds had ever been tamed, it certainly wasn't any more. Wood pigeons fired out of the heights on clapperboard wings, and starlings and jackdaws burst indignantly from nest holes as I approached beating back the brambles and bashing trunks with my precious stick.

It was here that I first met a fox. It wasn't really my own discovery. Old Bob, pulling leeks for the kitchens, slicing the tops with a single swipe of his hook-bladed knife as he spoke, had told me that there was an ancient oak stump at the top of the Broadwalk that was hollow. 'An ol' fox holes up in there,' he had announced. 'You can smell 'im as you pass by.'

I rushed to check it out. The huge oak had blown down and the trunk and branches removed decades before. Wind and rain had worked on the vast root plate, which had slowly subsided back to earth, leaving the stump sticking up at an angle. At my seven-year-old chest height, its rotted hollow was bigger and deeper than I had imagined, reaching further down into the cavernous roots than the end of my stick. I placed my head right into the hole and peered inside. It was completely empty and all I could smell was the fungally dampness of decay. I probed around its dark interior with my stick. Nothing. I wandered off and forgot about it.

A few days later I found myself passing the stump and thought I'd look again. I sauntered up confidently, expecting nothing, and thrust my head into the gaping void. Too late I realised that the rancid pungency that now assaulted my nose was markedly different from the time before, strangely alive and vital. The fox shot out like a jack-in-a-box, fur brushing my face as he fled, giving me such a fright that I fell over backwards into a clump of stinging nettles.

I would never forget that fox. It would mark a climacteric in my private, cerebral engagement with the natural world. I don't think I had ever touched a wild mammal before, except perhaps rescuing a drowning mouse from the rain butts or rabbits snared by the farm boys. But a fox was different. It was big and strong and very wild. I had seen its gleaming teeth and smelt its foetid breath. When I stood up I was shaking all over, trembling, not with fear – it had happened far too quickly for that – but with the suddenly triggered involuntary rush of adrenaline. For a stretched collision of time and space I didn't know what to do. My pulse was racing. I stood and stared at the stump. Questions swirled. Could it have bitten me? Savaged my face? Would I get into trouble if I told the grown-ups? Was there another fox in there? If there had been danger, it had passed me by, and anyway there was nothing I could have done to avoid it.

I approached the stump cautiously. This time standing well back, I knocked it with my stick several times before taking a closer look. It was empty, of course, but the cavern reeked of dark, musky animal, intimate and strangely prehistoric, belonging to another world. It was a smell I would never forget, a thrilling essence of excitement as sharp as vinegar, of danger, of adventure and above all a scent of wildness – alive and free.

3

The Manor House

If I ever get to be so old that I can no longer recognise my children; when I hear my name being called and it means nothing to me; when I cease to be able to name the birdsong I have known all my life and when the pageant of the season's turning fails to move me; when each day merges into the last and the next as a continuous fog and I hear people whisper, 'He's lost it, poor old bugger' – they will be wrong.

I shall be running free with the soft wind in my face, skipping through the shining grass of the damp Longbottom meadows, swiping with my stick at thistle heads to watch the downy seed caught and flown in eddies of sunlit breeze. I shall be straddling the old crack willow fallen into the pond where the moorhens built their soggy nest. I shall be under the ancient yew searching for tawny owl pellets, leaping the little box hedges of the ordered gardens and racing past the long glasshouses four in a row. I shall be heading out. The ancient flagstone floors will be cold beneath my bare feet once again and Nellie will be chasing me round the kitchen table with a tea towel. I shall be eight years old, laughter rippling through me till I ache, free as a cloud, embraced and held fast by the joy and the jubilation of careless youth. I shall be back at the Manor House.

As you headed out of the quiet Warwickshire village, past the little brick bridge over the weed-waving brook that burbles through the green, passing between Borsley's grocery store, the tart aroma from the block of cheddar cheese on the marble slab greeting you at the door, and Mr Anderton across the lane in his straw boater and a blue-and-white-striped apron, smile as wide as a valley, waving his cleaver over his butcher's block – 'Pettitoes not such a bad price this week' – you turned up Church Hill, past the long terrace of cottages on the right, slate roofs staggered like a rickety staircase.

Then past the Georgian vicarage, square, solemn and not a little smug behind high-boarded gates and an ivy-quilted wall. Opposite, on the south side of the lane, a low red-brick boundary wall to the graveyard led up to an oak-beamed and shingle-roofed lych-gate where the lugubrious Reverend Ferguson posted his notices every week. For years I thought his name was 'Vicar'. 'Morning Vicar,' was all I had ever heard. In the background the grey church tower stood square-shouldered against the sky.

The sweeping branches of ancient oaks and beeches trembled their shadows over the lichened gravestones of many of my ancestors, barely legible now. Far below, their bones and oak coffins were sifting down into archaeology in sure and certain hope of everlasting oblivion, earth to earth. Those trees seemed to me to be the very essence of antiquity. Their roots writhed silently beneath the tombstones and the flagged paths, tilting them drunkenly. The massive trunks powered upwards in plaited thongs of great strength, branched into an algal tracery against the sky where they clutched at the clotted nests of a hundred and more thronging, clamouring rooks.

A bit further on, on the other side of the lane and right at the end of the village, matching ornamental 'in-and-out' wrought-iron gates, both invitingly and forbiddingly painted bright white, were set a hundred yards apart. A dense privet hedge six feet high ranged between them like a green rampart. Behind the hedge, a long gravel driveway crunched through neatly mown lawns to link the two gates in a sweeping arc. Those gates announced the presence of a house that didn't need a name; it was and always had been the Manor House.

It was the home I longed for. Even now, sixty years later, it is engraved upon my soul. Not my parents' home at that delicate moment in my young life – my father was leading a peripatetic existence as he worked tirelessly to build a business and we had migrated to wherever he needed to be: Yorkshire, Bath, Devon, south Somerset; no, the Manor House was my father's family's long home to which we always gravitated as surely as bees return to their hive, however far afield the capricious winds of fortune had wafted us.

Family lore had it that Henry VII had made an ancient branch of our family Lords of the Manor, vassals to their feudal superior, Edward Plantagenet, Duke of Clarence and 17th Earl of Warwick in his magnificent medieval castle, around which the county town has mushroomed. In deference to this historical patronage many sons of our family had been christened Warwick, right up to the present day.

The house was built in the seventeenth century when fire ripped through the original Tudor oak-timbered manor house and razed it to rubble. Since then it had been added to seemingly endlessly, wings and extensions bursting out at every point of the compass and several in between, as if for centuries each successive generation had felt the need to append their own whimsical additions. By my time in the late 1940s, the original Jacobean oak-beam and straw-brick beginnings had been hemmed in on all sides by sprawling

Carolean, Georgian, Victorian and Edwardian wings, each apparently oblivious to any sense of architectural cohesion. The result was a jumble of gables and eaves on steeply pitched roofs with plunging valleys beneath a thicket of towering chimneys.

Getting around inside these ill-fitting extensions demanded long corridors leading to many external doors over countless steps, flights of stairs and varying floor levels more akin to a ship than a dwelling. And yet this random agglomeration of additions had awarded the house all the vernacular charm and mystique of a Cotswold village, in what seemed wilful denial of its much more formal intentions.

The house stood at the edge of a modest estate of farms and woods and was surrounded by broad acres of gardens and grounds. Close to the house they started off with the prescribed orthodoxy and the unmistakable Englishness of a country house, dignity upheld by manicured lawns, clipped box, privet and yew hedges and topiary, partitioned by walls and steps of ancient limestone intricately patterned with dark mosses and pale lichens. As you moved outward a network of flagged paths led you through a walled rose garden, the stonework dripping with bright aubretia, up stone steps and on beneath Japanese pergolas at the path intersections, smothered in tangles of rambling roses; then on past extravagant herbaceous borders and shrubberies bursting with scent and colour. Well away from the house, the walled gardens relaxed into much more casually arranged fruit beds of gooseberries, black and red currants, raspberries, loganberries, rhubarb and, finally, lurking discreetly in the distance, the ordered rows of vegetables.

Espaliered against the long south-facing wall, ten feet high, were pear, quince, plum, damson and apricot trees, where red admiral and peacock butterflies sipped the fruits' oozing and fermenting sugars and basked drunkenly in the sun. That wall was an important boundary, a physical and aesthetic barrier between the disciplined world of horticulture and formal gardening and an altogether wilder world beyond.

Passing through any of its several archways another world opened up, tamed perhaps but certainly not domesticated, another country where long ago nature had claimed primacy, despite periodic, half-hearted summer mowings and prunings of its rampant, inexhaustible verdure. It was a country of ancient orchards, luxuriant paddocks and copses, weedy ponds, nettle banks and marshy hollows, lime kilns long abandoned, fox earths and badger setts, rabbit warrens and thorn thickets where roe deer lay up during the day. Yet further, on to the pocket-handkerchief meadows of the Manor Farm, where the rickety old farmhouse and ivy-smothered labourers' cottages seemed not to have been built but to have grown organically out of the soil.

Behind the Manor House a discreet back drive led past the green-painted doors of the old coach house-turned-garages, to a veritable hamlet of outbuildings where the essential services of centuries of self-sufficiency had been performed: coach houses ivy-clad and a wide stable yard with a cast-iron hand pump and loose-boxes under a pan-tiled roof bursting with untidy sparrows' nests, the laundry cottage, servants' outdoor lavatories, wood and coal stores, pig stys, potting sheds, apple stores, saw mill, workshops, and four long, brick-based and white-painted glasshouses.

The Manor House was where, coming and going, we had been for centuries, and where my Victorian widower grandfather, born in 1873, now lived out his horticultural old age with my father's younger bachelor brother, Uncle Aubrey. Looking back now, I see that to have spent so much of my childhood at the Manor House and to have experienced that rarified, virtually unchanged Edwardian world was a particular privilege no longer attainable in modern society. To me, throughout the 1950s, it was Xanadu, a private kingdom all my own and everything a country child could hope for, even though at some point I became dimly aware that I was a tenuous and perhaps the final tendril emanating from a broader vine, the roots of which were planted elsewhere.

*   *   *

Properly, our family were Yorkshire folk. We had been in the West Riding since the reign of Edward III, whose heralds issued a grant of arms to 'Johannes Cay of ye lands and manors of Wodesham' in 1367, which, 150 years later, would emerge as the elegant, stone-built Elizabethan Woodsome Hall at Kirkburton, much as it stands today. As a confused schoolboy struggling to locate our place in history, I once asked my father what we were. 'We are Plantagenets,' he replied enigmatically.

I was always a lazy student of history, struggling with meaningless names and dates, but in early adulthood I began to understand that just as contemporary politics had severely impacted upon my immediate family, so down the centuries we had always been pawns in the grander machinations of power. To hang on to what we had, and even to survive, over the centuries we had been forced to duck and weave. As worthy (and opportunistic) Protestants we wisely ingratiated ourselves with Thomas Cromwell when Henry VIII set about dissolving the vastly wealthy Catholic monasteries. By some deeply devious political chicanery we came in for several thousand acres of rich glebe farms to add to our expanding Yorkshire estates. We leapt into Catholicism to avoid being burned at the stake by Bloody Mary, and bounced out again to appease her passionately Protestant half-sister, the virgin queen.

We were dashing Cavaliers in the court of Charles I – effusive supporters of the Royalist cause – and studiously kept in with Prince Rupert of the Rhine. One gallant ancestor, a knight called Sir John, was appointed Colonel of Horse to the king. He had helped raise 700 West Riding men to fight for the Royalists, for which he accepted a baronetcy in 1641. But in 1645 it all went horribly wrong when they were routed by Parliament's New Model Army under Sir Thomas Fairfax and Oliver Cromwell at the Battle of Naseby, the turning point of the Civil War. Sir John galloped away unscathed but would later forfeit everything to Cromwell's Republican parliament: titles, houses, estates and privileges – the lot. It was a sepulchral moment.

When by popular demand Charles II was restored to the throne in 1660, while the Republican signatories to his father's execution were being summarily hanged, drawn and quartered, we somehow inveigled our way back into favour. Our titles were reinstated and we were allowed to buy all our lands back, both in Warwickshire and Yorkshire, for a painful payment of £50 to the newly formed Cavalier Parliament, a pecuniary affront we never forgave, far less forgot. We had learned a bitter lesson. From then on we kept our political heads down and got on with looking after our own interests.

By the eighteenth century we had stumbled across coal underlying our Yorkshire land just in time for the emerging colonial markets and the incipient Industrial Revolution. On the mining profits and only a few miles from Woodsome Hall, enthusiastically competing with the fashionable expansion of the times, we built Denby Grange, a second, much more stately mansion which would become our principal family home. Its grand Georgian façade was attached to the restored shell of a twelfth-century Cistercian abbey that had been sacked in the Reformation. It overlooked the lush Colne valley, and was where, when I was born in 1946, our close cousin, Sir Kenelm, still lived in arthritic bachelor grandeur. But my great-grandfather had been a second son, not in direct line of succession for the Yorkshire estates. Instead, in 1856 his father had awarded him the Warwickshire manor and its adjoining lands as a wedding present. My grandfather had been born just down the east passage from my bedroom, so had my father.

It was only after Clement Atlee's 1948 socialist government nationalised our collieries, removing in one eviscerating Act the family business and capital holdings it had taken us 250 years to develop, that the deeply disillusioned Sir Kenelm debunked to Mullingar in Ireland to live out his days shooting snipe and raising racehorses, while the share-holding family elders took the tough but ultimately prudent decision to up sticks and abandon Yorkshire altogether. The titular heartland then shrank back to our medieval association with Warwickshire, where, on his share of coal profits, my great-grandfather had founded a cement works, later the Rugby Portland Cement Company.

When, many years later, I was old enough to look back down the drama of the centuries I found that we had somehow managed to produce a colourful, if never illustrious, array of *dramatis personae*: a few prominent courtiers; a mistress to James I; several swashbuckling soldiers; various undistinguished MPs; an adventurer who travelled the south seas with Captain Cook; a celebrated Lord Mayor of York who built the Mansion House and whose coat of arms still hangs on the Micklegate Bar; a chaplain to George II who became an outrageously greedy pluralist clergyman and Dean of Lincoln Cathedral; an ivory, then slave trader; one of Britain's first female industrialists; an opium dealer; a bevvy of sporting parsons; several masters of foxhounds; a Groom-in-Waiting to Edward VII; another king's mistress; a couple of naval captains; a fraudster and card sharp; several Lords Lieutenant; a pioneer Canadian cattle rancher; a successful racehorse breeder of classic winners; an eminent cricketer and a cement manufacturer. There was also quite a procession of probably dull but thoroughly worthy citizens, but, alas, no writers, nor any hint of a naturalist.

At six years old I knew none of the above. Small children are blissfully unaware of who they are or where they come from. To me the Manor House was a paradise enhanced by the strange, unstoppable passage of time. All I knew was that it was the home where I always felt we belonged, my sister Mary and I, or perhaps I should say where it never occurred to us that we didn't belong. It was never clear to me whether something *we* had done meant by us, the living family, last week, or last year or even by my grandfather, who seemed to me to be as old as Noah, or whether it had been done centuries before. One spring, jackdaws blocked a tall chimney with twigs and debris, which proved particularly tricky to clear. Staring up at men struggling with rods and brushes on the roof I heard my grandfather say, 'We didn't think about jackdaws when we built it so tall.' Later I discovered that *we* probably built it in about 1620.

We had become a generic collective, embracing more generations, more individuals, more loves, fears, hopes, dreams, tragedies and joys than we could ever know or count. Not even the graveyard could list them, except the very recent ones, such as my grandmother, Emily, cut down at sixty-five by a sudden heart attack in 1944. Tirelessly she had marshalled the ladies of the village to produce fruit and vegetables for the war effort while filling every available cranny of the house with hungry evacuees from the Blitz hells of Birmingham, Coventry and London. She had over-stretched herself, people said, and the firebombing of the old Coventry cathedral had broken her heart. Her stark five-foot limestone cross now stood beside the low graveyard wall in the shade of a vast beech whose huge branches clutched at the sky.

Traumatic experiences he would never discuss had made my uncle Aubrey a shy and private man, turning quickly away if anyone mentioned the war. They had changed him and his life forever. He had served with the Oxfordshire and Buckinghamshire Light Infantry and was taken prisoner on Dunkirk beach in May 1940. The Nazis marched them 500 miles to the notorious Stalag VIIIB Lamsdorf POW camp in Poland. When their boots wore out, they were forced to continue barefoot through a cruel winter. Feet bound in rags, black, frostbitten toes rotted and fell off as they hobbled along. They were starving. They had to beg raw potatoes and turnips from peasants along the way. Many died en route. Although my grandmother sent him food parcels every week for three years, Aubrey never received one. In dire health he was finally released in a prisoner exchange in 1943. He returned with suppurating malnutrition ulcers all over his legs, ulcers that would never heal, although he would survive as a virtual recluse for another thirty years. I once barged into the bathroom and surprised him changing the dressings. I have never forgotten the sight of raw flesh.

*   *   *

In common with many very old houses, the Manor House possessed a distinctive personality, an aura weighted far more heavily with the past than the present, with mythology as much as with reality, with the ghosts and shadows of those long-forgotten souls in the graveyard more than the living family and retainers, all of whom lived and moved in constant obeisance to the inescapable echoes of an unrecorded history. I loved it with a passion bone-deep and in all its unruly ramifications: its hidden cupboards and alcoves, its dingy corridors, its chill, feet-polished flagstone passages and its staircases leading upwards into shadow and mystery. Charged with an over-active imagination, exploring them became a never-ending adventure, the stuff of boys' comic annuals. To me the house exuded a happiness that was alluring, confident and ever present, and I rested upon it like a cushion.

There were rooms where instinctively I sensed that small boys were not supposed to be. Rooms I tiptoed through, furtively glancing over my shoulder in case the ghosts of the past stepped out from behind the door. Long stone-flagged passages where steps had been hollowed by centuries of bustling feet. It was a house into which small children could vanish for hours on end, exploring a seemingly endless succession of rooms leading into more rooms and more passages, up flights of steps, across landings, down again, through creaking doors revealing yet more rooms and corridors, ever more and more enticing.

In the front of the house the formal reception rooms were big, although my grandfather had taken my grandmother's death badly and had cut himself off from the world, refusing to entertain. He had retreated up the long west passage to the child-forbidden sanctuary of his study, known as the smoking room, only emerging for afternoon tea in the kitchen or dinner in the sombre Jacobean dining room, oak-panelling as dark as chocolate, dimly lit with half-shade sconces around the walls and candles flickering in silver candelabra on the long mahogany table.

The spacious drawing room with its finely carved cornice and chimney breast, where the iron fire basket stood four square like a bulldog in the empty grate, was temporarily closed down. Dark portraits of unsmiling ancestors glared loftily from the walls. Dustsheets covered the furniture and the blinds of wide French windows leading out onto the south lawn were permanently drawn, lending the whole room the air of long sleep, as though a spell had been cast upon it – time not just standing still, but altogether banished.

From the broad Jacobean hallway paved in large black and white marble chess-board squares, the elegantly curving main stairs bordered by high semi-circular alcoves, each one housing a large Imari bowl of rose petal potpourri, led up to more passages and bedrooms named after former occupants, mostly long dead. Great Aunt Amelia's room, at the end of the longest corridor with the squeaky floorboards, was also shut down and locked, but with the heavy key left in the lock. I had to use both hands. The door squeaked open into a pallid gloom, sun-faded blinds drawn tight so that, tiptoeing cautiously in, it took a while for my eyes to adjust.

No dustsheets here; a room intact as if the old lady had just walked out, as no doubt she had before collapsing into a border of heavily scented damasks and mosses in the rose garden a few years before I was born. They said she was dead before she hit the ground; sun hat, scissors, trug and cut roses theatrically arrayed around her like the pre-Raphaelite J.E. Millais' painting of Ophelia, and, when they found her, Bif, her little Yorkshire terrier, loyally sitting among her billowing skirts.

Her big brass bed still had a floral quilt counterpane and an eiderdown neatly spread over case-less pillows of blue and white ticking, and square folded blankets ready to be made up as though she was expected back any day. The glazed chintz curtains were part drawn; on the sills small tortoiseshell and peacock butterflies lay dead, brittle wings closed in a rigid clinch.

Her ivory-backed, family-crest-engraved hairbrushes still held strands of her platinum hair, tortoiseshell comb and silver-topped pots and trays for kirby grips, powders and creams laid out on her dressing table, and ornate flasks, too tempting to ignore. I eased the glass stopper from one little phial and recoiled, quickly replacing it. The perfume, rich and luscious, powered over me. It was as though some deeply personal element of her inner being had come back to life and escaped into the stillness of the room, the genie out of the bottle. Flushed by guilt, I felt that I had rudely invaded her privacy, made more poignant by the engaging stare from the silver-framed, fading sepia photograph of her handsome young officer husband killed in the Battle of Gallipoli in 1915. I quickly retreated, quietly locking the door behind me.

But it was the labyrinthine service areas of the house that I really loved: the separate world of kitchens, sculleries, dank slate-shelved larders, the old servants' hall, game-larder, laundry and sewing room all ruled by Nellie West, the house-keeper, whose 'I got my eye on you, young Jack' made me wonder why she didn't use both eyes. And where the almost completely toothless cook, Mrs Barnwell, with pouting lips like a goldfish and hair in a net, and Sally Franklin the scullery maid, with a backside like a shire horse and who daily threatened, 'If you don't look out I'll skin thee alive' together with deaf Ada in the laundry, whose surname I never knew, and old Bob Bryson, a retired gamekeeper then working on as a gardener, with sunken eyes swimming in bloodshot pools and whose pipe protruded through a double gap in his lower teeth, as well as a few other daily worthies, all lived out the merry backstairs pageant of everyday life. To my child's feasting eyes everyone seemed happy and content; they all got on with their various tasks, gaily teasing each other as though they were all members of the same family.

Uncle Aubrey was often to be found there too, bandaged legs always in black wellington boots, his proximity revealed by a perpetual acrid fog from chain-smoking his filter-tipped Kensitas cigarettes, only removed from his lips to replace with another. As the staff numbers had dwindled during the war years and never been replaced, so Aubrey, once rehabil-itated, had taken over the management of Moloch, the vast anthracite boiler in the outer scullery, where he also boiled up the daily bouillabaisse of bran mash, kitchen left-overs and vegetable peelings for the chickens in the paddock. For the rest of the day a rich aroma of barley meal edged with the sharper, earthy essence of hot bran and potato peelings pursued him through the house.

To me the front of the house seemed lifeless, most of its occupants dead and gone, enhancing the daunting possibility of ghosts and the lurking fear that accompanied territory forbidden to us children, as though there must have been something sinister there to hide. The adults who did pass through, including our parents, always seemed to live in a bubble of orgulous best behaviour, a strictly observed correctness that vanished once through the green baize door, where the servants' rooms and corridors bustled with life and ribald laughter.

4

The Dun Cow

It was in the oldest Jacobean quarter of the house that one of the most mysterious relics of local legend, the Dun Cow rib, was permanently housed. On a few links of rusty chain at either end the rib was slung from two square iron spikes driven into a black beam crossing the ceiling of the servants' hall. Like all ribs, it was curved with an angled head at one end, but this rib was exceptional. It tapered through four feet eight inches in an arc of dark, heavy bone. No one knew how long it had hung there. Some said 400 years, from the time of King James I, others claimed a much more ancient origin stretching back through former dwellings now crumbled into history, back a thousand years to the misty days of peasants, feudal overlords and Saxon kings. As a child I stood and stared up at it with a mixture of fear and awe.

I was first told its unlikely legend by my father when I was five. He picked me up in his arms. 'Run your fingers along it,' he whispered, as if to heighten its mystery. It was as rough as the ancient oak beam from which it hung, and patchily dark, its many centuries staining it almost black in places, quite unlike any bone I had seen before. And it was heavy, heavier than me at that age, although I would not hold its full weight in my arms for many years to come.

It was an inauspicious moment. George VI had just died on 6 February 1952. The whole nation was in mourning, the national newspapers edged in black. I can clearly recall the bold headline 'THE KING IS DEAD' and the chill of shock and disbelief permeating round the entire house. Across the lane the church bell tolled, and from its tower the St George's Cross rippled at half-mast in the winter breeze. My grandfather and father dressed in black suits. They wore black ties for days. With long faces and lowered voices the grown-ups talked of nothing else. Around the kitchen table Nellie, Mrs Barnwell, Sally Franklin and Ada pored over the newspapers, and special issues of *Picture Post* and the *Illustrated London News*. On the day of the funeral, 15 February, they crowded around the old wireless set on the sideboard to listen to the Home Service coverage, the doleful brass bands, wailing pipes and muffled drums of the procession from Buckingham Palace to Windsor, and the sombre commentary by the young Raymond Baxter. Nellie was in tears most of the day, sobbing into her tea.

It was only a few days later that my father took me to see the rib. The funereal mood and pall of death seemed to lurk in the darkest corners of the house. He told me that it had never been taken down since an unknown hand nailed it there all those centuries ago. His words struck chill into my heart: 'It must never be moved, and when it is, there will be bad times, and death will visit the family,' – although I'm sure he added that bit for dramatic effect. It worked. My imagination whirled like a top. I could see the headline, YOUR FAMILY IS DEAD, with a black edge all its own. The rib's image, hanging there on its old chains, went in deep and has remained, stark and vivid, to this day.

The legend of the Dun Cow is well known throughout middle England. There are many pubs called the Dun Cow; villages such as Dunchurch and Ryton, Bourton, Stretton and Clifton, all still have the historical appendage '-on-Dunsmore' attached to their names. They surround a once wild and barren heath known as Dunsmoor, bisected by the Roman Fosse Way. A second almost identical rib hangs in Warwick Castle ten miles away, and to this day many versions of the legend persist throughout the Midlands. Our own family narrative, written up by a Victorian maiden aunt in the mid-nineteenth century, runs like this:

About 900 years ago, in the reign of the Saxon King Athelstan, a herd of wild cattle roamed a heath in the middle of England. The Dunsmoor villagers lived in fear of these ferocious beasts. One cow grew to enormous size; four yards high it stood and six in length. This monstrous beast took to raiding villagers' crops and gored anyone who stood in its way. When several folk had been killed, the villagers turned to the lord of the manor. 'You must rid us of this menace,' they cried angrily. Straightaway the noble knight mounted his charger and set out for the heath with his lance and his broadsword. But when the great cow loomed out of the mist it was so huge, and so terrible was its bellow, that he turned and galloped away as fast as he could.

Greatly humiliated, he set off for Warwick Castle to find another knight who was renowned for slaying giants and dragons. Together they rode out to kill the cow. But when the beast flared its nostrils and tossed its huge horns at them, once again they fled. Concerned for their reputations, the two knights hit upon a plan. Off they went to find an old witch who lived in a cave on the edge of the moor. They plied her with gold until she agreed to cast a spell on the cow.

In the evening twilight the witch appeared from behind a rock and muttered her incantation. The great beast fell quiet beneath the spell. She produced a sieve from under her skirts and began to milk the cow into it. The cow turned its huge head and saw its precious milk draining away into the moor. Slowly it lumbered away into the mist and died of a broken heart.

Both knights took a rib from the dead cow and returned to their villages, each claiming that he had slain the cow, but the witch had cursed them for their lack of courage, saying that if ever they parted with the ribs their families would die out. So to this day one rib hangs in Warwick Castle and the other remains in our family.

It's a con. The ribs are not ribs at all. They are the two sides of a minke whale's lower jaw: two very large and uncannily rib-like bones. When in the 1970s we had ours carbon dated, it proved to be over 950 years old. Far from illuminating the Dun Cow legend, this revelation greatly deepened its mystery. It would appear that at some point in the far distant past some wag or prankster thought the legend deserved to be immortalised by producing the hard evidence of the cow. It was a cunning ploy. The ribs were very convincing – they could only have come from a huge beast – and for many centuries local people had believed in the colossal cow, utterly convinced by those awesome bones.

*   *   *

Separating the servants' quarters from the formal dining room was a long disused butler's pantry. During the war years it had become a cluttered store for a random miscellany of intrigue, like a bric-a-brac shop. Running the full length of one long wall were full-height, built-in cupboards, floor to ceiling. Teasing open their cobwebby doors was like opening huge windows into a distant past. Carefully and dutifully arranged on plain pine shelves was the china and glass of an Edwardian era of extravagant house parties, grand dinners and hunt balls.

There were Coalport and Dresden tea sets, whole Crown

Derby and Minton dinner services with vast meat platters
– big enough, I gaily imagined, for a glazed boar's head with
an orange in its mouth, steaming haunches of venison or a
whole salmon with a cold, staring eye, such as I had seen
in illustrations of medieval banquets. There were soup
tureens, sauce boats and vegetable dishes with ornate porcelain arrangements of tomatoes, marrows and turnips bulging
across their lids, and an ancient, chipped and faded, blue and
white service of family crested ware.

When I opened those cupboard doors, I fancied I could
hear the bustle and hustle of a busy household, the laughter
of family and guests, the merry gossip of servants, and the
chink of china and glass. When I closed them, the silence
of the empty house settled around me again so that I hurried
to open the next one.

It held rows of dusty cut-glass tumblers, twisted champagne flutes, sherry, port and wine glasses and rummers;
ranks of decanters, carafes, claret jugs with silver lids and
handles, Bacchus' bearded face glaring from their lips like
gargoyles; glass flagons and demijohns encased in woven
wicker; flower vases of every configuration and size, and
then, in the end cupboard, several large, plain blue-and-white
or floral-patterned china pitchers and ewers for marble-
topped bedroom washstands.

On a last lower shelf stood a row of large china slop
buckets with wicker-bound handles and lids smothered all
over with brightly coloured rosebuds, as if they might
somehow divert attention from their practical function. At
floor level, tucked away, there were rows of floral potties
and heavy bed-warming bottles of beige stoneware and some
curiously wedge-shaped white china vessels I puzzled over.
Much later I discovered they were slipper bedpans.

Closing the cupboard doors shut off the past, trapping it

back in the dark, no longer a real part of my life or the life of the house. The room returned to what it had been forced to become during the lean and wearisome years of the war, a dumping ground for duller stuff – two old wooden ironing boards and a wash-board, big cardboard boxes piled up, a canvas golf bag with a few wooden shafted clubs, two broken wicker carpet beaters, ancient black-initialled leather suit-cases with ships' labels and stickers from foreign parts, broken lampshades, gut-stringed tennis racquets in square wooden presses, a broken bagatelle board with the balls missing.

A cluster of tea chests was crowded into a corner, packed full of folded blackout sheets like satanic shrouds. Another contained the headphones, consoles and wall-mountings of several wireless sets dating from the early days of radio before the First World War. There were long-handled copper warming pans, an umbrella-stand full of walking sticks and feather dusters on long canes and, most perplexing of all, a rattan-backed mahogany commode in the form of an armchair. When I lifted the seat lid I found a gaping oval hole. I had never seen such a thing before and I peered into it, finding only a plain wooden shelf beneath. I struggled to comprehend why anybody would want to sit in a chair like that, so I spent fruitless hours balancing uncomfortably and hoping that by doing so its purpose might become clear. When I showed it to my sister, Mary, she said, 'It's a lavatory, silly. What did you think it was for?' I spent the rest of the day wondering why anyone would seek to deposit their daily doings on a wooden shelf.

On one such exploration I found, tucked away in an old cabin trunk, several wartime gas masks, unused, still in their original cardboard boxes. There were two types: some were black rubber masks which fitted snugly over your face with a clear cellophane panel to see through, white webbing straps round the back of your head and a khaki canister of filtration crystals hanging immediately in front of your mouth. The others, called GS Respirators, were clearly superior: whole head masks with round glass eyepieces and a twenty-eight-inch-long expanding rubber tube like an elephant's trunk leading from your nose and mouth to a separate canister carried in a khaki haversack at your side. These were much more sinister, with all the shock effect of an invader from outer space; it was impossible to tell who was inside.

Wearing one of these superior masks, I stalked the servants' back corridors searching for victims. My first was Sally Franklin, swabbing the flagstones with a bucket and mop. I crept up behind her and stood still. She swabbed slowly backwards toward me until all I could see was her voluminous backside encased in a wrap-around floral pinafore. I reached forward and tapped her bottom. She spun round. A muffled 'BOOO!' issued from inside the mask. Sally shrieked and leapt away, kicking over her bucket and sending her mop flying. I ran and ran, back down the corridor and out into the stable yard. I hid the gas mask in a manger and sauntered back into the scullery as though it was nothing to do with me.

Sally was sitting at the kitchen table, tears streaming down her face, Nellie doing her best to console her with a cup of tea. 'You're in trouble, young Jack, you are,' Nellie scolded. 'Look what you done to poor Sally. You nearly gave 'er an 'art attack. You wait till I tell your father.' But I knew she never would.

Nellie West was my friend. She was my grandfather's housekeeper. Her father, economically known as West, had been his chauffeur and valet, and her mother, Elsie, had worked in the laundry. Both had died in service before I was born. Slowly growing mould, West's dark green and gold braided livery still hung in a wardrobe in the old coach house. Nellie had started life as a chambermaid in her teens and gradually progressed to become a prominent member of the staff. After my grandmother's sudden death she had found herself at the head of the much-reduced post-war household. She would rule the Manor House with absolute dedication and my grandfather would come to depend upon her for the rest of his life.

A smile twinkled permanently in her blue-grey eyes and about her bunched cheeks, lips ever ready with a facetious quip: 'There's no lunch today, young Jack, cos I've heard you've not bin good enough.' Or 'I'm thinkin' of putting you under the pump cos I can see dirt behind your ears.' Yet she often spoke with a sigh and an inner sadness, saying, 'Do you really think so?' as though she were unworthy of her own opinions. She had greyed early and grown more than a little plump beneath her habitual navy blue or grey tunic dresses, always adorned with a floral pinny, and she was not surprisingly single.

Born in the first few years of the century her timing couldn't have been much worse. Turning fifteen at the end of the First World War, most of her potential seventeen- to twenty-year-old suitors, and many much older from her tiny rural community had failed to come home. They were the lost generation. In common with thousands of village girls the length and breadth of the country, Nellie's life chances at marriage had perished ingloriously in the trench hells of Verdun, Arras, Passchendaele and the Somme. By the time I was seven she would have been approaching fifty and she had accepted her spinsterhood with grace and cheerful dignity.

To me, Nellie and the Manor House were synonymous. She had always been there, a steadfast bulwark of my earliest childhood memories. I could not have enunciated so ardent an emotion back then, but I loved her, second only to my mother. Without it ever being acknowledged by either of us, Nellie West had entered my inner consciousness as a fixture, an anchor point of deepest security, as much a pillar of my brief existence as the Manor House itself. Whenever we arrived to stay, while my father always set off in search of my grandfather in his smoking room or his workshop or one of his precious glasshouses, I ran to the kitchens to find Nellie.

Those gas masks sparked an endless burst of imagination. Better than any cowboy hat or cap gun, they were real and tapped into a constantly creative vein. I could be a Martian invader or a horrid German paratrooper prowling the woods and fields, or I could be the hero hunting them down. I could be a burglar raiding an imaginary bank or a high-wayman like the Dick Turpin I had read about, leaping out from behind a tree to halt an imaginary carriage and pluck rings and necklaces from rich ladies' necks and fingers.

Wooden swords in hand, I persuaded my sister to wear a mask too, so that together we could prowl the corridors seeking out a fearsome ogre whose den was known to be the game larder. We approached with extreme caution. Then, stepping boldly forward I kicked the door open and shouted, 'Come out and fight, you ugly beast!' Only to find that he was not in, but the stark, bloodied evidence of his fearsome power hung in rows from the beams – hares, pheasants, duck and partridges, all his victims impaled by their beaks or their feet on rusty hooks, blood dripping to the flagged floor. Once, old Bob was in the larder quietly plucking pheasants. When I burst in to accost the ogre, I got such a fright at finding someone there that I ran for my life, mask or no mask. I rushed to the kitchen to tell Nellie. 'Now that serves you aright, young Jack.'

My father had installed a television for the Queen's Coronation in June 1953 – small, a bit fuzzy, and black and white, of course. Although viewing was strictly controlled, I was allowed to watch Westerns, my favourite by far being *Stagecoach* – proper cowboys and indians – repeated every Christmas for years. I used to sit cross-legged on the floor, entranced, my face only a few inches from the tiny screen. As influences waxed and waned so I variously became Davy Crockett, Daniel Boone, Kit Carson, the dashing Wells Fargo agent Jim Hardie, and inevitably I was gripped by *The Lone Ranger*, but never the oh-so-smooth masked hero in his white Stetson, polished boots and creaseless britches, on his spotless white horse 'Hi-Yo Silver!' Oh no, it was Tonto I wanted to be: the moccasin'd indian with the tracking skills of a leopard who leapt onto his horse bareback and was usually the one who did all the dirty work (played by the brilliantly named Mohawk actor Jay Silverheels). I tied a dishcloth band round my head and wandered the woods muttering *'Kemo sabe'*, possessing not the first inkling that its translation was 'trusty scout' in Potawatomi. I longed for a sheath knife like Tonto's.

It was not a sheath knife, but my grandfather gave me a shiny black clasp knife for my eighth birthday. It wasn't new, it had been his, and that made it more precious still. It had two blades, one large and one small, a bottle opener and a hook for getting stones out of horses' hooves. To me it was also like being awarded a latch key; a tacit acknowledgement that at last I was old enough to venture out, to whittle my own sticks, to essay, raid and foray, returning like Robert

Louis Stevenson's 'hunter home from the hill'. Armed only with the knife and a four-foot hazel stick my father had cut for me, and clad in the new dark green gabardine 'windcheater' from my mother, with patch pockets and a zip fastener (still a novelty in Britain), I ventured forth into the great unknown.

That stick possessed magical powers: it could be Robin Hood's bow or his sword or staff; it was Huck Finn's pole, rafting downriver; with a length of string it became a whip, or, with the thicker end tucked into my armpit, a gun, accompanied by the 'Pwrrch! Pwrrch!' from pursed lips with each imagined shot, as I prowled the hedgerows. My stick and my knife were essential props I carried everywhere – my armory, my badges of office, my power beads. Into the shaft I carved notches and rings for imaginary villains I had gunned down or defeated in breathless hand-to-hand encounters.

These two items had located the violent core of my inner self, a Pandora's box of hyperactive pre-pubescent imagination, slaying enemies without mercy, hanging, drawing and quartering the Sheriff of Nottingham, gunning down and beheading innocent victims in my rush for power and domination. Without them I was nothing, as helpless as a highwayman without his mask and pistol or a knight without sword and shield. I became permanently attached to my stick, beside my bed at night, never heading out without it. Then, one day, in a fit of pique because I had refused to take her with me, my sister snapped it in two. I was devastated and a secret murder boiled in my heart.

I have often wondered whether those years and the wildness that seemed to flourish within me were a direct result of my mother's illness and absences, or whether they were a natural outpouring of youthful exuberance given the freedom to expand unchecked in the splendid Elysian fields of the little Manor House estate. Had she been there I don't think my mother would have been able to exercise any more control than Nellie. The potential for escape was always too great, the horizons too wide, and my energy and determination too deeply rooted. She possessed neither the strength nor the will to hold me in check. In truth, I had no idea either then or for many years to come how seriously ill my mother was. I was gloriously out of control.

Those early years of discovery were often hazardous, even dangerous, but always exhilarating. As a fuller awareness of my expanding landscape slowly dawned, so I think I began to realise that its possibilities for adventure and excitement were limitless. But that first brush with the fox had changed me. From then on, with the immutable tidal wash of destiny, natural history and wildlife would always be the most likely ingredients of fulfillment.

I can't now remember precisely when, but probably by the age of seven or eight, my exploration of the self-contained world of the Manor House had begun to burst at the seams. It was expanding out of doors. While the house's labyrinthine interior still held endless opportunities for adventure, the extensive out-buildings were new and exciting. Some, such as my grandfather's large workshop, were firmly locked.

It would be several years before I was allowed to try my hand at carpentry; years before I could be trusted with belt-driven lathe and band saw, planes and chisels honed on whetstones until they were as sharp as a sabre. Both my grandfather and my father were highly skilled practitioners, way beyond anything that might be described as a hobby. They were that rare combination of professional men and amateur craftsmen. Although until the Second World War the little Manor estate had employed men and women to perform most everyday functions of country life, there existed among the family members an unspoken moral principle broadly interpreted as 'never ask anyone to do anything you can't do yourself', and which seemed to honour a centuries old tradition of manual dexterity and self-sufficiency in English country life, a tradition of which they were rightly and properly proud.

I was allowed to stand and watch, occasionally to help out – 'Hold that end, boy, for the last cut. Don't let it fall.' It seemed there was nothing they couldn't turn their hand to: making and repairing hand tools, barrows, carts, garden furniture, or hanging doors and re-roofing sheds. Often it was mechanics, spanners and wrenches for nuts and bolts or metalwork, grinding on the engineer's wheel: 'Stand back, boy, and get your goggles on.' Sparks showered in dazzling arcs and then at the brick forge a lump hammer ringing on the anvil, 'Pump those bellows, boy, we need more heat,' before welding in the fire.

Later, when I was considered old enough, I was indoctrinated in those same skills: 'Whoa! Steady now. Slowly, slowly. Never force it. Let the saw do the work.' Or 'Hold the hammer at the end, boy, not halfway down.' And the first time I rushed to pick up a piece of steel still hot from welding and smelt the roast beef aroma my own burning flesh the observation would be: 'Well, you won't do that again.' Words spoken not with any sense of reproof – far from it – they came with that age-old, firm but all-embracing warmth of loving instruction from master to pupil, from father to son, that had served so well down the generations, always couched in the same proudly principled tenet of independence that bound us all together.

Other buildings were not locked. Dark, cobwebby interiors of potting sheds, apple stores, wood stores, stables and various annexes to the old coach houses were an endless source of mystery and delight. Games of hide and seek with my sister always ended in tears because we could conceal ourselves so completely and so unfathomably that either the seeker gave up in frustration and wandered off or the hider lost patience, became bored by never being found and emerged insisting, 'You're useless!'

It was often after such frustrations that I was abandoned and left to devise my own entertainment. Wonderful though it was, the Manor House was a cut-off world still roundly entrenched in Victorian values. We children had no local friends and village children did not venture into Manor House territory; had they done so I suspect we would have been actively discouraged from associating with them. Not that I was ever lonely – quite the reverse, I loved being left to explore on my own.

Beyond the line of ancient trees at the top of the gardens lay a large pond ringed with crack willows, some of which had broken up in winter storms and fallen into the water. Further on again was an orchard of ancient apple and pear trees, gnarled and pruned to distorted configurations, neatly spaced in ordered rows and perfect for climbing. Those old fruit trees taught me to be an expert tree climber and when I fell, as often I did, it was never very far, landing ruffled but unhurt, cushioned by the long grass below.

The pond was a favoured haunt. Wings thrashing, mallard often rose from the water rasping their alarm as I approached and every year moorhens laboured back and forth to create a nest of soggy weed among the twigs of a fallen willow as it lay across the surface of the water. I thought it might be possible for a small boy to clamber out along the fallen limb to a position just above the nest.

In those days many country boys collected birds' eggs.

My grandfather and his father before him both had cherished collections in specially made wooden cabinets of drawers, the precious blown eggs carefully labelled and housed in partitioned sections on beds of cotton wool – *Linnet, Hawthorn thicket, Ryton Wood. 24.4.26* – many dating back to the Victorian era. It had been a fashionable and entirely acceptable pastime, many amateur collections proudly maintained to museum standards.

The cabinets stood in my grandfather's smoking room, a room we dared not enter. My father had also had a collection of his own when he was a boy. He showed me the drawers of eggs, drawer after drawer, row upon row. Eggs of birds I had never heard of: hawfinch, redstart, corn bunting, whinchat . . . I longed for a collection of my own.

The bottom drawer of my grandfather's cabinet housed the intricate paraphernalia of professional egg collecting: a set of special drills twirled between forefinger and thumb for cutting the perfect round holes in the end of the eggs, minuscule for wrens and warblers, much larger for geese and swans; slender blow pipes of several sizes for inserting through the hole and gently blowing out the yolk and white; a little phial of surgical spirit for cleaning and disinfecting the shell, inside and out, and a glass pipette for administering it; a wad of lint for lining the drawer sections and a roll of cotton wool in dark blue paper; a pair of fine pointed scissors; tweezers and a soft paint brush; crystals of silica gel in a tiny pot and another containing crystals of naphthalene for keeping mites and other bugs at bay.

That spring I sat quietly on the bank and watched the moorhens heaping up their weedy pile. They worked fast and diligently, both birds ferrying back and forth with beaks crammed with any old weed they could find. The pile grew well clear of the water, so much so that one bird had to remain on the mound while the other passed the weed up to it. Then she sat.

I couldn't keep away. Every day I visited several times, the bird always firmly parked on her nest. I longed to see into it, but I couldn't. Even when she came off I still couldn't see in from the bank. I climbed a tree nearby but however I craned my neck it was no good. Very stealthily I ventured out along the fallen branch. Immediately it shook the nest; the hen took fright, springing away into the water with a sharp-edged yelp. She half flew, half skedaddled across the surface, cutting a dark trail through the bright green duck-weed to the far side, where she disappeared under an overhanging thicket.

I saw my chance and stepped boldly out along the branch until it began to wobble under my weight. Then I dropped to my hands and knees, clinging on to slender, twiggy laterals as I crawled forward. At last I could see into the nest. There, glowing with heat, were seven stone-coloured eggs speckled with rusty dots and squiggles. They were magnificent. At that moment I wanted one of those eggs more than anything else in the world. I wanted to take one home and show it to my father and my grandfather to persuade them that I needed to start a collection of my own – my own cabinet of drawers, my own carefully inscribed labels, my own toolkit, my own trophies.

I crawled forward again. The branch flexed alarmingly under my weight, but there was still a long way to go. The nest was woven into the flimsy extremity of twigs well out from the main stem. I lay down on the branch and inched forward like a snake stalking its prey. I could still hear the moorhen squawking anxiously from its hideaway. Another five feet to go – with a sickening snap the dead branch broke and I crash-landed in the water.

It wasn't deep, only about three feet. I quickly righted myself, hauling up on the branch, dripping and spitting foul water like a ducked witch. My wellingtons found the bottom and I stood up and wiped the weed from my face. I'd cut my lip and blood flowed freely down my sodden shirt. Stinking of rotten eggs, bubbles of marsh gas were percolating to the surface all round me. Then I realised that I was sinking. I tried to raise my feet one at a time. They wouldn't budge. I was sinking into deep, cold, evil-smelling mud. Nothing for it but to abandon my boots and haul myself out on the branch in soggy socks. I took a long last look at the nest, still out of reach, before hauling back along the branch to the bank.

I limped painfully home, cringing with every step. I crept in the back door to the scullery desperate to find Nellie before anyone else saw me. 'Oh my lordy Lord,' she cried, wringing her hands in her pinny. 'I knew you was up to no good.' Water trickled down my legs and pooled muddily on the flagstones at my feet.

'Please don't tell,' I begged. I knew she wouldn't.

5

Ye hunter's badge

I can no longer remember when I first became aware of the significance of wildlife. Born into the woods and pastoral landscapes of England, I had gradually become familiar with the existence of foxes and badgers, otters, weasels and stoats, several species of deer and many birds, but no such rarified and thrilling excitement as a wildcat existed either in the cultural heritage of my background or out there in the English countryside.

The sporting tradition of the eighteenth-century country squire, of huntin', shootin' and fishin', lay at the heart of that heritage. The staring, snapping and snarling relics of the chase adorned many of the Manor House corridors and rooms, an enduring cultural ingredient immortalised in lurid taxidermy. Fox masks with slavering tongues leered as I crept past, otters curled their bristly lips and the mad, goggle-eyes of hares stared out from passage walls, all mounted on glossy mahogany shields, duly dated and referenced on ivory plaques, like gravestones, *Killed Paulton Way. 17.11.29*, with the initials of the family member who had ridden home rejoicing.

Other trophies were scattered about the house so that I never knew what was going to confront me as I rounded corridor corners. At first their strange language bewildered me, a codified lexicon of their own, which, to enter the enticing world of conformity, you had to know by heart: foxes lived in 'earths' and their silver mounted bushy tails were 'brushes'; otters lived in 'holts' and their thick, tapering tails were 'poles'; badgers dug 'setts', their long-clawed paws 'pads'; and you didn't say deer hooves, you said 'slots'. On white and gleaming frontal bone, red deer antlers possessed their own full glossary – important to know your tines: 'brow', 'bez', 'trez' and 'tops'; 'hummel', 'switch', 'ten pointer' or the complete, majestic spread of a twelve-point 'Royal' stag – or full mounted heads of fallow 'bucks' with broad palmate antlers, or roe 'bucks' with 'pearling', or the freakish malformation of a 'perruque', all haughtily eyeing me from on high.

A whole 38 lb salmon with the glassy eye of a crazed convict stared malevolently from above the butler's pantry door. In the hall, above a cast-iron umbrella stand bursting with thumb sticks, walking sticks, croquet mallets, ram's horn crummacks, silver-knobbed canes and old black Briggs' umbrellas with knobbly handles, something deeply scary called a 'ferox trout', all 12 lb of it, with mouth agape and multiple jagged teeth, shark-like, bared for the snap and snatch, floated its menacing grin through the rigid weed of its glass case. All these relict lives were alarmingly life-like; I tiptoed past them as much in awe as in fear that those teeth might still bite.

At the far end of the smoking-room passage was the gunroom, where immaculately oiled and polished guns and rifles gleamed alluringly from their glass-fronted cases, securely locked away from the prying fingers of small boys, territory from which I was expressly forbidden. 'Now don't you let me catch you nowhere near,' Nellie would wag her finger at me, but that made it a certainty and I sneaked off there as soon as no one was about.

That long corridor, with its threadbare red runner and squeaky floorboards, lined with bookshelves, also led to my grandfather's indoor sanctuary, his study, known as the smoking-room, which was always locked if he wasn't there. I would not have dared even try the brass doorknob. But that corridor held an irresistible magnetism for a small boy. The whole place reeked of antiquity, the irrepressible incense of a past when nothing ever changed: tobacco, gun oil, the tangy scent of cordite, all blended with mansion polish and a whiff of mothballs.

Every August for most of his adult life my grandfather had taken off to Scotland, in the 1930s it was in his elegant, long-bonneted convertible two-litre Lagonda Tourer, driven by Nellie's father, West, who performed the triple roles of chauffeur, personal valet and his loader. Top quality English side-lock shotguns came in pairs: Purdeys, Holland & Holland 'Royals', Boss, William Powell, Churchill, there are many makes, always in beautiful flat leather cases, embossed with names, initials or family crests, each piece of the dismantled guns – stock, barrels, fore-end – bedded in their own scarlet or royal blue felt-lined compartments. There would also be fitted slots for a small phial of Rangoon gun oil, two steel snap caps, a special ebony handled screwdriver which exactly matched the slot on the engraved side-lock screws, a ramrod with knurled ebony handle and threaded cleaning mops. A matching leather magazine contained the cartridges.

Such English shotguns were then and still are universally recognised as the best guns in the world, nowadays costing more than an expensive car. They are also works of art. Their steel side-lock plates always intricately and beautifully engraved with acanthus leaves or sporting scenes: pointers, retrievers and spaniels, or pheasants, snipe, partridges, duck or woodcock, and the highly polished stocks sculpted from Spanish walnut root. But those guns were also de rigueur, an essential hallmark of class and wealth, a social shibboleth and a passport to the finest sporting estates in Britain. You were expected to own them and to bring 'your man' with you.

While shooting across most of England was principally about pheasants and partridges, in Yorkshire and Scotland it was grouse – the red grouse – one of only two (with the Scottish crossbill) endemic British bird species. Grouse were then and still are shot walking up 'over dogs' – pointers or setters – or 'driven' toward the guns by a line of flag-waving beaters. They fly fast and low in coveys of up to twenty or thirty birds at a time. To maximise the 'bag' requires skilful sharp-shooting with two double-barrelled shotguns – hence the pair – and a loader to stand behind and reload each gun in turn, smooth and well-rehearsed handovers between the two men in rapid succession. Nellie often told me that the expedition to Scotland for six weeks each year was the highlight of her father's calendar. The entire household turned out to wave them off.

They were headed for Lennox Castle in the Campsie Fells, north of Glasgow, lying between the Kilsyth, Kilpatrick and Gargunnock hills, the Scottish lair of my grandfather's greatest sporting ally, Captain Billy Kincaid-Lennox, Chief of Clan Lennox, whose purple grouse moors stretched into the heathery uplands to the north. It was an annual August migration; 'the Glorious 12th' an absolute fixture in my grandfather's diary.

After the grouse, in September they moved further north to the far-flung borders of Sutherland for more grouse and for stalking red deer in the high hills, sports which, together with fly-fishing for Atlantic salmon leaping upstream to spawn, had defined the Scottish Highlands ever since Queen Victoria and Prince Albert established the famous triad of patrician sports – grouse, deer and salmon – at Balmoral in the 1850s, later immortalised by Sir Edwin Landseer's *Monarch of the Glen* and by John Buchan as a 'Macnab', when you achieved all three in one day. When Captain Billy and my grandfather had stalked their stags, they turned south again just in time for the partridge and pheasant shooting season in England.

Heading down through Yorkshire, they always stopped off at our family's ancestral seat, Denby Grange, where our cousin, Sir Kenelm, ran a celebrated shoot, before ending up at Captain Billy's home pheasant shoot at Downton Castle in Shropshire. Flicking through the pages of both Sir Kenelm's and my grandfather's game books, I see that before and immediately after the Second World War, among the names of dukes, earls and other titled gents who attended shooting parties at Denby are Sir Aymer Maxwell and his brother, Mr Gavin Maxwell, of whom my grandfather observes in his looping copperplate hand, 'shot extremely well'. Many years later, after becoming a celebrated travel writer and adding 'global best-seller' to his name, Gavin would tell me that the grey partridge shoots at Denby were a cherished feature of his upbringing.

When so many gamekeepers and estate workers, as well as their officer-class employers, went off to the world wars, these seasonal migrations temporarily halted, but the tradition was deep-rooted and by the time I was born immediately after the war it had begun to pick up again exactly where it had left off. I'm not sure how long my grandfather continued these annual shooting expeditions – he was seventy-three when I was born, and West died in 1943 and was never replaced – but throughout my formative years the enticing echo of those predatory days resounded through the corridors of the Manor House.

As I grew older and was swept up in the shooting culture myself – I was given my first gun at thirteen – so I was allowed to inspect the game books and to listen spellbound to my grandfather reminiscing with my father about those pre-war expeditions, about their extravagant bags of hundreds of grouse in a day, always, for some arcane reason, counted in 'brace'. Talk of shooting until the gun barrels were too hot to hold; of blunt and characterful gamekeepers who ruled their estates with forthright opinions; of pointers, terriers and retrievers; of walking up ptarmigan in the highest hills or stalking roe deer in the woods; of crawling through mountain bogs with a tweed-clad stalker to close in on a stag. I was enthralled and longed for the opportunity to travel to Scotland myself, to partake of this grand, glowing Highland tradition.

At some point during those impressionable years I had found in the library at the Manor House a fine green cloth-bound volume with a gold thistle embossed on the cover, entitled *Wild Sports and Natural History of the Highlands* (1848) by Charles St John, the younger son of Viscount Bolingbroke. Beside it, also in handsome green cloth bindings in two volumes, embossed with 'Ye Hunter's Badge' of the heads of a red deer stag, a sea eagle, a salmon and a seal, all enclosed within a heraldic shield, was John Colquhoun's *The Moor and the Loch* (1880). Both were best-sellers of their day; the acknowledged sporting handbooks of the period, which graced the library shelves of every sporting lodge and country house in Britain.

Inspired by my grandfather's tales of the Highlands, I took the books down and studied them wide-eyed with awe. Eventually I would inherit them. Recently I looked them out again, blew the dust from their tops and plunged back into their rough-edged pages. I not only wanted to refresh my memory, but was also on a journey to revisit the old buzz I had gleaned from them so long ago. I wanted to try to figure out just how they would have influenced my form-ative awareness of the bizarre contradictions and conflicts that then existed – and for many still do – between 'sport', natural history and nature conservation.

It was in those celebrated tomes that I first encountered the Scottish wildcat. Both books contained a chapter dedi-cated to the species, accompanied by crudely effective pen-and-ink illustrations of what the artist imagined a wildcat should look like. The results certainly look wild, but that is where the resemblance ends – not so surprising since both authors freely admit that the wildcat is very rare, so it is most unlikely that their illustrators had ever seen one. But John Colquhoun and Charles St John certainly had. They both claim proudly to have hunted down and killed many wildcats. More than this, St John openly advocated the *extir-pation* of wildcats as heinous vermin.

I remember heaving down the weighty two-volume Webster's dictionary to discover the meaning of *extirpate*. As a ten-year-old I was shocked. '*To root out, to destroy totally, to EXTERMINATE.*' Why, I struggled to comprehend, would anyone seek to wipe out such an exquisitely beautiful wild animal? I read on.

St John insists: 'the damage they would do to the game must be very great'. He then recounts the demise of one wildcat he happened upon while fishing in Sutherland. Armed with a stout stick he pursued her with his terriers

until she took refuge in a corner of the rocks . . . As soon as I was within six or seven feet of the place she sprang straight at my face . . . Had I not struck her in mid air as she leapt at me, I should probably have got some severe wound . . . she fell with her back half broken among the dogs, who, with my assistance dispatched her.

Then in slightly more conciliatory tone he adds, 'I never saw an animal fight so desperately, or one which was so difficult to kill.'

Colquhoun, writing thirty-five years later than St John, opens his short treatise on the wildcat by firmly stating, 'The wild-cat [sic] is now rare in this country.' He goes on to say, 'Although I have spent a great part of my life in the most mountainous districts of Scotland, where killing vermin is . . . my own recreation, I have never seen more than five or six genuine wild-cats.' He then describes them with creative hyperbole thus: 'the hair long and rough, the head exceedingly broad, ears short, tusks extremely large' and 'the great length and power of the limbs'. He builds a picture of a truly fearsome beast. 'Lambs, grouse, hares, are all seized with equal avidity . . . The female fears nothing when in defense of her young, and will attack even man himself.'

Much of this is sensationalist baloney, which begs the question whether Colquhoun was exaggerating to excite his readers, or even whether his claim to have seen and killed wildcats was actually true. That question might also be fairly addressed of Gavin Maxwell in the early chapters of *Ring of Bright Water*:

Wildcats grow to an enormous size, at least double that of the very largest domestic cat . . . Once I caught one accidentally in a rabbit snare, a vast tom with ten rings to his tail, and that first year at Camusfeàrna I twice saw the kittens at play in the dawn . . . there was no hint of the ferocity that takes a heavy toll of lambs and red-deer calves.

Although laced with his enchanting lyricism, much of the rest of Maxwell's anecdotal record rings largely implausible:

The males sometimes mate with domestic females [entirely true and now a very real problem for the species] but the offspring rarely survives [certainly not true] either because the sire returns to kill the kittens as soon as they are born [highly unlikely] and so expunge the evidence of this peasant wenching, or because of the distrust in which so many humans hold the taint of the untamable [appealing, but sadly also untrue]. It is the wild strain that is dominant, in the lynx-like appearance, the extra claw, and the feral instinct; and the few half-breeds that escape destruction usually take to the hills and the den life of their male ancestors.

Yes, the pure wildcat is markedly bigger than a large domestic tabby, but certainly not 'at least double that of the very largest domestic cat'. And it has marginally longer limbs and a broader skull also with fractionally larger canine teeth, but 'the great length and power of the limbs' and 'ten rings to his tail', 'the lynx-like appearance' and 'the extra claw' are all pure myth. Now having first-hand experience of many wildcats, both alive and dead, there is no extra claw and I have never seen one with more than six distinct rings to its tail, and many have only four or five.

Other writers and observers have chosen to perpetuate this feline mythology – the wildcat's fierceness, its fangs, its untamable reputation, its size and dramatic strength – but much of it is simply fabricated or dramatic exaggeration.

The obvious and overriding fact is that the animal is *WILD*. Of course it is fierce. Of course it is strong. It is a predator and needs a vicious bite to secure and kill its prey, just as do the fox and the badger, the otter, weasel, stoat and pine marten, if you are daft enough to test any of them on soft human flesh. And in common with all of the above, if cornered or attacked by man or dog, all of them will struggle and bite as fiercely and as savagely as any wild animal. I know very well how strong the wildcat is.

When I first came to live in the Highlands in the 1970s, I had a collection of ornamental wildfowl – ducks, geese and swans of many different species. They were secured in a large enclosure fenced to six feet with stout netting to keep out foxes and badgers. During the first few years I was puzzled to find that birds as big as geese were disappearing without any obvious indication of the culprit; ducks and geese vanishing off their nests but never any sign of a struggle. So I set a large cage trap baited with a dead wood pigeon. In the morning I found myself staring into the flaring green eyes of a wildcat. I drove it to Glen Affric twelve miles away and released it into the ancient forest of the Caledonian Pine Reserve. Soon the predation started again. I reset the trap. Again I caught a cat, another large wildcat tom, hissing, spitting and angrily flicking its bushy tail. Off I went to Glen Affric again, marvelling at the strength of a cat that could snatch a weighty Canada goose from its nest and then climb a six-foot fence with the bird in its teeth, leaving scarcely a feather behind.

As Gavin Maxwell relates of his Highland home in the 1960s, back in those days wildcats did not seem to be rare on the west coast or in the remoter reaches of these glens. On winter nights we would often catch sight of their burning green eyes in our headlights. Gamekeepers on surrounding estates regularly hunted them down. Every year we heard of wildcats being shot or snared. In the 1970s, a local keeper known only as 'The Blue Charm' (after a much-favoured salmon fly) told me that in snares and gin traps he killed 'ten or more wildcats every year'.

As a child and well into my teens I barely questioned this gratuitous killing. It was what was done – the norm, part of the accepted culture of sporting estates the length and breadth of Britain – together with trapping, snaring and shooting of every hooked beak, every weasel, stoat, polecat, pine marten, hedgehog, otter, badger and fox, even herons and gulls; every creature, in fact, that might have the temerity to take a game bird, or its egg or its chick, as well as many innocent species that didn't. It was killing that those game-keepers were specifically employed to undertake, their success displayed on macabre gibbets, totems of murder, where the wind- and rain-shrivelled corpses of 'vermin' were proudly arrayed. To quote Maxwell again, 'the estate . . . had long waged war upon the wildcats, and a tree . . . was decorated with their banded tails hanging like monstrous willow catkins from its boughs'. I had seen many such gibbets in the woods around my English home and was drawn to them out of morbid curiosity, astonished by the numbers of birds nailed there: rows of jays, crows, magpies, sparrow-hawks, owls, kestrels, merlins, hobbys and buzzards, among the hapless weasels and stoats in their dozens.

The world has moved on significantly since then; protection laws have emerged and most people's values have shifted towards conservation, although there are still plenty who would put their 'sport' before any aspect of nature conserva-tion. Maxwell, I am pleased to record, writing in 1959, makes his own views entirely clear: 'the wildcats are (now) protected . . . Under this benign regime the number of wildcats has marvelously increased.' If only that were still the case today.

We all live by the instilled standards of our time. My grandfather certainly did, and I doubt whether he would have questioned the killing of wildcats. But extirpation? That's another matter, and I would like to think that he would have pulled back, as, interestingly, did the redoubtable John Colquhoun, who firmly advocates trapping against poisoning, whereas Charles St John heartily advocates *strychnia* as a tool of vermin control.

Illegal poisoning of birds of prey on sporting estates is still a very live issue in nature conservation circles, arguably worse now (2017) than it has been for most of my career. But surprisingly, and to his great credit, Colquhoun decries exterminating 'vermin' altogether. In a telling aside he states unequivocally:

> Clearing off the vermin by poison has been much in vogue in recent years. But, to say nothing of murdering all the dogs in the neighbourhood, it seems a pity to treat the now rare and interesting rovers of the desert like rats. This . . . may find favour with the man whose only pleasure in Highland sport consists of butchering game. For my own part I would rather trap one fine specimen of . . . the wild-cat or the marten, than shoot one hundred brace of grouse.

For all his killing, I fancy I hear the muffled beat of a conservationist heart, heavily disguised by the cultural mores of his day. In a later essay in Volume II, entitled *The Natural History of Sport*, he beats a drum familiar and endearing to my ears.

> A passing glimpse at the wilder and more interesting British animals is every year becoming less common,

since the cultivation of moorlands . . . draining, tree-planting etc. has, in many districts, driven away the aboriginal beasts of prey from haunts where they have prowled for centuries . . . When a schoolboy I remember how often the hen-roosts were plundered by pine-martens or wild-cats, which nightly crept forth from this sanctuary and the superstitious awe with which I listened in the calm twilight of summer to the cry of the tiger-cat to its fellow . . . For years this habitation of wild beasts has been swept away as if it had never been . . . call it improvement if you will . . . as an old sportsman I protest that some of our best fishing rivers have been ruined, our wild sport curtailed and our very climate modified . . . by these same labours of the improver. As the Indians fled before the white settlers, the remnants of our nobler predatory animals have sought refuge among remote Highland wilds, but they will find little sanctuary even there . . . [as] every . . . mountain and rugged moor are sought out and set apart exclusively for grouse and deer. Keepers have been commissioned to destroy the 'vermin' by exterminating as many as possible of our rarer and most interesting beasts and birds of prey; so that the eagle, the peregrine, the kite, the marten, the wild-cat . . . are fast receding . . . to make way for such real vermin as droves of pheasants, which afford no better sport than barn door fowls.

Well said, Mr John Colquhoun! Would that his words had been heeded by the sporting fraternity. We might still have some wildcats out there and some unsullied habitat for them. A hundred and thirty-five years after those words were written our task is immeasurably harder.

6

Rheumatic fever

For the first eleven years of her life my mother was a normal healthy child, a non-identical twin with her sister Margaretta. Then it happened. At 12.35 p.m. on Friday, 16 October 1931 the shining white-hulled 14,000-ton Royal Mail Ship *Corfu* eased away from the passenger boarding berth at London's Tilbury dock. It was the Peninsular & Orient liner's maiden voyage, off on the London to Hong Kong run via the Suez Canal, calling at Southampton, Port Said, Aden, Bombay, Colombo, Penang and Singapore. On board were 170 first-class and 211 second-class passengers; among them were the twins, Margaretta and Helen, with their eight-year-old sister, Priscilla, and their parents, bound for Port Said.

It was the girls' first experience of foreign travel, off to Cairo and on up the Nile to Aswan, where their father was to take up his post as a consultant engineer. During the passage through the Med, Helen developed an angry sore throat. Two weeks later, as they disembarked to travel upriver, she was running a high temperature. Glandular fever, the English ship's doctor had declared. He was wrong. So began the problems that would direct the course of her whole life.

*   *   *

Rheumatic fever has nothing to do with rheumatism. It derived its misnomer because some symptoms mirrored rheumatism. Commonplace in Britain during the world wars, it remains widespread in developing countries, especially those without ready recourse to antibiotics. It almost always affects children between the ages of eight and fourteen, eleven being the median norm, girls suffering more than boys. Caused by a bacterial *Streptococcus pyogenes* infection of the throat, nowadays it is easily treated with penicillin. If allowed to persist, it triggers an auto-immune response, which dramatically shifts the consequences of the disease from a fever to a far more devastating chronic condition. Early diagnosis and treatment are vital if the infection is to be prevented from sliding into full-blown rheumatic heart disease.

The infection causes the body's immune system to produce antibodies whose function is to attack the *Streptococcus* bacteria. The sore throat goes away, but in the process those same antibodies are corrupted, unable to detect the difference between the bacterial infection they are supposed to be attacking and other important parts of the body, such as the lining of arteries, heart valves and the heart muscle itself. It is known as 'antibody cross-reactivity'. Untreated, what appears to be just a nasty sore throat becomes a life-long, life-threatening illness.

The mitral valve is the most commonly affected, developing a thickening of the flaps, known as *mitral stenosis*, eventually failing altogether. The mitral and the aortic valves sit side by side. If the mitral valve doesn't close properly the blood flow to the aorta, the main artery to transport blood round the body, reduces, affecting the rhythm of the heartbeat and slowing the whole circulatory system down. But the auto-immune attack doesn't rest with the mitral valve, it spreads to the aortic valve, causing it to falter too. In severe cases the other two valves, the tricuspid and the pulmonary, also become damaged.

Even that isn't the end of the story. Patients experience shortage of breath and energy and develop a heart murmur – the Carey Coombs murmur – caused by the blood regurgitating back and forwards between leaking valves. The heart is forced to work harder, dilating its muscle tissue, causing an overall increase in the size of the whole organ. The risk of severe strokes from clots passing to the lungs greatly increases.

Rheumatic heart disease is not just a horror that afflicts young children. The corrupted antibodies go on gnawing away at the heart valves and muscles for decades, gradually affecting its victims more and more, taking between ten and twenty years to reveal itself as a serious, chronic and ultimately life-threatening disability.

*   *   *

Helen was taken to hospital in Cairo too late. The chance to kill off the infection had been missed. Antibody cross-reactivity had set in and she was irrevocably doomed to a life profoundly complicated by heart disease. Yet, true to form, those complications would not properly emerge for a further ten years, by which time she would be an attractive young woman just married to a tall and dashing Englishman.

Initially at a French convent in Zamalek, the affluent district of Cairo, genteel and cultured nuns had schooled her and her sisters. She was a bright, cheerful child, always smiling with a ready, rippling laugh and an irrepressible desire to please, secure and happy in their lush Gezira island-in-the-Nile home among flowering jacaranda, banana and golden mohr trees, and scented datura, whose white bell flowers swayed in the hot afternoon winds. But there was another side to her education.

On regular walks to Giza along the glittering Nile, egged on by her much more precocious twin Margaretta, hand in hand they explored the dim and aromatic alleyways of that ancient crowded city, always listening, watching and learning. Their pale peach skin, bobbed hair curling in just below their ears and held back with matching satin bows on kirby grips, their identical gingham dresses, waistbands with bows at the back, brown sandals buckled over white ankle socks, and their nursery-taught, delicately mannered British coyness – 'Be sure to say Please and Thank You to everyone you meet' – hovered over them as their guardian angel. It was an ancient Arab world that had changed little since Ptolemy wrote the Almagest. On these daring expeditions they made unlikely friends with the fierce-looking *thobe*- and *kibba*-robed Bani Rasheed tribesmen tending their donkeys and camels on the desert edge of that vast city.

The Bedouin were filthy and stank like goats. Fearsome curved *khanja* daggers were thrust through their braided robe belts. But the twins loved the haughty indifference in their hooded eyes and written deep into the creases on their hot-wind and sand-leathered eagle-beaked faces which stared out from beneath *kufiya* turbans. These rough-hewn men of the desert in their flowing *disdah*, *thobe* and *kibba* robes fascinated my mother. Over the following years she would spend hundreds of hours in their company, sitting quietly, observing and absorbing their always volatile and often violent exchanges, yet never feeling frightened or threatened. She would never forget those sharply etched nomads and their camel trains vibrating through the heat haze, slowly emerging or disappearing into the burning sands.

Those romantic images were not the only unforgettable influences from Egypt and the Bedouin. The tribesmen taught the girls to spit and belly laugh and to swear in Arabic. *'Imshi y' Allah! Yla'an haramak! Ibn himar!'* – an unladylike skill my mother retained all her life. Throughout my childhood she muttered curses at those who offended her, knowing full well that the chances of anyone in England understanding 'Clear off! Son of a donkey!' were always likely to be slim. In extreme cases she would resort to *'Ornak sharmoota!'* – 'Your mother is a whore' – followed by some far more lurid instruction beneath her breath. Proudly she wore the zigzag scar of what must have been a vicious camel bite on her upper arm.

My mother was a Romantic as much by instinct as by inclination. Later in life, in hushed reverence she relived her precious memories of the Sphinx of Giza, Luxor, the Aswan High Dam and the Nag Hammadi Barrage, Lake Nasser and Wadi Halfa, of lateen-sailed feluccas on the Nile, of water buffaloes along the banks tended by little Egyptian girls with gold earrings and long cotton *djellabahs*. During the Suez crisis in 1956 she wept bitterly when Gamal Nasser's resistance fighters dynamited the statue of Ferdinand de Lesseps, the French creator of the canal, and tipped it into the water. But the images most dear to her were the frankincense, cinnamon and cardamom-scented souks and the long, roped camel caravans carrying cargoes of dates and myrrh resin, undulating rhythmically through the desert like a convoy of ships rising and falling on the tide.

The remaining ten years growing up were spent almost exclusively overseas in Egypt, then Persia and on to Turkey when her father moved to Karabük as consultant to the new steel works British engineers were building on the dusty plain surrounded by the foothills of the Kolu Daglari

83

mountains. Helen and her sisters enjoyed a carefree child-hood laced with the exciting advantages of being raised at each posting in the rarified exclusivity of the secure and vibrant 1930s British ex-pat community.

Small crinkly-edged black-and-white photographs from the albums of her late teens reveal smiling and laughing gangs of young men and women at picnics and *chukar* partridge shoots in the hills, setting out on impromptu horse-back expeditions, and at barbecues and tennis parties at the large British encampment.

That she was thought to be a 'delicate' child did nothing to dampen her enthusiasm for life. She was bright, vivacious, unsnobbish and fun, always with confident opinions wrought of high principles, a natural linguist who loved music, ballet, opera, theatre, literature and, above all, people. Always with a ready smile, as much flashing in her blue-green eyes – the blue-green of blackbird eggs marbled with dove grey – as spreading across her high-boned cheeks. By eighteen she had grown to be shapely and attractive – a striking young woman – always spiced by her unassailable Romanticism and a quick, intuitive intellect, ever locating the best in people and endlessly redeeming their muddles, and by her characteristic silvery laugh. That cheerful positivity was an indomitable trait that would deliver great fortitude in the testing years ahead. At Karabük she became very attached to one of those young engineers. One man in particular, very tall, strong-featured with a centre parting and a wide moustache, appears with telling regularity in her photographs.

Her childhood had been full of adventure. She had been well; her health marred only by the occasional lack of energy. The rheumatic fever had been largely overlooked. She had apparently recovered fully and showed no outward signs of disability. The family had ceased to worry.

As a child Helen would have had no idea of the true gravity of her condition and, besides, by nineteen she was in love and engaged to marry the tall man in the photographs, John Christopher, the man who would become my father. He was twenty-six and well made. Six foot six, lanky and leggy, with a powerful upper frame. He had rowed for his university college, was an accomplished horseman and an excellent shot. He makes a comical figure in the photos, with his horizontal handlebar moustache and a trilby hat at a jaunty angle, a spotted silk cravat, hacking jacket, breeches and long riding boots, the embodiment of an extrovert character straight out of P.G. Wodehouse, always with a strong-jawed throwaway charm.

My father was quite definitely *not* a Romantic or a linguist. He was a hard-shelled pragmatist and an empiricist, a man with excellent hand and eye coordination who could make almost anything he turned his mind to, while the Arts, including music and literature – the whole creative canon – remained an impenetrable mystery to him. He was a man of rigid principles dictated by custom and instilled tradition, ever diligent with sound judgement, and never shying from hard work. I remember him only ever dressed formally, with a neat but unadventurous style, almost always in a tweed or worsted suit with a plain shirt and tie. He never possessed a pullover or a cardigan, condemning those who wore them as 'sloppy'.

The instincts that ruled his character were in unequivocal monochrome, black or white, with a resounding sinkhole between the two. There was right and there was wrong, good and bad, honourable and dishonourable: Nelson was good, Napoleon bad, degrees veering only to extremes. Churchill embodied everything noble, Hitler everything evil, no nonsense, no debate. He harboured immutable war prejudices against all Germans, while freely acknowledging their engineering expertise. For the same reasons he admired Holland – anything to do with water or the sea he would announce, 'Bring in the Dutch!' The French he dismissed as frivolous and unreliable, the Italians devious and untrustworthy, and the Spanish and Greeks 'bone idle'. Americans were loud, extravagant, vulgar and late. And yet, to his endearing credit, when events proved him wrong, he would laugh at himself and declare openly, 'Well, well, blow me down! I would never have guessed it.' Convention permanently hovered over my father's facial expressions, often revealed in an undecided conflict between form and a mischievous sense of fun that made him good company, his humour inclined toward irreverent and ribald.

Those carefree days in Turkey came to an abrupt end in 1939. The outbreak of war meant a chaotic dash back to England on what the London *Times* described as the 'last safe boat out of Istanbul'. Thunderous war clouds brooded over the whole of Europe, but at least the young couple had each other and their own future looked bright.

As a qualified civil engineer – a wartime 'reserved occupation' – my father was barred from enlisting, despite his pleading with all three armed forces. Instead he was seconded to Lord Nuffield's disastrously unproductive Spitfire engine factory at Castle Bromwich. Out of touch with the reality of war, Nuffield knew how to make motor cars – his was the Morris empire – but Britain needed aero engines far faster than he had ever made cars. My father often spoke of the extreme frustration among the young engineers that Nuffield had refused to adopt modern assembly line procedures. In 1940 Winston Churchill personally intervened. Nuffield was summarily sacked and replaced by the far more bullish Lord Beaverbrook as Minister of Aircraft Production.

My father was rapidly promoted and tasked with building munitions factories in the Black Country. He remained very proud of his contribution to the war effort for the rest of his life.

War changed everything; weddings were famously austere. The amateur photographs show my mother in a corduroy suit with peplum shoulders, her dark hair long and waved to her collar, tumbling down from the fashionable 1940s heart-shaped coiffure above. My father, hair slicked down from his habitual centre parting and neatly trimmed moustache, stands tall in baggy cavalry twills and a tweed sports jacket with leather patched elbows and cuffs. They were married on 7 March 1942 in Westbury-on-Trym parish church on the outskirts of Bristol, where my mother's parents had settled. She is clutching a bunch of daffodils.

Fifteen months later she fell pregnant with my sister Mary. As the pregnancy progressed so the doctors picked up a heart murmur, not from the baby's heart but from her own. The sinister growl of rheumatic heart disease was beginning to make itself heard. The Carey Coombs murmur. A succession of check-ups confirmed the worst. Her mitral valve had become stenosed, failing to open and close so that blood could be heard gurgling backwards and forwards between the two chambers in her heart's left ventricle. It was working overtime. She should not have tried to have children, the doctors said. Too late for that.

Evidently she was made of tougher stuff than they feared. The baby girl was born without complications, and mother and child flourished. But back came the dire warnings – strictly no more children. If a second birth proved difficult and her heart couldn't cope, she would almost certainly die. Quite probably so would the baby. I was being written off even before I was conceived.

In the 1940s doctors and surgeons were universally viewed with veneration. The profession, particularly those as rarified as cardiac specialists – the high priests of both medical and surgical disciplines – sat on pedestals, unchallengeable and unaccountable to their patients, way beyond the reach of ordinary mortals who accepted what they were told without question. Diagnoses, prognoses and decisions were delivered in solemnity and received with almost religious reverence.

Open-heart surgery, in so far as it existed at all, was still in its experimental infancy and would not be an option for another eight years. Besides, Helen felt well enough, perhaps a bit breathless now and again, but no significant chest pain, nothing unduly alarming. And the doctors must have been hugely encouraged that she had apparently sailed through the birth of my sister. Did my parents attempt to assess the risks of a second pregnancy? Or because it was wartime and everyone's future hung in the balance, did they do what every other young couple was doing, taking life day by day, week by week, hoping for the best, dodging the Blitz and shrugging their shoulders, '*Que sera, sera*'?

I am now astonished that in adulthood I never had these conversations with either of them. But the world was different then; some things were never discussed, emotions were reined in, seldom displayed. Fears and anxieties weren't analysed, rarely even revealed, awkward questions ducked. A redoubtable British stoicism ruled and kept lids firmly shut – the counselling culture would not be invented for another thirty years.

There were whole chapters of life's spicy cocktail that simply weren't mentioned. Sex was an absolute taboo to my parents' generation, not just unmentionable but unthinkable too. Even well into adulthood there was no breach in the wall, no chink of insight to the tender intimacies of their private lives. In our adolescence it was a denial that proved unhelpful; no one to turn to when blindly we stumbled and fumbled our way into the sexual morass. Years later I used to chuckle to myself when sitting watching television with them both. When a steamy embrace or a bed scene appeared, up went the newspaper and my father vanished from view, suddenly deeply attentive to the day's stock market wobbles, while my mother pretended not to have noticed and busied herself with her embroidery.

But I know from their letters that the *actualité* was very different. They were ardent lovers, full-blooded, bonded, rapt. Helen was an unshakable Romantic, loving and demonstrative by nature, and my father, although reserved, even aloof by inclination, was unquestionably all male. And they were in love. From the haze of distant hindsight I am struck by how little I really knew of my parents.

What I do know is that my mother was as soft as eiderdown, kind, gentle, forgiving and always blessed with an inextinguishable positivity. Her personality was ruled by the soaring gift of a generous spirit, not just to her children but to the whole world, always tempered by an invisible core of steel. She had no time for self-pity – although, dear God, she had cause enough – not in herself or in anyone else.

My father was a very different animal. He struggled to express any emotion at all. A brusque and laconic exterior gave an entirely false impression of uncaring insensitivity; in fact, I think he felt things very deeply but was unable to express them, no doubt the product of an austere Victorian upbringing by nannies and governesses. His response to a problem was instinctively pragmatic – find a quick and practical route to fixing it. If there was none available he fell silent, erecting a shield of denial that made him look as though he didn't care. It took me years to work out that his inability to share deeply-felt solicitudes was a burden he carried all his life. I never kissed or hugged my father, although deep down I never doubted that he would be there for me in a crisis. From his marriage to his death he was an unshakably stolid husband and father, a diligent provider and extremely hard worker for his family. We shook hands and we smiled and nodded to each other for my entire thirty-six years until his premature death. Such serious conversations as we ever had were brief and superficial, skirting around contention, awkwardness deftly avoided.

★ ★ ★

I was conceived in Yorkshire at the beginning of September 1945, only five miles from my family's deeper ancestral heartland. These were times of great national jubilation, despite all the grievous losses, including my mother's younger sister Priscilla, killed a year earlier while driving an army staff car that skidded on black ice. Hitler was dead; our boys were heading home. The war in Europe was over and at last Japan had conceded defeat. The world's first atomic bomb, 'Little Boy', had been dropped on Hiroshima on 6 August, and the second, 'Fat Man', on Nagasaki three days later. The Japanese Instrument of Surrender was signed on the deck of the USS *Missouri* in Tokyo Bay on 2 September 1945.

I shudder to think that I might have been conceived in the mood of exultation after such apocalyptic devastation, but, in fairness to my parents, the national relief must have been overwhelming after five years of deprivation and mayhem, and it is unlikely that until much later anyone in Britain had any real idea of the holocaust those two bombs visited upon those tragic cities' blameless civilians. Like many millions of others, my destiny was to be born a 'baby boomer'.

But such exhilaration as there might have been was to be shortlived. Only three months into the second pregnancy rheumatic heart disease's unwelcome overture re-emerged. At seven months my mother was admitted to hospital, struggling to carry the burden of a big baby. Worse, her placenta and her well-developed foetus were demanding more and more blood, causing the left ventricle to pump harder and the audible regurgitation through the now badly leaking mitral valve had thrown her heart into arrhythmia – an irregular and worryingly erratic heartbeat. Her whole bed was shrouded in an oxygen tent.

My birth was a close call. Her heart struggled valiantly yet horribly; the pressure in her left ventricle rose to the level of extreme danger. The chances of cataclysmic heart failure must have been very high indeed. But the gods were bountiful, and I emerged into this world a little blue but soon wailing loudly. I was whisked away, but my mother remained in dire distress, doctors and nurses fighting to save her life. She would remain at high risk for three weeks, with a nurse beside her day and night, and under close observation on a post-natal ward for a further six. Nobody knew the extent of the damage to her heart, but it would become evident soon enough. She would never be the same woman again. It would be a very long time before I knew it, and even longer before I properly understood it, but I had almost killed her.

*   *   *

Who can say when a child's awareness begins? Awareness needs a time, a place, events, sounds, smells, people, words, things done or not done, placed in order, fitted and received, all the essential marker buoys along the treacherous channel into comprehension's safe harbour. All children awaken to the world around them in fragments, a baffling mix of receptivity and inattention. Awareness waxes and wanes, like waking from sleep and drifting off again, clouds floating in, seen, then gone again until the next one wafts through. In *Cider with Rosie*, Laurie Lee's famous *First Light* was grass, 'each blade tattooed with tiger-skins of sunlight'. Mine was a table leg. A big old kitchen table. In the absence of a playpen in those immediately post-war days, I was imprisoned under that table and a sheet strung round all four legs, fencing me in. That's all there is to it. Just that. A first flickering of memory.

Then a three-year blank. A long, drawn-out blank of no memory at all, a blank of months yawning into years of staring out while all-uncomprehending, the world revolved around me, a world of immediate preoccupation with the mud-pie moment, a world without place or a name. I saw trees, birds skimmed through, sights with and without sounds; leaves trembled and flashed, light gave way to dark, sun to rain. Nameless voices garbled incoherently, footsteps came and went. Doors banged. My hands and chubby knees knew the grainy chill of flagstones. Buckets clanked, water gushed. A cockroach crawled across my hand. Months passed like the wind turning pages of a book, unread and silent, telling of nothing. Events flooding over me as a bright stream flows over stones, unremembered and lost, a dim and watery oblivion, life obscured behind a feral haze.

Then suddenly, without any warning, everything changed. I am sure I understood nothing of it at the time, but my mother became dangerously ill. In the way that you know instinctively that something is wrong, I had divined that she was the problem. Her illness was never discussed, certainly not in front of us small children. She disappeared to London. We lived our days with the dark vacuum of silence and absence. 'We've arranged for you to go to a new school,' she told me in a strange voice when she came back. I was not quite six and had no idea what was coming next.

What I can recall only survives as the disjointed fragments of some allegorical medieval fresco uncovered on a church wall, the gaps leaving us guessing at the parable. But those fragments have lived on, unsullied, as sharp and bright as a sunlit dawn: school outfitters to buy uniform; name tapes; wondering why on earth I needed number 18 on everything; trying on new black lace-ups which were too big and made me walk in a clumpy way; watching my trunk being packed, each item ticked off against an inventory – all clear signals that my life was about to change, but still no clue how. Most of all I remember how my mother clung to me, choking back tears, the day she was taken back to London. Not once did it cross my mind that the reason I was being sent away to boarding school was because a dark shadow had fallen across our family.

As a pre-prep, Hampton House School was probably unexceptional for the 1950s. I had never boarded before. It was just something that happened to me, like bad weather – no preparation, no reasons given, no option. My father drove me there in silence. New navy blue blazer with white bindings, a grey flannel shirt and blue tie, grey short trousers and long grey socks with blue turn-down tops and my navy cap with white HH monogram above the peak, I sat on the back seat's shiny leather the colour of ginger biscuits. I remember fiddling with the rotating Bakelite ashtray under the window; it popped in and out as you pushed it.

He smoked his pipe as he drove and if I close my eyes I fancy I can still see the frantic flick of the windscreen wipers and hear the distinctive whine from the old Riley gearbox. I don't believe I had formulated any clear picture of what was happening or where I was going, or even why. Yet those memories I have retained are as vivid as yesterday's, made sharper and in stronger relief, I now realise, by just two things – looming fear of the unfamiliar and the cold slap of loneliness. Everything else has washed out. I was suddenly there without any idea that something was horribly and permanently wrong. Children didn't get explanations back then.

He carried my old battered trunk, his and his father's before him, in from the car. Other arriving boys and parents bustled around me as I watched with the detached indifference of watching a bad film. Then 'Goodbye, dear boy. Don't forget to write.' We shook hands. He turned on his heel and was gone.

7

Hearts and minds

In 1903, twenty-eight years before my mother's fateful journey to Cairo, in a modest middle-class home in Clapham, London, Herbert Brock's wife Elvina gave birth to their fourth child, Russell Claude, in what would eventually be a family of six sons and two daughters. Herbert was a 'master photographer' specialising in weddings, portraits and commercial photography. They can never have dreamed that their son would become Lord Brock, the world's most celebrated heart surgeon of his day.

Aged eighteen, Russell elected to read medicine at Guy's Hospital Medical School, passing up with an arts scholarship. Five years later he graduated with honours and distinction in medicine, surgery and anatomy. Aged only twenty-five, Russell Brock could display LRCP (Lond.), MRCS (Eng.), MB, BS and FRCS after his name. He was on his way.

That year he won a Rockefeller travelling fellowship to work in St Louis, Missouri, with the great American thoracic surgeon Evarts Graham – the first surgeon to successfully remove a lung and the first to attribute lung cancer to cigarette smoking. Graham had also attempted open-heart surgery in a bold effort to resolve the commonest of valve complications, mitral stenosis. He failed. All his patients died. It was a pivotal moment in the young Russell's career and he would never forget Graham's distress. The experience had handed him a cause forged by the best possible tutelage, and he knew it. In 1936 he returned to London and was immediately appointed consultant surgeon to both Guy's and the Royal Brompton Hospital in Chelsea. Cardiac and thoracic surgery was now his chosen discipline, both areas of extreme challenge at the cutting-edge of medical science. In 1938 he was honoured with a Hunterian Professorship, the highest accolade in medicine. He was only thirty-five.

By 1947, a year after I was born, Russell Brock had established a thoracic surgical unit at Guy's and turned his full attention to resolving problems with heart valves. He argued that stenosis could easily be rectified by surgery if only techniques could be refined to keep the patient alive. Surgical grandees at the apex of the profession disagreed. Russell was not deterred. He was on a mission, determined to find a way of performing successful open-heart surgery.

Even at that tender age Russell Brock's force of character – never taking no for an answer – had established a potent work ethic. He was a perfectionist and unquestionably driven, but always meticulously fair, while famously intolerant of others who didn't share his absolute dedication – or his views. He abhorred pomposity and sloppiness, and could be abrupt and incisive to a point of rudeness, as well as coldly dismissive of those he considered unequal to the task in hand; but such was his reputation and his unswerving loyalty to those colleagues he valued and respected that his pioneering procedures were very rarely challenged.

He had chosen to focus all his considerable intellect and skills upon the correction of mitral stenosis. He began a series of operations in September 1948, using his finger to break the restrictions in the valve flaps, a procedure he named *mitral valvotomy*. But he was a consultant surgeon, a wielder of scalpels. All good surgeons need to work with equally

gifted physicians. Accurate diagnosis and the medical preparation of a patient for some weeks before what was always
a life-endangering procedure was essential for success. In
1950 a brilliant young physician took over as director of the
cardiology department at the Royal Brompton Hospital. Dr
Paul Wood was forty three, four years Russell Brock's junior.
His textbook, *Diseases of the Heart and Circulation*, had gained
him immediate worldwide recognition as *the* European
authority on heart disease.

Paul Wood had specialised in studying rheumatic fever
and its concomitant heart complications. He pioneered the
analysis of pulse signals from arteries in different parts of
the body and the irregular rhythms of heartbeats, reading
the murmurs within the heart vessels in order to achieve
accurate diagnosis of precisely which valves were causing
the problems. His skill became legendary. With little more
than a stethoscope he could build an accurate picture of
what state a diseased heart was in. It is no surprise that to
this day the cardiac unit at the Brompton Hospital is named
after him.

As a man Paul Wood was the antithesis to Russell Brock,
an opposing polarity that would bring them together as
inseparable colleagues and firm friends. Paul was an extrovert, revelling in his own individual brand of sarcasm, often
witheringly funny, and a taskmaster who took no prisoners.
If Russell Brock didn't suffer fools, Paul Wood shredded
them, and yet his students adored him. He could tease out
a diagnosis with the analytical incisiveness of Sherlock
Holmes, dazzling his audience.

A slight figure, he was balding with a domed forehead
and a sharp nose like a beak. Blue eyes boldly flashing, he
spoke quickly and with total confidence. He never engaged
in tact and pulled no punches, simply not his style. If he

was critical of a procedure or a colleague, regardless of rank, he could be fiercely combative, never backing down. And yet in his patients he inspired confidence and absolute trust – a vital psychological as well as clinical preparation for the terrifying uncertainty his patients had to face.

Russell Brock took to him immediately. It was a meeting of minds and causes, a marriage of Titans, the world's leading heart surgeon partnered with the world's top authority on hearts. Arriving at the Brompton to work with Russell Brock had handed them both a unique opportunity to develop their skills jointly – to become the finest cardiac team the world had ever known.

* * *

In 1936, the year of Russell Brock's appointment to the Royal Brompton, my mother was a happy sixteen-year-old skipping about Turkey with her twin sister, having fun at picnics and tennis parties and galloping off into the hills on horseback. In the ten years leading up to my birth she had become a fulfilled wife and mother. She can little have guessed that everything was about to change. I wouldn't understand it properly until adulthood, but giving birth to me had strained her heart badly and brought into stark focus her heart's seriously deteriorating condition – an irrational culpability I have felt keenly ever since.

After my birth she remained in hospital for three months, but even after being allowed home she suffered constant breathlessness and lack of energy. By 1950, the year Russell Brock and Paul Wood started working together at the Brompton, her disease had rapidly worsened. My mother was seriously ill. She was closing down. The problem, as yet formally undiagnosed, was the gradual malfunction of her mitral valve. The heart muscle was struggling badly. She was at imminent risk of total cardiac failure. Without urgent surgery she would die.

*   *   *

It is difficult now to piece together the events of the next few years. Up to the age of five, of course, I remember virtually nothing, but what I can recall very vividly was the sense that something was wrong, or perhaps I should say *missing*. In truth, of course, my mother was missing – not all the time, but regularly – and even when she was at home and with us, she was often unwell. She got up late and was forced to lie down in the middle of the day; she couldn't carry her small children or run and play with us. Whispered parental anxieties framed our days, and the coming and going of doctors was an accepted feature of our lives.

She would go away for several days, but we were never told where. 'Mummy will be home soon,' became an apologetic mantra wheeled out over and over again. Either silenced by worry or just an Edwardian ineptitude with small children, our father was studiously mute. It was as though the grown-ups had enjoined a conspiracy of non-explanation – that children didn't *need* to know. It was all we got, and it hurt without ever knowing why. A hollow emptiness consumed me when she was absent, and when she came home I lived out a fear, like a perpetually nagging ache, that someone would whisk her away again. I had no concept of how very ill she was, but the dark spectre of the Dun Cow rib would not go away. Somewhere deep inside, in some hidden recess of my collective consciousness, a primeval animal instinct was nurturing the seeds of mistrust.

Then came the sudden and unwelcome event that would harpoon itself into the delicate flanges of my memory forever – school, boarding school. I was still only five. Every morning I sneaked into her bed to cuddle up to my mother, the scented sanctum of ultimate warmth and security. The memory vivid. She had hugged me tight, unwittingly increasing the force of its impact. 'We've arranged for you to go to an exciting new school – a boarding school.' There was a tremor in her voice, an uncharacteristic hesitation despite the forced smile and the hug. I am sure she was clinging to me as much to conceal her own swirling emotions as it was a desperate attempt to shore me up.

I knew well enough what school was. But *boarding*? 'What's a boarding school?' I asked from the echoing chasm of innocence. She did her best to soften it but the answer came as a shock. 'You'll have your own bed with friends of your own age in a dormitory.' Another new word. 'It's just a big bedroom,' she tried again.

I had never given any thought to sleeping anywhere except at the Manor House or at home, in my own room, with my sister in hers across the landing and my parents at the end of the passage. Even being taken on shopping expeditions to buy uniform and equipment did nothing to help me understand that from now on, aged barely six, for three-quarters of the year I would be living somewhere else with complete strangers. Nor did I have the faintest clue that I was being sent away because she was going to London for someone to slice open her heart with a scalpel and that there was an odds-on chance she might never come back.

'The boy will be fine,' my father said.

* * *

It would be years before I knew, far less understood, what my parents had gone through. Now, with the benefit of access to her letters – carefully guarded secrets not discovered until after my father's death – I have been able to piece things together.

Death from rheumatic heart disease was commonplace in the '40s and '50s and it was widely known that the route to surgical correction was studded with the gravestones of those who never made it. Our parents will have been in no doubt how fraught with complications the new and revolutionary procedures were. My mother writes in one of her letters to my father, *'Dr Wood has told me that the chances of a severe stroke are very high.'* Paul Wood's reputation for plain speaking preceded him; he had left her in no doubt.

Two letters, written immediately before that first surgery, lay out her fortitude and her fears. The first, written from her Brompton Hospital bed on 5 September 1953, twenty-four days before the operation:

> *My dearest Christopher,*
> *I slept better last night. I really feel happier knowing that possibly something can be done – what about you? I hope your faith doesn't allow you to have fears about my making the grade! Nothing will be done until it is all thoroughly chewed over. Mr Brock will see you and put all his cards on the table – I thought it was all going to be so simple, but apparently not so – well, we've come so far, we will just have to face this. Paul Wood is coming to speak to me on Tuesday. I shall know much more then.*

There followed an unexpected insight into both my mother's endlessly caring personality and a gentle sideswipe at my father's inadequacy with his children:

> *Felt rather worried after Saturday. I thought dear Jay sounded*
> *so tired and sad. Give him lots of love, darling, he seems such*
> *a tough little guy, but he needs lots of love – an occasional*
> *cuddle from Daddy won't do him any harm.*

The second letter, written in fountain pen in her elegantly fluid hand on the day of the operation, is much more revealing:

> *My own darling Christopher,*
> *I can't thank you enough for your wonderful words of encour-*
> *agement. I feel wonderfully calm and am quite prepared for*
> *the pain I shall have to endure . . . I have everything on my*
> *side and so much to get well for – the best husband ever and*
> *our wonderful children. Thanks to God's help and your great*
> *love, I have been able to face up to this thing. Alone I couldn't*
> *face it. Never forget that I love you now – and always will.*
> *Helen.*

8

Hampton House

We were twenty-two boys aged about six to eight, and a few dayboys – Daybugs – whom we boarders viewed as a wholly inferior caste. At eight years old we would be expected to ascend to the Junior School, a full-blown boarding prep school a quarter of a mile away down an avenue of ragged Scots pines. But at six, eight was still light years away, an unimaginable seniority I could only view with that hollowing-out dread of the deep unknown. By day and night the spectre of fear loomed unbidden in my heart. It surrounded me in every direction and was contagious. I could sense it in the other new boys' faces: fear of older boys, fear of teachers, fear of being late or being in the wrong place or wearing the wrong clothes, fear of being laughed at, but the greatest fear of all was yet to come. It would be many weeks before it finally dawned that home would never be the same again.

His name was Bettesen, David Bettesen, if after all these years of neither remembering nor trying to I can scrape together such crumbling flakes of detail. We were required to use surnames only, but nicknames stuck best. I recall a timid and sensitive boy with a round button mouth and a hesitant smile that was always there, hovering around his lips, but which never quite made it to his cheeks. If I close my eyes I can see him clearly – a thatch of wheat-sheaf hair and pale blue questioning eyes behind wire-framed glasses, a troubled face where diffidence ruled over any hope of conviction. The sort of child you look at twice to make sure he's all right. A boy without vice who wore his vulnerability like a delicate flower. We called him 'Betty'.

We were new boys and immediate friends in an amity of torment, born of an unspoken but equally shared homesickness, a sickness that clamped down upon us like gathering storm clouds at nightfall and was still firmly parked on our chests when we awoke in the morning, an inner desolation that held us permanently teetering on the precipice of tears. Every night I fell asleep aware that in the next bed Betty was silently sobbing into his pillow, a choking intimacy of despair. It was a misery I felt keenly but was unable to evince by day with anything more than a perpetually repeating sigh and a longing I couldn't revoke.

In my sponge bag my mother had lovingly placed a tiny white handkerchief with a lace border, dabbed with her one and only perfume, sandalwood with a note of hyacinth. She must have known I would be unhappy, but events had closed in on us all and given her no choice. Years later she told me that she'd felt a terrible traitor agreeing to send me away, an enforced betrayal wholly counter to her loving instincts. In bed I put that handkerchief under my cheek so that I could wallow in its fragrance. She and the scent permanently fused. It intensified the emotion, bringing it close to anguish. It was an unshielded, unadrenalined pain, fiercely resolute, which raged unchecked like a fever through every pore of my being. If I bit hard on my bottom lip I found that I could focus it, bringing myself to the very edge of crying out, and then, letting go, spinning briefly and blissfully into the surging wave of relief. I did it over and over again until exhaustion dragged me into unconsciousness. Sometimes it drew blood and I would awake to find the pillow spotted and smeared like a medieval bride's nuptial sheet.

Betty's bed was next to mine in the corner of a dormitory of ten uniformly black iron hospital beds with squeaky springs, bars and knobs like knuckles at the joints, head and foot, mattresses of bristly black horsehair unlike the hair on any horse I'd ever seen. On dark-stained floorboards they stood in two perfectly spaced rows of five beds, feet to feet like a ward, separated by a highly polished brown Lino aisle down the middle, at the far end a big cream-painted cast-iron radiator with sharp vertical ridges. In our leather soled house shoes we could sprint halfway down the aisle and then skid as if on skates, slamming right into the radiator. One afternoon Betty forgot that gym shoes wouldn't slide. He was fast. His dash catapulted him head first into the radiator and smashed his glasses. Blood spurted out of the top of his head in a six-inch fountain. It wasn't serious and he quickly recovered, but the image was permanently fixed. I'd never seen anything like that before.

Each bed was robed in a blanket of pillar-box red. These were topped with a travelling rug of our own. Some boys' rugs were bright tartan, others of more sombre hue, mine a country weave of black and white hounds' tooth, yet others of plain camel or grey herringbone. Every morning before breakfast we had to fold our rugs into a measured rectangular bolt across the foot of the bed, slippers placed with military precision beneath.

The school was run by a well-rounded lady in her forties called Mrs Warmley, who, all these years later, I still view among the angels with a disposition as sweet as a peach. I can see her now, a gently spoken soul with lines tickling the corners of her kind eyes, sympathy inscribed in runes, and a fizzing goldfish tank in her large study bedroom. Her overshot lower jaw seemed somehow to be detachable, to swivel sideways like a camel's, clicking as she spoke. A man in RAF pilot's uniform smiled from a photograph on her sideboard, but never any mention of Mr Warmley. We guessed he might have been killed in the war.

She had meticulously flowing handwriting, always with a Waterman's green-and-gold-marbled fountain pen with royal blue ink; the pen vertically clipped to the front of her dress, nestling between her large baggy bosoms so completely that when she sat down it vanished altogether. It fascinated us. We giggled about it, waiting for it to pop out again. She taught us English and French. '*Ou est ma plume?*' she would ask the whole class and we giggled again.

Before bed she read us the Chronicles of Narnia with her spectacles on the end of her nose, knitting as she read from a big winged armchair, needles and jaw gyrating and clicking in unison, fountain pen nowhere to be seen. Teeth cleaned, hair brushed, and in our dressing gowns and slippers, we sat cross-legged in a semi-circle on her carpet. Trenchard Minor was allowed to sit on a cushion. Later we learned he had just been circumcised. We called him 'Snipit'. I imagined Mrs Warmley had written the chronicles herself with that fountain pen and I loved her for that. She made boarding slightly more tolerable. If it hadn't been for Betty and Mrs Warmley, I would have run away.

We were nearest the dormitory door, Betty and I, beside the rows of pegs where our camel dressing gowns hung in more perfect spacing on either side of the door. A floorboard in the passage creaked as Miss Beech, tall and skinny, hollow cheeked and flat chested, hair in a mean knot at the back of her head, crept up to listen for talking after lights out. We dubbed her 'Twig'. She was in charge of us juniors. She ruled our days and nights with malevolent and despotic zeal.

At the time we just accepted Twig as a hovering dread in our lives, an ever-present foreboding of trouble. It preceded her like a bad smell, there whether we deserved her ire or not. Looking back, I now feel a twilit glimmer of sympathy for her. In childhood or as a young woman I realise that life had dealt Muriel Beech a bum hand; she was plain and had learned it painfully when some acid circumstance had soured her against the world. We were her only outlet for that bitterness and she couldn't conceal it. It seeped from every pore.

Beside the door, we were sentries. I could detect her shadow eclipsing the crack of light under the door. 'Cave! Twig!' flew round the dorm, whispered from bed to bed. If she heard us she burst in like a tidal wave, snapping the lights into dazzling glare and brandishing a gym shoe. 'Out of bed!' she'd bark. 'You, you and you. Bend down and touch your toes.' She spat out the words, seeming to pick her victims at random. Then she walloped them.

The rest of us lay and watched her swinging into the task. *Thwaap!* went the gym shoe, *thwaap! thwaap! thwaap!* onto small, tight, thinly pyjama'd buttocks. The boy's sharp intake of breath at each blow, the leap back into bed and the struggle to hold back tears. Behind her glasses her eyes were cold and grey; the left one was a few degrees off kilter and wandered aimlessly so that you never quite knew where she was looking or whether it was you she was addressing. When she was angry it gyrated like an aspen leaf in a breeze, her whole unhappy presence shedding fear as a flower sheds scent.

If one of those eyes spotted someone's slippers not placed correctly beside the bed leg she'd wallop him too. She picked on boys she didn't like; Sutton got thrashed over and over again. When he contracted poliomyelitis and left, she switched her ire to Hobson. But she also had favourites, a goody-goody called Holdsworth whom we branded a sneak, and Shawcross, a small boy with blond curls and cinnamon freckles dusting the bridge of his nose. They never got beaten, wherever their slippers were.

We feared Twig. I was convinced she was Narnia's White Witch in disguise. At night I imagined her riding in the sleigh, shrieking orders at the slavering wolves running alongside. She aroused in us dark and troubling emotions we had never encountered before. Hatred sprung sweet and shocking in such tender human breasts. We were too innocent to understand that her nocturnal assaults had little to do with discipline – her spinsterly frustrations made manifest and visited upon us in violent raids of spite.

Every night before lights-out we were made to kneel at our bedside and say our prayers while Twig stalked up and down the aisle peering to see if our eyes were closed. I prayed silently for deliverance, for Aslan to invoke the Deep Magic so that he could spring out from behind a rock with an ear-splitting roar clawing Twig to the ground, fangs plunging into her neck, blood squirting out of the top of her head like Betty's.

Aslan, it seemed, might have been listening. Once, in the dead of night, a boy named Hewitt jumped out of bed, downed his pyjama bottoms and fired an uncontrollable explosion of diarrhoea into the middle of the Lino aisle. Wailing, tears flooding down his cheeks, he stood barefooted with his dung-drenched pyjamas around his ankles, surrounded by an expanding morass of evil-smelling excrement. Someone flicked on the lights. We sat up blinking and recoiling at the overpowering stench that quickly filled the dorm. 'Better get Twig,' they said.

She appeared in her flannel night attire with a woollen

shawl thrown round her shoulders. The harsh light shone back from a greasy white cream applied liberally to her cheeks and brow, making her ashen and ghostly. We'd never seen her hair untied before, hanging in ragged cats' tails onto the shawl. She looked older than usual and, for the first time, powerless. She gasped at the sight in front of her. 'Stay where you are,' she snapped at Hewitt. Then she turned and disappeared. He began to wail all over again.

Twig returned with Mrs Warmley in a long blue candlewick dressing gown, white curlers in her hair like breaking surf. 'Get a bucket and a mop,' she told Twig. 'And you'll need Jeyes Fluid.' Then she took Hewitt by the hand, helped him step clear of his pyjamas, wrapped him in a towel and whisked him away. We could hear the bath running. Some minutes passed before Twig came back, now incongruously dressed in tracksuit bottoms, gumboots, rubber gloves and an apron, carrying two buckets of hot water and a mop.

By now we had woken up properly and the first glimmer of entertainment was rising within us like a winter dawn. We lay doggo and silent, our noses clenched into the top sheet like a row of Bedouin in a sandstorm. Were we really going to witness our nemesis reduced to cleaning up shit? The suspense was unbearable, gripped by agonies of delighted reckoning. Twig set to, clanking the bucket handles in ill-concealed disgust, down on her knees, hauling in the faecal mess with a towel and wringing it out in the hot water. Betty and I threw each other glances. Our faces creased and we sniggered. The acrid reek of Jeyes Fluid caught in our throats and slowly overcame the stench.

For twenty minutes, retching and recoiling, the subject of our direst loathing was utterly humiliated before our eyes. The force of the eruption had splashed Hewitt's tartan rug and the end of his bed. She had to strip it back to the mattress, carrying the offending bedclothes away with her. We felt triumphantly bewildered, trapped between the urge to laugh out loud and jeer, and the fear of terrible retribution if we had. She avoided our eyes, only snarling 'Go back to sleep' as she swept out.

Mrs Warmley returned the white-faced Hewitt to his remade bed. 'Please try and make it to the lavatory if it happens again,' she implored as she tucked him up. 'Now straight back to sleep, please, boys.'

In class Twig was vile. We dreaded her lessons; longed for the gentle caress of Mrs Warmley's kindness. I was a precocious reader, taught on my mother's knee. At six I could read well. I loved books. 'You'll never feel lonely with a book,' my mother had said. Mrs Warmley had smiled generously: 'I hear you love reading. That's marvellous.' But it was Twig who took us for reading lessons. 'We'll see,' she had sneered.

In one of her first lessons she had handed out an early-reader picture book about a Mr Fox with a narrow snout and long whiskers, pointed black ears, slanty eyes and a long bushy tail. He lived in a burrow house with a green door set among the roots of a huge tree on a bank. The five or six lines of text on each page were large, printed below extravagant and jaunty illustrations. Night after night Mr Fox snatched chickens from a farm until the farmer called in the hunt. It chased him over the hills and far away; a timeless country tale made all the simpler to comprehend because I was a country boy and so familiar with it. I read it in a flash, flicking through the twelve pages to the end. Twig saw me close it.

'Open the book,' she screeched.

'I've read it,' I answered, unwisely.

'Oh, he's read it!' she jeered to the whole class. 'Did you

hear that, boys? Well, you'd better come up here and read it out loud to us all.' I got up and shuffled forward. 'Face the class.' She spat the words at me.

I had read it, diligently, right through. It began 'Beneath an old oak tree on the edge of the wood . . .', but that first large capital letter 'B' of the first word on the first page was not a proper letter. It didn't resemble anything I had ever seen in an alphabet. It was a fox slouching against the bank with its legs crossed and its body and tail fashioned into an ornate and indecipherable B. I couldn't recognize it as a 'B' at all. Or anything else. And the rest of the word in normal script 'eneath' meant nothing to me. So I left it out, starting 'an old oak tree on the edge . . .'

'Start at the beginning.' She cut me off, voice edged with malice as sharp as vinegar. Her wobbly eye zoomed off on its own. I faltered, battling with tears prickling my eyelids. 'Come along,' she insisted. 'Read.'

'Please, Miss Beech, I can't read that first . . .'

'Oh, you can't read, eh? Did you hear that, boys? He can't read. I thought you said you'd read it all.'

'I have, Miss Beech, honestly, but I can't . . .'

'But you can't read. That's it, isn't it? You were lying. You can't even read the first word.' The tears won. 'And now you're blubbing because you've been caught out. Get back to your seat and don't you ever lie to me and the class again.'

At the end of the lesson she told me to go to her room. 'Bend down and touch your toes.'

9

London

'Mrs Warmley wants to see you,' Twig growled as we filed into the dining room. 'Go to her room after breakfast.'

'What for?'

'You'll find out soon enough. Now stop dawdling.' She stalked away. Fear flooded in, edged and bitter in my throat. Was I in trouble? What had I done? What was happening?

I asked Betty. 'Dunno,' he whispered with an empty, unhappy face, immediately afraid he was in trouble too.

Every once in a while there was a random inspection of our tuck boxes and lockers, usually by Twig. If we'd been given sweets we had to hand them in – bull's eyes, sherbet lemons, humbugs, toffees and barley sugars – to be pooled and shared out on Sundays. Sweet rationing had only just been lifted; sugar and cocoa had been unobtainable throughout the war. To many boys they were almost a novelty, certainly a luxury. My mother had made me some peppermint creams in little screws of greaseproof paper. She had written loving messages on each one encrypted with a code: *ILY*. It was our secret. I hated handing the sweets in, but had to. Every Sunday I looked out for them on the tray as it was passed round. They never appeared, but I knew where they had gone.

A few weeks earlier I had been summoned to Twig's room for some minor misdemeanour. I stood staring at the floor while she dressed me down. 'Yes, Miss Beech,' I heard myself mutter, 'Sorry, Miss Beech.' My eyes strayed to one side. There were the dreaded gym shoes on the floor beside her waste paper basket. I found myself staring down at several of those precious screws of paper with my mother's handwriting clearly visible – *ILY*. Tears welled up. 'Oh, do stop snivelling,' she had sneered.

'Sorry, Miss Beech.'

'And stop saying sorry when you don't mean it. Go away.' Bursting with rage and antipathy I ran to the lavatories to dry my eyes. Hurt and anger were flaring in my head like a Roman candle, the hurt of injustice and the anger of a child's utter impotence. I kicked the lavatory door and then ran to tell Betty.

'She's a pig,' he said.

I wondered why clean clothes had been put out for me that morning. Grey flannel shirt, long socks, my Sunday short trousers and blazer. Timidly I knocked on Mrs Warmley's door. 'Ah, good. Come along in, John.' Her voice was calm; a velvet kindness issued in waves, like a tropical breeze. The dangling fountain pen was strangely reassuring. Tension avalanched away. I was still puzzled, but I knew it wasn't trouble. 'My goldfish need feeding.' She moved a chair over to the fizzing tank. 'Would you like to do it?'

'Yes, *PLEASE*.'

'Hop up here.' She handed me a little tub of flakey, multi-coloured food. 'Now just a pinch between your fingers – that's it – spread it around a bit to make sure they all get some. That's enough. You mustn't overfeed them because it makes the tank smelly.' I could hear her jaw clicking beside my ear. The fish mouthed 'O's at the flakes and darted away, returning again almost immediately. I was fascinated. 'Jump down,' she spoke gently, but the breeze had shifted, chill slithering in. Something was wrong. She sat down and the fountain pen vanished into its mammary crevasse. 'Now, John, your father is coming to collect you at eleven o'clock. I'm afraid your mother is not very well.'

Not very well? What did that mean? She was often not very well – everyone knew that. Had she caught a cold or was it the 'flu I'd heard so much about? I didn't like to ask. It didn't seem very unusual or very important; besides, a burst of sunlight had shafted through – I was going HOME. The joy of it was pinging around in my head like the bagatelle mother and I often played together. I wanted to shout out, *Yippee!* But I didn't. School had engendered a dampening sense of decorum. Mrs Warmley was Mrs Warmley, the headmistress, and I liked her. I liked her all the more because Twig was so vile. And this was her room. You didn't shout *Yippee!* in Mrs Warmley's room, even if you thought you were going home.

She saw my face light up and hurried to soften the blow. 'You'll be away for the weekend. Your father will bring you back on Monday. Matron has put some overnight things in a bag for you.' She nodded towards a small holdall near the door. I stared at it. I'd never needed an overnight bag if I was going home before. 'What's that for?' The words were out before I could stop them. She sensed the bewilderment straightaway. She stood up. There was the pen again, its marbling catching the light, wobbling as she spoke. 'You'll need it for where you're staying in London.'

'London? Why am I going to London? Aren't I going home?' Hope teetered like a jogged vase about to fall.

'No, I'm afraid not. Your mother is in hospital in London, John. You're going to see her there.'

'Oh.'

*   *   *

My world had imploded. Not because she was in hospital but because I wasn't going home. I was used to her being away. No threat there, that was normal. But *HOME*, that was different. Home was freedom: the unfettered freedom of gardens beneath scudding clouds, woods and fields, catching minnows and sticklebacks in streams. The rough caress of tree climbing; the velvet nose of the old grey mare in the orchard twitching and slobbering against my hand as I fed her slices of apple; the moorhens' soggy nest on the pond; turning stones for great-crested newts like miniature dragons. Home was the prattling chitter of starlings and sparrows nesting in the Manor House stables' roof; newborn kittens in a manger of sweet hay; finding the fox in the oak stump or peering into the dank gloom of a badger sett in the paddock bank. 'Mr Brock lives down there,' my grand-father had said. 'Can you smell 'im?' I knelt on the sandy mound of their diggings, bent to the hole and breathed deeply. 'He's all right, Mr Brock is. He's a grumpy old blighter, but he minds his own business.'

My father arrived. 'Hullo, old chap. Jump in.' Tobacco as rich as cinnamon; the flickering indicator that stuck out of the side of the car. The Bakelite ashtray again – out-in-out-in. 'Damn and blast!' he cursed when a bus pulled out in front of us as we swept into a town. I was relieved when we hit country again. Woods and fields I knew and understood.

'How much further?'

'Not long now.'

Suddenly more buildings than I had ever seen. Taxis. Buses. People walking and on bicycles. Earls Court on a sign. 'South Ken,' he said as though I ought to know what it was. A hotel – De Vere . . . something? A bell-boy in a maroon uniform and a pill-box hat carried my bag. 'Look sharp, old bean.' Up some carpeted stairs, two at a time. He gave the maroon lad a sixpence. A room with two beds, flat wooden bars head and feet, and a marble washstand with a mirror; bath and lavatory along the corridor

'Can we see Mummy now?'

'All right, old thing. On our way.'

Small hand clutching huge, we stepped out into the street. Traffic again. Red double-deckers, people in raincoats, crowded pavements, long queues at bus stops. Men in bowler hats with umbrellas, striding out. Pigeons in the gutter. Half-running to keep up. 'Taxi! – Brompton Hospital, please.' The cab rattled. Brakes squealed. I noticed his fingers were raw round his nails, one thumb was bleeding and my father kept sucking it. 'Three bob, please, gov.' The taxi rattled away. Then steps and a brass handrail. Steps with shiny metal edges, down, down, down and round and down again, into a tunnel.

I can see that tunnel clearly. Its walls were cream and its ceiling domed in a complete semi-circle, pipes and cables pinned to it, wartime posters on the walls. One showed a smiling nurse. 'Make nursing your . . .' The bottom bit torn away. Another said 'Don't forget your gas mask' underneath a picture of someone wearing one just like ours. He tugged me along. The steel plates on his brogues' heels rang out on the concrete floor. Nurses in royal blue capes with scarlet linings and stiff white caps, blue bands crisscrossed in front, came toward us in twos and threes, laughing.

'Why are they laughing?' I asked.

'Prob'ly going off duty,' he replied distantly. 'Heading home.'

I wished I were heading home.

'Are we going home tomorrow?' A nagging hope surfaced.

'No. Sorry, old thing. Back to school tomorrow night.' My heart sank. Then he continued, 'But I'll tell you what – we've got a new house.'

'Oh,' I uttered, nonplussed. *Why do we need a new house?* I wondered. 'Where?'

'It's down in Somerset, a place called Martock. I need to be down there for work. You'll really love it.' I didn't know what to say. I couldn't imagine loving anywhere other than the Manor House. 'Will Nellie be there?' I asked.

'No, of course not, you silly old thing. Nellie's needed where she is.' The conversation died. Whatever my father intended by tipping in that bit of news had passed me by. If it was meant as a distraction it failed dismally, just another worry.

The tunnel echoed and seemed never-ending. 'We're under the Fulham Road,' he volunteered, changing tack. He could have said under Timbuktu or the Taj Mahal. I'd never heard of the Fulham Road – never been to London. 'If you put your ear to the wall you can hear the traffic up above.' I did. There was a sort of rumble, but I wouldn't have known what it was. 'We'll come up inside the hospital. Nearly there.' I ran ahead.

He tapped out his pipe on the wall and buried it in his pocket. A lift with clanky sliding gates you could see through – two gates. Inside smelt of Jeyes Fluid. I thought of Twig in the dorm. A smile flickered and died. Up, past more clanky gates without stopping, and more. A whining noise and a clunk. We stopped with a jerk. Clank-slidey-clank. Twice. A wave of heat and a bright corridor. 'Ward 6,' my father muttered. We followed signs, turned a corner. Nurses bustled past. A man in stripy pyjamas was pushed past on a trolley. His eyes were lost in sunken hollows and his toothless mouth gaped.

'Is that man dead?' I asked when he'd gone past.

'Hope not,' my father replied, glancing back. 'He's prob'ly just ill.'

So that is what an ill man looks like. I walked backwards staring at him as he was wheeled away. 'Have you ever seen a dead man?'

'That's enough of that. Come on.' He sounded cross, hand gripping tighter, almost hurting. Huge ribbed radiators lined the walls, painted cream like school, but bigger, much bigger. I ran my fingers along the ribs. Then a big sign: SILENCE.

Three beds in a row, my mother in the furthest from the door. We smiled lamely at the women in the first two. One didn't smile back. She looked really miserable. I broke free and ran. We hugged. I buried my face in her satin bed jacket. I breathed her in. Father leant over us and kissed her on the cheek. 'Hullo, old girl,' he whispered. He pulled up a chair. I clung on and on. She looked the same to me. Sounded the same. Smelt the same. Felt the same. Warm, soft, silky. Perfume like old roses and her bed at home. Everything was all right. Everything MUST be all right. I said, 'Mrs Warmley said you weren't very well.' Her silvery laugh rippled out as though I had made a joke. We all laughed, although I had no idea why. At seven you don't do irony.

For a few minutes my parents spoke almost as though they were strangers on a train. A stretched awkwardness seemed to pervade the ward, the very British awkwardness of stilted reserve, of buttoned-up decorum and constraint, of an inhibiting dignity and topical banalities aired between long, lofty silences. It was 1953, for God's sake. Princess Margaret wanted to marry Peter Townsend. A divorcee. 'Outrageous!' I heard my father say. The very suggestion. The Church had said 'NO'. 'Quite right,' he added crisply. God save the queen.

A little while later two men in long white coats came in and straight to her bed. My father stood up. 'Hullo,' said the nearly bald man with a beaky nose, smiling, stethoscope round his neck like a pet snake. 'I'm Doctor Wood. This is Mr Brock, our surgeon.' He was thicker set and wore glasses with dark frames, hiding even darker eyes with pinpoint irises that seemed too small for their whites. He looked stern, a face of serious intent and implacable distinction. They both shook hands with my father. 'How do you do?' said Mr Brock, stiff as a pillar.

'Shall we go?' my father asked.

'No, no.' Dr Wood insisted amiably, swinging the end of his stethoscope in a circle as he stuffed it into his coat pocket. 'Please stay.' He was nodding and grinning, his face bright with confidence and understanding. 'We just wanted to say hullo to your wife, a quick chat.' I began to warm to this doctor. There was something easy about him, a mix of kindness like Mrs Warmley but a jolliness too, barely suppressed. He turned to my mother. 'Are you comfortable, my dear? We won't see you over the weekend, but we'll be back in again on Monday. If everything's OK you'll be going up on Tuesday, first thing.'

I saw my father wince. He was sucking his thumb again. But she was beaming. 'This is my son, John,' she said, quickly changing the subject. 'He's at boarding school.' It sounded like an announcement, as if I was far more important than anything to do with doctors and hospitals. I felt a rush of blood, cheeks firing.

'Hullo, John.' A sunburst smile lit up his whole face. 'That's a very smart blazer you've got.' I liked Dr Wood even more. He stepped forward to shake my hand and made a little bow. And then, 'This is Mr Brock.' Mr Brock nodded. A quick flicker of a smile shot through and vanished.

'I know a Mr Brock,' I said. 'He lives in a burrow near our house.'

'Jay!' My mother sounded shocked. 'Don't be so silly.'

Doctor Wood leaned forward and fixed me with steely blue eyes. 'Would that be Mr Tommy Brock, by any chance?'

For a second and a half I was fazed. How did this friendly doctor in a white coat know about badgers? How did he know about Beatrix Potter's badger? Surely he didn't read children's books. But those blue eyes weren't intimidating in the least. He was waiting for an answer. I had to join in, drawing courage from the blithe self-assurance of the innocent. 'Yes,' I said. 'That's him. He's a smelly old badger and Mr Tod the fox tries to tip a bucket of water over his head while he's in bed.'

A great guffaw broke from Doctor Wood, head thrown back. 'There you are, Russell! He's got the measure of you.' We all laughed. I felt Doctor Wood was a real friend. A few minutes later Mr Brock asked if they could have a private word with my father. The three of them left the ward together.

That night, when he tucked me up in the hotel bed, my father spoke in a sombre voice. 'Mummy's going to have an operation next week.' The skin round his thumb was still oozing blood. He looked uncomfortable, rocked and not properly fitting into even his austere paternal skin, not quite sure whether to sit on the bed or not.

'Oh,' I said, not having the remotest idea what it meant, because it didn't matter. Nothing mattered. I had seen her, held her tight. She had laughed and kissed me goodbye when we left. She was OK. Nothing was wrong. She was the same old Mum, my mum, and that was all that mattered.

Bartonfield

Whoever built the Bartonfield farmhouse in the late sixteenth century had pretensions. Stonemasons with flair and skill must have been employed to erect the shell of the building to a particular design reflecting the vernacular vogue of the day – and then apparently dismissed. Whoever took the job over possessed neither a set-square nor a level or even a plumb line. It was as though the architect had said, 'Build us four stout walls and an elegant facade and we'll get the local lads to do the rest.' Not that it was shoddily built – far from it. With thick stone internal walls, it was a house to withstand earthquakes, but behind that designer facade the construction was a joke, an escapade, an adventure where no rules applied, come what may.

The house, nowadays officially listed as an historic building, much extended and gentrified, still stands. It is built in Ham stone ashlar, a warm, sand-coloured, ferruginous limestone from ancient Roman workings on Ham Hill, a local landmark only a few miles to the south, and for many centuries the favoured building stone for south Somerset. Its soft, warm glow awards both charm and an unmistakable vernacular distinction to the entire district.

Thought to have been built in the reign of William and Mary, Bartonfield's genteel pretensions extended to finely carved mullioned windows below a continuous string line and a classical portico with columns over an iron-studded oak front door – and no further. It was a powdered face, a cosmetically devised signal to the watching world, just that. Once behind that facade all pretense had been cast to the haphazard winds of functionality and, I imagine, budget.

The iron-studded oak front door opened into a wide passage with elegantly proportioned rooms off at the front, but which descended into virtual cellars and dungeons, dark and cramped, by the time it arrived at the back of the house. Forward-facing windows in the refined facade were matched, symmetrical and delicately constructed; to the rear they seemed to have been placed by whimsy, wherever someone thought a bit more light was desirable, the builders appearing to have competed amongst themselves willy-nilly for eccentricity of sizes, shapes and positions. Downstairs was floored in huge, uneven stone flags; doorframes were low and crooked. Upstairs, no bed, dressing table or chest of drawers could stand upright. Wide elm floorboards veered wildly across bedrooms, bucking and dipping as they went. Wardrobes leaned drunkenly. Ceilings lurched and curved into bulky black oak beams that had never witnessed a saw. Like surfacing whales, other beams emerged from plaster layered on like a child's icing on a cake, only to vanish again a few feet later.

Busy building a limestone quarrying empire – he would become a leading expert on Sir Christopher Wren's great buildings – my father had found himself managing several sites in the West Country at once: Portland, Beer, Maiden Newton, Bath. He needed a house central to them all. He plumped for Martock, on the southern edge of the Somerset Levels, in the 1950s very definitely a village, nowadays a thriving country town of 5,000 souls.

With the deeply embedded traditionalist and past-oriented

instincts that shaped his whole personality, he had searched the countryside for something old. Old, *old*, OLD. In Bartonfield he found it – a former cider farmhouse on the western fringe of the village, complete with dairy, stables and a two-storey cider barn with its press and vats intact, rampant wallflowers bursting from the cracks in crumbling masonry, surrounded by orchards of cider apple trees. These gnarled old veterans fruited local varieties of small, bitter apples such as Red Worthy, Lambrook Pippin, Dabinett, Coat Jersey and Cap of Liberty, bred in and around the village over many centuries.

Cider – scrumpy locally – was important to the medieval Somerset economy as the chosen grog to refresh the dusty throats of working men. Whoever the industrious apple-pressing souls who commissioned the house were, they lived well. It was set back from, but facing, the narrow country road looking across a swift-running brook, a minor tributary of the River Parrett, which rippled through banks lined with ancient pollard willows, where moorhens, red-billed and with flicking white under-tails, stalked among quilts of watercress and mare's tail, and to damp, buttercup-studded water meadows beyond, where shining galaxies of marsh marigolds thronged the many rills, beneath the ringing blue of those endless summer skies of my childhood.

I need not have worried. We didn't lose a home; we gained one. The Manor House was a fixture, and would remain so for many years to come, rooted firmly at the core of my consciousness. I dreamed its stone-flagged corridors at night and was constantly in trouble from Twig when in class she caught me daydreaming through its soggy fields. Nothing else in my short life's journey could supplant its superiority. So when my father told me that he had bought another house, I wasn't really interested. It didn't seem important.

When I saw it for the first time that summer holidays I might still have been six, or possibly just seven. We'd had other temporary homes before, as my father roamed about expanding his business affairs, but I do remember him collecting me from Hampton House – I thought to take me up to London again, but I was wrong. We turned south to the Mendip Hills and beyond to the vast waterlogged basin of the Somerset Levels.

I was given a small, narrow room at the back with a low window looking out over the cider barn and the stable yard to tall elm trees and the orchards beyond. I quickly warmed to the house's higgledy-piggledy interior, much smaller than the Manor House. Its beams and low ceilings made it feel more like a large cottage than anything grander, but it had a friendly, nonchalant aura about it as if, down its long centuries, it had seen just about everything a house was likely to witness and nothing much surprised it any more. But most of all I liked the outhouses, the old cider barn and its cobbled floor, the dairy, abandoned to us children as a den, and the clicking thumb-latches to the stables' doors, familiar from the Manor House. Up above was a long, cobwebby loft, accessed by a rickety ladder and quickly adopted and entirely taken over by fantail pigeons.

Like Kenneth Grahame's Mr Toad, our father was occasionally given to sudden impulsive flights of fancy. They emerged without warning, burned furiously for a few weeks or months, and then fizzled out. They appealed to us children, keeping us guessing and humanising his otherwise inflexible and overtly conservative persona. One evening he arrived home carrying a hamper. 'Guess what I've got.' His eyes gleamed with child-like excitement. He thrust his hand in. There was a brief scuffle as he chased something around. *Guinea pigs!* I thought. The hand emerged holding the purest white dove I had ever seen. It was exquisite, as white as a sunlit swan, soft plumed, with a glossy eye of black opal ringed in a perfect circle of leathery pink. I was instantly captivated. Two cocks and three hens.

We never discovered where they came from or why he wanted them. He spent the weekend constructing a handsome barrel dovecote, erected in a corner of the garden behind the house. A few days later, impatient to see them strutting and pouting their courtship displays around the house, he let them out – far too soon. They never went near the dovecote again. They had immediately spotted blissful pigeon habitat in the loft above the stables, secure and predator free, with rafter perches and wall-head nesting shelves all the way round.

By the end of that summer my father had lost interest. But we had many more fantails displaying in an ever-expanding fly-past, dipping and diving onto the roofs, the air burbling with their dulcian cooings from dawn till dusk. A year later we had dozens. I loved those birds, and they became mine, spending many hours in the loft, lulled by their gentle language and hypnotised by the males puffing up their chests, fanning their tails and bobbing, bowing and pirouetting to their hens. Some were very tame and would feed from my hand; others would allow me to stroke them softly on the nest while incubating eggs. But a few would have none of it and would strike out angrily with a hiss and a wing swipe at my hand.

Those pigeons presented my first serious dip into animal biology. By counting the days of incubation I could time the hatching, the egg rocking very slightly as the chick began to saw at the inside of the shell with the 'egg tooth' on the top of its bill. Then the crack, a hairline fracture; later a tiny hole and an angular fragment of shell breaking away, revealing the wrinkly membrane beneath. The whole process could take all day, so I would go away and sneak back an hour or two later, only to find that virtually nothing had happened. This first stab at avian life held me in thrall. I found it hard to believe that the cramped, screwed up chick, apparently so helpless and frail, could possibly break free from the shell and within a few hours transform itself into a baby bird covered in yellow down, ugly and reptilian though they were, with hideous bulging eyes, stubby wings and vulgarly distended bottoms.

Sometimes in those early days I became impatient and tried to hurry the hatching by picking bits of shell away, but all too often it would end in death because the chick hadn't properly freed itself from the yolk sack and the blood supply hadn't closed off. Bleeding freely from its umbilicus, the chick would weaken and within an hour or two it would be dead.

I had to learn these things the hard way. I don't ever remember either asking an adult or having anyone else around who might have given me guidance. My mother had a natural affinity with animals; blessed with patience and compassion in equal measure, she had reared whole broods of orphaned birds, lovingly mixing food and teasing it into tiny mouths with a curious glass syringe that delivered a worm of soft food from its nozzle. Once it was greenfinches, six of them all lined up along the verandah rail, all fluttering stubby wings, all squawking for food at the same time. Another time it was goldfinches, but also baby squirrels and rabbits, even field mice. Had she been there I am sure I would have asked her for help, but in those early days of the fantails she wasn't. She was in hospital.

I learned so much from those birds. Without knowing even the words, far less the science, I was imbibing the rudiments of bird biology and ethology. I watched the cock bird's insistent minuet spirals, the hen's coy submission, the mounting, the quick cloacal embrace, followed by the hen's satisfied ruffle of tail feathers and the cock's immediate collapse of ardour. My face only inches from the nest, I could witness the hens shuffling into egg laying, turning, heads tilted to gaze proudly at their work, the hot eggs wet and shining in the twiggy nest.

Then the hatching and the rearing. I watched the adult birds regurgitate a sticky 'milk' from the lining of the crop, rich in protein and fats, the chicks probing deep into each parent's gaping throat. I saw the strong squabs wax fat and the weaklings falter and fail – a downy corpse in the messy nest trodden flat by its careless sibling. Both sweet and shocking, I learned that nature takes no prisoners. I watched the stubby, blood-filled plumules emerge from the reptilian skin and gradually flower into the miracle of feathers. I saw the pale, soft beaks narrow, harden and shape to a proper bill. Then there were lice.

Out of nowhere an infestation of lice devastated our pigeons. At first I didn't know what was killing the chicks. Nest after nest failed. When I left the loft in the afternoon, well-grown, strong squabs would apparently be alive and well; by morning they would be dead in the nest. I told Mark. No one else around to tell.

Mark Cuff was a recently retired glove factory worker from the cottages next door. His wife, Isobel, appropriately known as 'Dizzy', was a porcelain skinned, bird-like creature in her fifties who lived on her own particular brand of nervous energy. She was supposed to help out in the house, and she did, after a fashion, but for some unexplained reason couldn't carry or move anything heavier than a feather duster, far less a bucket or a coal scuttle, so she would nip next door and drag Mark in to do it for her. My father was convinced this was a ruse, but after a while he gave in and employed Mark too. He arrived every morning to perform a routine of chores that included bringing in coke for the boiler, logs for the fires, emptying ash and sweeping the yard. He also cleaned my father's shoes.

Mark was small, shy and a man of eloquent silence. If he had something to say, it would be delivered with maximum economy. Puzzlingly, he called my mother 'Mum'. When he came in to do the shoes, he would hang his cap on a lobby peg and say 'Shoes, Mum,' disappearing into the boot room without waiting for an answer. He moved slowly and deliberately. I used to watch him at work, carefully placing the polish tin down as if it were bone china. The only rapid movement I ever saw was the back and forth of the cloth to complete the shine.

'Lice,' he pronounced when I told him the chicks were dying.

'What do you mean, lice?' I asked, astonished that he had an opinion at all. 'Lice is killing 'em,' without looking up. Zip, zip, zip went the duster. A long pause. 'What does lice mean?'

'Bird lice.'

'What *is* lice?' I pressed. 'I don't understand.'

'It's bird lice, Jack. I've 'ad it wi' me budgies. Y' need powders.'

My father gave me two shillings to go and buy powders from Brownes, the ironmongers down the street towards the church, my first independent purchase. 'And be sure to say thank you properly.' To a child, Mr Browne was very large and very frightening. He was goggle-eyed behind thick-lensed circular glasses and flat-faced with sagging jowls like a bloodhound. He also had no neck. His huge head seemed to be balanced on his shoulders, chin resting on his chest, and his gorilla-like belly bulged above and below a wide leather belt. I imagined that when it was undone his whole torso would avalanche jelly-like to the floor. He didn't speak unless he had to, but he did have just about everything in his shop – a proper ironmonger. Lined throughout with shelves crowded with bottles, packets, tins and tools; broom handles and willow-twig besoms stood in bundles in a corner; shining galvanised buckets were stacked one inside the next in a teetering ziggurat beside the counter. Shiny nails sold by the pound. The shop reeked with a nostalgically English cocktail of paraffin, creosote and mansion polish.

Suspended on a spring, the brass doorbell jangled angrily. I approached the long pine counter, grimy with age. Slowly, like a snail emerging from its shell, Mr Browne slid silently out from the gloom of a backroom. 'Please, Mr Browne, I need some bird lice powders.'

'Chickens?'

'No, pigeons.' He peered at me suspiciously before slithering off to a shelf a few feet away. Back he slid to plonk a tall tin on the counter. 'One and nine.' The sound emerged from vocal cords somewhere below his belt. I passed him the florin. Keys depressed like a typewriter, the large upright till pinged energetically and the drawer shot out, smacking him in the belly and bouncing off again. He handed me the three-penny bit without a word. I turned to go, then remembered. 'Thank you very much.' He nodded the tiniest, least-movement-possible nod you could imagine, so tiny it was almost invisible. I wasn't even sure I had seen it. I ran all the way home.

They did the trick. The rubbery beaks of newly hatched chicks gaped cavernously from every nest. Sometimes I left my bedroom window open and scattered a handful of corn on the sill. I would be awakened at first light by a fantail scrum, white wings flapping, clambering over each other and pushing and shoving like suckling piglets. Sometimes pigeons flounced into the room and perched on my wardrobe, where they cooed and bowed soothingly. But when they crapped on my new school blazer, they were summarily banished from the house and I was forced to pursue my pigeon fancying outside.

*   *   *

That first Bartonfield holiday was marked by the absence of our mother. Russell Brock had corrected her mitral valve in an eleven-hour operation on 29 September 1954 and straight back onto the ward – there were no intensive care units in those days – where Paul Wood had overseen her long recovery, first at the Brompton and later at the Brompton's cardiac convalescence unit at Frimley Sanatorium near Camberley in Surrey. What we didn't know, and wouldn't for several years to come, was that her aortic valve was also in trouble. But the procedure for aortic correction was still dangerously experimental, far too risky to attempt. Russell Brock and Paul Wood had seen it very clearly. They entered in her notes: 'Aortic regurgitation is occurring. She will need to return for AV correction in due course.' This was visionary, but also wishful thinking. There was no aortic valve correction available until the mid-1960s, but that last sentence in Paul Wood's handwriting is a clear demonstration that they intended it would be – if she survived that long.

The convention of silence had been religiously upheld. We were told only that she had had her operation. The option of going up to London to see her in recovery was never either discussed or available to us children. I'm sure my father went regularly, but we didn't. I imagine it was considered too disruptive for her and too distressing for us, the subject never broached. Either my father couldn't bring himself to talk about it, or perhaps his habitual inadequacy in communicating with children simply clammed him up. We would never know. Such information as we could glean came second and third hand from snippets overheard between adults or casual remarks from one of our minders. 'Mummy's doing really well,' I remember being told, and wondering at what? I knew she loved embroidery. Was she doing well at that? And she was really good at making friends – perhaps that was it?

We children knew nothing. In our brief, sheltered lives anything even approaching the reality of exploratory heart surgery had never been explained to us – its dangers, such as blood clots getting away to the lungs and causing devastating strokes, the horror of infection or the ever-present risk of her heart stopping altogether. To us it was black and white. She was either well or she wasn't; either she was alive, in which case we expected her to be exactly the same and coming home sometime soon, or, unthinkably, she wasn't. Yet somehow, out of that swirling black hole of ignorance, I had begun to grasp the hollowing out possibility that she might not – that she could die.

For me, the move to Bartonfield at seven years old was shrouded in those acid anxieties. Yet in the security of home, whether at Bartonfield or the Manor House, I was easily diverted. Blessed with the sanguine naivety of my age and the security engendered by home, I didn't lie awake at night worrying. There was always plenty to distract me and I absorbed my mother's protracted absences as a part of the pattern of life dignified by the twin blindfolds of ignorance and soaring hope. But at school, in the dormitory, it was different. Hearing Betty sobbing out his own private homesickness beside me, the spectre of doom crowded in and kept me awake. When sleep finally came I had only two dreams, both of which recurred over and over again. One was of seeing my mother in the distance, running to her but never quite getting there; the other was at the Manor House, entering the old servants' hall and seeing the rusty chains hanging empty, the Dun Cow rib nowhere to be seen – and then waking up sweating and with panic pounding in my chest.

I never told anyone about my fears or my dreams. Logic is absent or surfaces but slowly to a child. The terror that she might die was unspeakably private, something I was incapable of uttering for the added and illogical dread that if I did, it might somehow make it more likely. My whole school existence became a dungeon of despair, manacled by those fears, a captive utterly beyond hope. All I could do was bury the terror within myself, a gritted propitiation of silence and loneliness.

Finally, several months later, we were allowed to go to see her at Frimley Sanatorium. Excitement bubbled inside me until we arrived, then the long hurt of estrangement over-came me with an illogical, withering shyness. She was standing at the door to greet us. I let Mary go first, studying my mother's face as if I expected her not to look quite like herself. But in seconds it was familiar all over again. Everything was all right, the same smile, the same hug, the same sweet voice, the same scent. The only change seemed to be that she had a walking stick and was a little unsteady on her feet. We spent the afternoon with her in the gardens and had tea with several other inmates in an overheated lounge that reeked of old socks and disinfectant. She gave me a lollipop. Then we left. 'When are you coming home?' I asked.

'Not long now,' she nodded reassuringly.

11

The dragon's den

My ninth year, 1954, started well but soon spiralled out of control. My mother had come home in time for Christmas at Bartonfield. She seemed much better – that is to say, better than before the operation. She had more energy, so she could do more with us, although she still tired easily and I now know she suffered chest pain, although she never, ever made a fuss about it, accepting her lot not just with stoicism but with the same gritty determination she had declared in her letters from hospital.

We soon forgot that she had been away at all. She made paper chains with us from strips of coloured paper and hung them all round the house with her glamorous twin, Margaretta, who wore dangly Mexican earrings and smoked Marlboro cigarettes in a long holder, and proudly showed off her new-fangled Zippo cigarette lighter with a click and a zing as it snapped shut. She had married a GI, gone to live in Texas and mysteriously now sported a Southern drawl like Dolly Parton. She came to us for Christmas to celebrate her sister's recovery.

When Margaretta and my mother were in the kitchen lost in childhood reminiscences of the Bedouin and their camel trains, I became bored and wandered through to the sitting room. On the mantelpiece I found the Zippo. Flicking it was irresistible. Its enticing zing made me do it over and over again. The benzene flame leapt and flared like a beacon. I held it up and ran torch-like round the room, passing too close to a paper chain. It caught, blazed and immediately broke the chain, both flaming ends falling vertically to the floor. The flames shot up the chains to the beam they were pinned to. I had two fires burning fiercely on opposite sides of the room.

Panic surged in. I snatched up a wicker wastepaper basket and tugged the flaming chains into it. Then I had a fire raging in a highly flammable basket. Trailing a column of smoke, I ran to the boot room sink and dowsed cold water into the fire still flaring angrily in the wrecked basket. I abandoned it in the sink and rushed back to the sitting room. The beam was black anyway, so the burns didn't show, but the room was thick with smoke. I flung the windows wide and fanned the door backwards and forwards. But it was no good. The smell of smoke and the absence of the paper chain were far too obvious. It was a miracle I hadn't burned the house down.

Mother was cross, but Margaretta, a rebellious maverick by nature and always an ally when I was in trouble, persuaded her it was a genuine accident. 'Please don't tell Daddy,' I begged. We all feared his legendary wrath, capable of lasting for hours. Never violent and never for one moment laying a finger on us, he compensated by raging like a tiger with toothache. If we broke something important to him, either by accident or through carelessness, he would explode pyrotechnically. I once knocked an Anglepoise lamp off his desk and bent its delicate arm. 'Smash! Smash! Smash!' He had fumed all round the house, his handlebar moustache twitching like the tiger's whiskers. 'All you children ever do is smash my things. If you have to smash things, go and smash something of your own and leave mine alone.' Mary

scuttled upstairs to her bedroom as fast as a frightened rabbit
and I shot outside to the pigeon loft, not venturing back
until long after the storm had abated.

Our parents inspired entirely different emotions in us,
each to our own marque of filial affection. To me our father
was as the splendid sun, distant but fierce, untouchable yet
solid and reassuring, a constant presence to be worshipped
from afar and a glowing ring of security. Despite all her
problems I viewed our mother as entirely other: she was
our *Terra Mater*, the all-embracing mother earth, Venus and
Ceres interwoven, in which our roots were nourished, intimate, warm and sustaining.

My plea had touched an inherent weakness. Mother and
I had a history of secrets. I had told her about Twig and the
ILY peppermints. She had been deeply indignant – as close
to real anger as she ever came – and wanted to pen a sharp
rebuke to Twig, but I persuaded her that it might make life
even more difficult, and besides, I didn't want Mrs Warmley
to think ill of me. Our little secrets were private intimacies
as much to do with her guilt at illness-imposed absences as
with my obvious delight in commanding her attention. Her
endlessly generous and forgiving nature won through and
she agreed not to mention the fire, trying her best to be
stern but failing dismally. We ended the afternoon happily
making a new paper chain, back in place before my father
came home.

★   ★   ★

The previous autumn Betty and I had ascended to Hampton
Down Junior School. Sad to desert Mrs Warmley, we both
cheered loud and long to be escaping from the execrable
Twig. Hampton Down was a large, fully-fledged prep school,

run on English public school principles by a bombastic extrovert headmaster called Bernard Forbes. To his face the boys never called him anything but sir, but behind his back he was 'Bernie the Dragon' to just about everyone.

The school was composed of a large country house of which the south-facing block was the Forbes family's private abode, with its own gravel drive and neatly mown lawns adorned with several pairs of strutting peacocks – in an unguarded moment I had overheard Mrs Warmley say they complemented his ostentatious personality – and a longer wing to the rear, entered across a broad tarmac quadrangle, the school's matrix, buttressed by a double rank of barrack-like single-storey timber classrooms and expansive games fields beyond.

Mother had been allowed out from Frimley so that both my parents could take me to the new school for the first time. Mr Forbes came out to greet us. He was tall with a swarthy complexion, dark hair swept back from a prominent brow and a bellowing voice fit for a town crier. He dressed immaculately in a navy blue blazer above fawn cavalry twills and a white shirt with a brightly striped silk cravat, an invariable uniform of authority we came to know well and which I now recognise as determined power dressing. With a flourish of his hand, he boomed to an older boy by name – 'John!' The boy approached. 'Michael, would you take John off and show him round?' I was deeply confused. The boy smiled. 'Follow me,' and off we went. Mr Forbes whisked my parents away to his private quarters for afternoon tea.

A little while later I met up with them again and walked to the car to see them off; they were heading straight back to Frimley. 'Mrs Forbes is very nice,' my mother said, 'but I'm not sure I like the headmaster. He's pompous and very pleased with himself, cocky as a bantam.' I wasn't sure what pompous meant, but if she had said it, it had to be true. Along with the enduring image of a bantam cockerel, one I never managed to dispel, I locked it away in my memory bank.

I didn't really like being called John. My mother and sister had habitually called me Jay, a familiarity primed with affection, and to Nellie I had always been Jack. When I'd asked her why, she had smiled and sighed with an ancient sadness. 'Now I should really be callin' you Master John, but I knows how naughty you is and that puts me in mind of my brother Jack who never come 'ome from the war, so there, it'll be Jack, whether you likes it or no.' Both Jay and Jack made me glow inside, and my grandfather had always called me 'boy'. I liked that too. Only my father called me John and then only when I was in trouble. Usually I was 'old boy' or 'old chap', or, persuasively, 'Look sharp, old thing.' In my new-boy misery at Hampton House John had been imposed on me whether I approved or not. It sounded formal and threatening in a slightly sneery way. I used to lie in bed in the dark and mutter JOHN to myself over and over, *JOHN, JOHN, JOHN* . . . until it no longer sounded like a name but just a peculiarly uttered animal noise.

Betty and the other Hampton House boys had always called me 'Liss', which was fine. But I was immediately confused about this other, soft-spoken John with wavy hair and freckles across the bridge of his nose as if he'd been dusted with nutmeg. I was too diffident to ask him why he was apparently called both John and Michael, so I chose to call him nothing at all until I saw his name on a house list.

Michael John was my first encounter with the Welsh, and a total delight. I loved the gently subtle intonations in his lilting accent and the way he raised one eyebrow when a question loomed – a feat I strove for but failed to achieve.

He had been nicknamed 'Dylan' after the celebrated Welsh bard who had recently drunk himself to death just as he was being catapulted to global fame. *Under Milk Wood* was first broadcast that year. Despite being a year older than me, my Dylan was to become a resolute friend. The school was split into four houses. I was in Jefferson, Betty in distant Westerdale, an imposed apartheid from which our friendship never fully recovered.

It would be a long time before I properly understood what pomposity really was, but I quickly discovered from other boys that Mr Bernard Forbes was both feared and respected in the way that one instinctively views a Rottweiler. He was autocratic and unquestionably in charge. No one challenged his authority, certainly not to his face, and I think that everyone knew that had they done so they would have been summarily quashed. It would be tempting to label him a despot, but that wouldn't be entirely fair. He was a strong and assertive leader – necessary attributes for a good head-master – but I now perceive that as so often happens with despotic rulers, even benignly motivated ones, power had inflated his readily susceptible ego. In Bernie's case he was able to support his unassailable autocracy with the authority of God.

What we didn't know back then was that he had very nearly chosen the cloth – had in fact set out on the route towards full ordination into the Church of England. In jumping ship to become a schoolmaster he had spotted a way of combining the authority of the pulpit with a more financially lucrative and flexible career, altogether more fitting for his flamboyant personality. So he had become a firebrand lay-preacher instead, as we very well knew to our yawning repletion in chapel every Sunday.

Trying my hardest to recount this fairly, if never objectively, I do not think Bernard Forbes was a bad or cruel man; rather, to damn him with faint praise, I would say that he usually meant well. But in common with those who cannot see or admit fault in themselves, he was possessed by that dangerously corrosive self-righteousness which, combined with a headmaster's supremacy, roughly equivalent to the divine right of kings, made him aggressively intolerant of anything or anyone he didn't like, raging and ranting like a dragon. An irony that would make me chuckle long after I had recovered from the events I shall soon describe was that his favourite moral text for sermons was on the importance of *humility*.

*   *   *

Summer and winter, every day started with a bracing cold bath – in and out again in seconds – but we had to submerge completely, head and all, for the count of five. We removed our pyjamas in the dormitory, wrapped a towel round our waists and filed barefoot into the communal bathroom where several baths were pre-filled by a duty master or matron. Prefects and senior boys went first. They threw their towels aside, leapt in, ducked under, held for the mandatory five seconds, and leapt out again, water swilling in all directions. Extrovert boys with something to prove would stay under for longer, sometimes ten seconds, emerging to cheers from friends and derisory boos of 'Look who thinks he's a hero!' from others.

Some of the seniors were twelve, one or two thirteen years old, about to ascend to public school. They sported what seemed to me to be unnecessarily extravagant genitals topped by a flourish of pubic hair, something I had never witnessed before. Deeply intrigued by this diverting phenomenon I secretly examined myself under the bedclothes with a torch, relieved to find that nothing had changed. I remember wondering whether it would happen overnight or whether I might receive some advance warning of this apparently unavoidable metamorphosis.

Discipline was focused on a system of 'pluses and minuses'. A chart on the school noticeboard listed every boy's name, against which marks were awarded or subtracted every week, a score to be aggregated for the whole term. Plus 8, very rarely awarded, attracted special praise at school assembly; minus 8 was reserved for particularly heinous sins, there in red for the world to see and which meant a summons to the headmaster's study to be caned – the much vaunted 'six of the best' by Bernie the Dragon. When a boy did get minus 8 word quickly travelled round the whole school in a fizz of excitement – mostly, I think, out of grisly curiosity, but there was genuine sympathy too, for the bright red welts across his buttocks, later turning to a grid of purple bruises, would be highly visible at cold bath time. Boys would crowd into the bathrooms to witness the unfortunate victim's wounds to cries of 'Crikey! Bernie really laid into you!' Or 'Blimey! I bet that stung.' At the end of each term your pluses and minuses were totalled to reveal the trend in your behaviour.

A popular spare time recreation was roller-skating in the quadrangle. Good skaters were viewed as an elite. Dylan was an ace. He could skate backwards at great speed, weaving with ease and grace in and out of the melee of teetering less-accomplished boys, chopping and changing to forwards and back again in mid-flight without losing speed at all. I was spellbound by this Olympian skill. I had achieved a respectable competence going forwards, but not the art of reverse and certainly not the flying change. Dylan offered to teach me, a natural generosity of spirit not widely present among boys of prep school age. I flourished under his tutelage, raking in kudos and envy as we flew round the quad together.

One afternoon I was practising backwards. Dylan urged me on, faster and faster as round the quad we sped. Just then a geography mistress called Miss Mackenzie emerged from the main doors and was crossing the quad with an armful of books. By the time I saw her it was too late. I crashed into her, knocking her over, books flying to the winds. She was understandably furious, pushing me away when I tried to help her up. I apologised profusely, but she was having none of it. 'You're a ruddy little hooligan!' Dylan whizzed up and helped me gather her books. To my dismay, that evening I found that she had given me minus 7. While not quite the ultimate sentence, it was sufficient to trigger a summons to the dragon's den.

Above his door there were two lights: one red and one green. Red meant do not disturb, green it was OK to knock. But at eight years old the universality of red and green signals had not really registered in a brain much more receptive to pigeons and moorhens. The red light was on. I pondered the logic: *Does it mean go away, or just wait? If it means wait, how does he know I'm here?* But I had been summoned – my housemaster had told me I was in trouble and to go straight to the head's study. Hesitantly I knocked on the door. It flew open. 'Can't you see the red light?' Bernie roared. 'Wait.' He slammed the door before I could say a word.

I waited for what seemed a very long time, while dread pooled in my black lace-up shoes, leadening my legs all the way up to my gut. Finally the green bulb lit up. I knocked again. 'Come!' The big room was furnished like a sitting room, with leather armchairs and a sofa, a large leather-topped desk across the corner and a huge bookcase against the wall.

'You wanted to see me, sir.'

'Yes, I did.' He rose from his desk and stalked to the window. Staring out over the lawn with his hands clasped behind his back, he asked, 'Are you aware that you hurt Miss Mackenzie very badly? She could have easily broken an arm or a leg.'

'Yes, sir. I said I was sorry, sir. It was an accident.' Past him I could see a peacock parading its glowing iridescence across the lawn.

'It was not an accident. It was utter self-indulgent carelessness and a total disregard for other people.'

'I didn't mean to, sir.'

He spun round to face me. 'Are you aware that if Miss Mackenzie had given you minus 8 I would be bending you over that armchair and giving you six of the best with that cane?' He pointed to a stout cane knuckled like bamboo lying across the corner of his desk.

'Yessir.'

'Let this be a lesson to you. I will not tolerate such behaviour again.'

*   *   *

When we broke up for Christmas, we always headed straight for the Manor House for my grandfather's birthday on 19 December, a ritual attendance required at the beginning of the Christmas holidays. As soon as we arrived I would rush to find Nellie in the kitchens.

'Well, now, if it isn't Master Jack. My! How you've growed.'

'It's *GROWN*, Nellie, not growed.'

'Well, it's growed to me and always will be. I never was much for schooling, not like you. Now I knowed you was coming so I've baked some scones for tea.'

'It's *KNEW*, Nellie, not knowed.'

'Well, is that so? My! My! I never knewed that afore.' It took me years to realise that she did it on purpose. Her scones were as soft as eiderdown and slightly salty, dripping with creamy butter from the farm dairy and her own strawberry jam.

Two things stand out about that December visit. First, my Manor House bedroom was a former dressing-room off my parents' room, connected by an adjoining door. My father habitually rose early to make tea, bringing it back to my mother on a tray. The next half hour would be spent talking. If the door was slightly ajar, I could hear most of their conversation, often mundane stuff about the abhorrent politics of the day. One morning I overheard my name and crept to the door. Over the next few minutes I gleaned sufficient to take in that my parents were worried. My first Junior School end of term report had arrived and evidently signalled alarm.

My father kept all my school reports meticulously filed in an archive, so years afterwards I was able to revisit the precise text of their anxiety. From my housemaster:

John is always in trouble . . . If there is a disturbance he is usually in the thick of it . . . His classwork is satisfactory but he needs to occupy his free time more constructively to avoid such bad marks.

And an overview from the headmaster: 'His aggregated score this term is a disgraceful minus six out of plus eight. This <u>must</u> improve.'

'What does minus 6 mean?' my mother asked, sounding worried.

'It tells us he's always in trouble.'

'What sort of trouble?'

'It doesn't say. Perhaps you should speak to him.'

It was typical of my father to duck this responsibility. He knew he wasn't good with children and he had always deferred to her, as he did with any domestic situation. Mother, on the other hand, was utterly non-confrontational and always avoided awkward conversations with us. I suspect that she was so burdened by what she wrongly perceived to be her own health-imposed inadequacies that the last thing she wanted was to criticise her children. She never did raise it with me, but I logged it away as a gradually expanding cancerous hatred of Mr Bernard Forbes.

The second distinction was the discovery of the Manor House cellars. Up to that point all my explorations had been above ground or outside. I knew of the existence of the cellars and knew that they were accessed by a locked door off the school room corridor.

One breakfast at the kitchen table, while downing Nellie's glutinous porridge made delectably stickier with honey and cream, she announced, 'I got to get a bottle o' port from the cellar cos Mrs Barnwell's doin' a jugged hare for your grandfather's birthday dinner tomorrow. We got to steep it overnight. That's 'ow he likes it, he does, but ooh, 'ow I hates goin' down to that cellar.' She wrung her hands on her pinny. 'Will you come with me, Jack, case I falls?' Sensing adventure, I agreed readily.

A dank chill and the stale miasma of mould assaulted us as Nellie turned the key in the heavy door. A bare light bulb lit the fourteen steps down the side of a damp brick wall, down into the foundations of the oldest part of the Jacobean house. Wet cobwebs brushed our faces. At the bottom another bulb dimly lit a large room with a vaulted ceiling and an uneven brick floor. Rows of rusty iron, double-sided wine racks occupied the bulk of the cellar, most of them empty, but the one nearest the steps held a few cases of claret and port, some ancient brandy and a few of Champagne. Most of the paper labels had long since perished and a coating of slimy dust obliterated what was left. Only wired-on lead labels could identify the contents of each rack; the name and date in white wax crayon.

'My ol' dad used to keep all this,' Nellie revealed, wistfully. 'But no one comes down here now 'e's gone on. Only me.' She drew a bottle from the rack. 'Come on, Jack, let's go afore we catches our death.'

'Wait a minute, Nellie, I've seen something.' In the middle of the floor beside an open drain sat the most enormous toad I had ever seen. It was almost five inches across, cold and clammy, with warty bumps all over its ill-fitting skin – altogether gloriously ugly and wrinkled all over, like a toad should be. It eyed me from bulbous amber eyes with sinister black slanting pupils and made no attempt to move away. It just sat and let me pick it up. 'Nellie, come and look at this, it's amazing.' I held it up to the light for her to see.

'Ooh, I don't like they,' she cried, recoiling. 'Take it away.'

I had every intention of taking it away. I wanted it for a pet. We stumbled back up the steps, she with her bottle and I with my precious, magnificent toad. I kept it in a box in the game larder until the end of the holidays, when I returned it to its drain. I fed it on cockroaches caught in my hands behind the scullery sinks and little brown slugs from the kitchen garden. I knew enough about toads to be sure that because of its great size it was bound to be female, but I named it Bernie.

12

The pain of injustice

Butterworth had been given a Parker 61 for Christmas: the smart fountain pen of the moment, sleek and glossy with a shiny gold nib and a 'no mess' capillary filling system – and very expensive. No other boy in our class possessed such an icon of opulence and Butterworth made the most of it. The rest of us were stuck with traditional dip pens and blue-black ink from inkwells in our desks. As if to press home this superiority, Butterworth insisted that he had to use royal blue Parker Quink and that the school ink – a powder mix – wouldn't work in his precious pen.

Our teachers seemed to tolerate this precociousness, but we wigged him mercilessly, dubbing him 'Penny' and 'Parkerworth'. In truth we were deeply envious – but damned if we were going to admit it. The pen lived in his desk in its velvet-lined box with a sprung lid. At the beginning of every lesson he brought it out and provocatively arrayed it for us all to see. The box snapped shut with a loud 'clop!' He did this over and over again, as if to rub in the emergence of this irritating prop to his vanity, the bottle of Quink very obviously displayed on the desk.

In the petty way that school children fall in and out of favour with each other, at that juncture I didn't like Butterworth and he didn't like me. I thought he was an odious, spoilt child. I have long since forgotten why, but I think it must have been something to do with the small clique of boys I had made good friends with. If he had friends of his own, I can't remember them. He was short, slightly tubby and an only child, unkindly said to be a 'mummy's boy'. Most of us were good at games; he was not. Butterworth's parents were perceived to be very well off and probably were.

Children seem to have a pack mentality at school, an apparently natural behavioural division into groups and types based on many differing and usually illogical criteria: age, abilities, interests, looks, accents, backgrounds, whether perceived or actual. Snobbery is as fickle as fashion; it waxes and wanes. We excelled at it.

While parental cars such as Jaguar, Humber, Hillman, Rover, Austin, Morris, Riley and Wolseley were common enough, Butterworth's father drove a very expensive, hand-built Bristol 405, a four-door sports saloon in glossy maroon with a long, sleek bonnet and an oval radiator vent like a goldfish mouth. It was the talk of the whole school, divided into those who thought Bristols and their owners were amazing, and those who were snobbishly jealous and dismissed them as 'flashy'.

My father had always driven good solid British marques such as Riley and Rover, but secretly I thought the Bristol 405 to be both beautiful and alluring. I was envious – no question – but because my clique of friends fell resolutely into the flashy camp, writing off both the Parker 61 and the Bristol 405 as ostentatious extremes of conspicuous consumption (although we would never have heard of that epithet nor had a clue what it meant), and despising the wretched Butterworth for it, I kept my envy to myself. In an attempt to curry favour and win me round, one Sunday after chapel he asked me out to lunch with his parents. I knew it would mean a ride in the beautiful Bristol. I longed to go, but to my shame – and I blush to record this – I declined purely on the grounds of snobbery and because I knew my friends would jeer. He was affronted by this unmerited slight and never forgave me for it.

One morning at the beginning of a maths lesson he opened the box and removed the Parker pen. A howl of anguish broke from his lips. Someone had stabbed the elegant nib into something hard, cruelly crumpling it beyond repair. The maths master, a stern but respected Mr Dennis, inevitably known as 'The Menace', demanded to know what the fuss was about. Tearfully, Butterworth showed him the pen. A row ensued and it was reported to Bernie. At assembly he threatened detention for the whole school unless someone owned up. No one did.

Later that afternoon I was summoned to Bernie's study for the second time. The light was green and I knocked timidly. I had no idea why I had been summoned. The Menace and an angry, red-faced Bernie stood together at the fireplace. In full dragon pose, Bernie fired first: 'I am led to believe you were responsible for breaking Butterworth's pen.'

'No, sir. It wasn't me.' I shook my head vigorously.

'Are you lying to me, boy?'

'No, sir.'

'Why do you think we believe it to be you?'

'I don't know, sir.'

'Well, I'll tell you why. You don't like Butterworth, do you?' I hesitated, but only for a split second.

Then Mr Dennis spoke. 'Isn't it true that Butterworth kindly asked you out to Sunday lunch last week?'

'Yessir.'

'And you declined?'

'Yessir.'

'Why did you refuse his offer of friendship?' I was stuck. I didn't have an answer. I looked at the floor, tugged at my sleeve, shuffled my feet. I had been snared.

Bernie lunged. 'I think you are lying. I believe that for some silly reason, probably jealousy, you don't like Butterworth, so you decided to break his Parker pen.'

'No, sir. I didn't.'

'And now you are trying to lie your way out of it.'

'No, sir.'

A long silence ensued while he glared at me as though by doing so he could dissolve me, break me down. Time folded into itself in an ugly, strained vacuum. At last he spoke. 'Are you going to own up, or aren't you?'

'I didn't do it, sir.' Another gruelling pause while both men stared at me. I looked down.

'You may well hang your head,' Bernie sneered scornfully. I shook my head again. 'Look at me, boy. Look me in the eyes and tell me you did not break Butterworth's pen.' He amplified his formidable voice and marshalled the full force of his pulpit authority.

Emotions swirled and fizzed inside my skull, confusing me. My head was spinning into a morass of helpless unknowing. I was frightened. I had winced at the sight of other boys' buttocks bruised to the colour of plums, far worse than anything Twig's gym shoe had delivered. I did not want to be caned. I was certain Bernie didn't like me and I was equally convinced that he longed to vent his wrath upon me. As the Bible says, I was 'sore afraid', but the gods of fairness and justice had deserted me, vanished behind a glowering cloud. I felt trapped. Terror clutched at my bowels and fear tramped painfully through the landscape of my mind, all paths to propitiation fenced and overgrown.

I had no idea why I was being blamed for this; I hadn't

lied and I was affronted that Butterworth or someone else had named me as the culprit. Taut with antipathy, the room spun. I felt sodden and heavy, everything a child feels when angry and silenced by authority; the whole world an overpowering insult. I wanted to cry out, to shout and stamp my feet. I wanted to run at Bernie, punch him and kick him. I hated him – but I couldn't do any of those things. I was trapped between powerlessness and something akin to rage that crouched inside me like a wildcat ready to spring. While it lasts, rage is intoxicating, blocking fear and freeing up otherwise padlocked inhibitions, releasing an uncertain, rainwashed calm. Marshalling powers known only to my instincts, I did what I now realise must have been total abhorrence to him – the proverbial red rag. I took the only escape route open to me, the last resort of the angry, humiliated child. I confronted him. Slowly I raised my face and looked him straight in the eyes. I glowered with silent, sullen resentment.

He pressed again: 'Well? Are you going to own up?'

Factual and defiant in the teeth of woe, I spoke slowly and deliberately. 'No, Mr Forbes. I did not do it. I had nothing to do with it and I think it is very unfair that you think it was me.'

A kind of furious darkness gathered in his face. His lips tightened into a thin line and I could see his jaw knotting and flexing while he struggled to contain his composure. I felt sure he was going to cane me anyway. The Menace looked embarrassed and shuffled his feet, but I was glad he was there. Seconds ticked by. At length Bernie spoke again: 'Very well, but if I find that you have lied to me and Mr Dennis, I will give you an immediate minus eight and you may be sure I will speak to your parents about this. Now get out of my sight.'

I turned on my heel and left. I walked stiffly away from

the study and broke into a run down the main corridor. I
burst through the swing doors and out into the quadrangle.
I ran down the drive, down the long avenue of pines and
up the rise to Hampton House. I ran in through the side
door and bounded up the stairs to Mrs Warmley's room. I
thumped on her door with my fist. The door opened. 'John!
Whatever are you doing?' I opened my mouth to speak but
no words came. A dam burst into unstoppable tears.

For several minutes she held me in her arms, my head
cradled against the cushion of her matronly bosom. 'There,
there,' she cooed as she hugged me. 'Come and sit down
and tell me all about it.' With an irony neither sought nor
understood, I could feel the cool shaft of a fountain pen
against my cheek, issuing a strange and naked peace.

*   *   *

An hour later I was walking back to school greatly cheered
by that generous-spirited, compassionate woman whom I
had embraced as my surrogate mother figure and always
secretly adored. For three years of my short, bewildering
school life, without ever evincing any outward sign of affection toward me, in my head Marion Warmley had fulfilled
the dual roles of Nellie and my mother, filled the absence
of both with an unspoken loving kindness that was an essential quality of the person she was. I didn't know that she
intensely disliked Bernard Forbes and had been openly critical of his headmastership. Nor, of course, had I any idea
that I had just compromised her.

Weeks passed and the Easter holidays approached. My
weekly marks worsened and had stuck resolutely at minus
seven, however hard I tried to improve them. I just always
seemed to be in the wrong place at the wrong time.

One of the ongoing competitions among the boys was the search for brightly coloured peacock feathers. There were only five or six cock birds strutting the lawns displaying their ludicrously extravagant tail fans and brilliant green-blue iridescent necks and breasts. All birds moult their feathers. Some do it all together, like wildfowl, becoming flightless for a few weeks while they grow new ones, and others, such as peacocks, moult theirs one by one, usually after the principal mating period each summer. We all kept an eye out for these beautiful feathers because they had become a school currency.

A fine long 'eye' tail feather commanded a price of sixpence, as long as it was unbroken and in reasonable condition. Broken tail feathers were thruppence and neck or breast feathers fringed with glossy irridescence were tuppence each. We all watched out for them all the time. I made a point of nipping out early in the mornings and running round the main building, scouring the lawns for these valuable pickings. I had built a reputation for finding them and selling them on.

One day a senior boy cornered me in the quad. 'I say, Liss, my sister would really love one of those long peacock feathers. She'll pay a shilling for a good one.' This above-market offer played on my mind. At night the peacocks were housed in a fox-proof shed in a corner of Bernie's private garden, strictly out of bounds. I eyed it from the distance and wondered if it contained any feathers. I felt sure it should. I knew from my pigeons that birds preened themselves extensively, often before roosting at night. The pigeon loft floor was always littered with white feathers. I decided to mount a night raid.

A soft spring dusk settled over the school. The bell to end prep sounded at eight and we had to be ready for bed by nine. I had an hour in which to effect my plan. The night was deep and moonless. I had a pen torch my mother had given me and, carefully sneaking round the outlying buildings, I took a circuitous route to the smartly mown lawn in front of the house. Bernie's quarters were a blaze of lights. I stood in the shadow of a large laurel. The whole building seemed to loom and sway as though I were watching a film. Somewhere far away the fading two-tone whistle of a train echoed out of the darkness. I saw Mrs Forbes draw some upstairs curtains and I caught a glimpse of Bernie crossing from his study, through their front hall and on into their sitting room in the front of the house.

I was on an adrenaline high. Excitement rimmed with the fear of being caught, made more exciting by the overpowering sense of reparation – that I was somehow striking back at Bernie. *It must be like this to be a poacher or a burglar*, I thought. The stealth appealed hugely. The realisation that I was invisible but could observe the Forbeses' every move fired me with a fierce and brooding sense of power.

I could see the back of Bernie's head as he settled into reading a newspaper. Mrs Forbes came in and joined him. This was thrilling. The school clock struck eight-thirty with a single ponderous chime. Half an hour left. Satisfied that the Forbeses were settled, I nipped across the lawn to the shed on the far side. I eased the bolt back and slipped inside. The peacocks were lined up on a perch four feet off the ground, breasts settled down onto their feet, with their long tails cascading down behind them, just clear of the ground. They didn't move. I flicked the torch beam around the floor. No feathers. Not one, not even a broken one. I was gutted. I slunk out and carefully closed the door behind me.

That night I lay in bed and pondered my failure. Even though it was fruitless, I had loved it, especially spying on Bernie. I hated him. It was as if I had begun to get my own back: raiding his private domain felt like a redemptive counter-strike against his zeal to entrap and cane me. A deep, glowing justification urged me on. I was determined to try again.

My mother had given me a vanity pack in a leather case with a zip fastener. It contained a hairbrush and comb, a nail file and a pair of sharp nail clippers like wire cutters. Under the bedclothes with my torch I examined the clippers. Snipping a chunk off my toughest toenail with an audible click, I knew that the clippers were capable of slicing through a peacock quill.

Two nights later it was overcast with a thick, disorientating darkness. I could feel the excitement funnelling up inside me as it neared eight o'clock. When the bell sounded, I ran to my locker for the clippers and the torch. Then I sauntered out into the night and down between the classrooms. I bumped into Dylan heading back to the main building. 'Hey, Liss, where are you off to?'

My hands were sweaty, heart thumping like a bass drum. 'Nowhere much, just mooching.'

'Fancy a game of ping-pong?'

'No, thanks. It's my bath night, so I'm heading up in a minute.'

'Oh, heck! Yes, it's mine too, I'd forgotten. I'll see you in the dorm.'

'Blast!' I muttered to myself as he walked away. Do I go on, or do I abandon the plan for another night? But the adrenaline had already kicked in. Besides, I was on a mission. The peacocks were the embodiment of Bernie. Pompous, my mother had said. I still wasn't sure exactly what it meant, but it didn't matter – I had a score to settle.

The same approach, same wait under the laurel, shadows humming with tension, the night air softly rippling through invisible spaces. Bernie there again in his armchair and through drawn curtains I could see the silhouetted figure of Mrs F moving about upstairs. I slid across the lawn and into the shed. Now my heart was really pounding and I had to force myself to stand still, eyes closed, breathing deeply.

The torch clicked on. The nearest bird shuffled and then, to my joy, it flicked round on its perch, sweeping its long tail over the rail so that it flowed down in front of me. Torch off. *Settle*, I thought. *Come on, settle, you stupid bird*. More deep breathing. *Steady now, don't rush it*. Seconds floated past. Torch on. Settled. *Good!* Torch gripped in my teeth I reached for the nearest feather. The bird didn't move. I ran my fingers gently up the shaft until I could feel the naked quill close to where it emerged from its body. Taking great care not to touch the body, I slid the clippers into place. A deep breath and squeeze . . . Snip! The feather came away in my hand. The bird shook its ludicrous tail and settled again. *Wow!* I thought, *This is easy. I'm sure it won't miss another one* . . . Snip! *Why not take three while I'm at it?* . . . Snip!

The peacock didn't flinch, body perfectly still, only its ridiculous bobble-crested head gyrated slowly from side to side as though it knew something was happening but couldn't work out what. Very slowly I moved to the next bird. Snip! And another snip. *Gently now, don't rush. Easy does it* . . . I had a whole handful of glorious feathers. *I may as well take a couple more*. Snip, snip and snip again. I had ten feathers more than three feet long. Beautiful, glossy, shining 'eye' feathers flashing in the light of my torch. *Five bob in the bag*.

Out of the shed. As I started out across the lawn the front door opened and the Forbeses' fat Welsh corgi waddled out onto the gravel drive. I froze. Fear rocketed up from deep inside my gut. Mrs F was a hard silhouette in the yellow light from the porch, a sinister effigy of dread. 'Hurry up,

Blodwyn,' she called out. The dog was staring in my direction on the edge of the pool of light. I shrunk back towards the hut. It was a mistake. It detected my movement and advanced, yapping furiously. 'Bloddie! Bloddie, what is it?' she called out. Turning back to the house, she shouted, 'Bernard! Come quickly, Bloddie's seen something.'

Bernie leapt out of his chair and appeared in the porch beside his wife. He strode out into the driveway and flicked on a large lantern. The beam swept across the lawn to the dog and then to the peacock shed. 'I bet it'll be that bloody fox again.' His voice charged the night air with dread. 'What is it, Blod? What have you got there?' The dog came ever nearer, still barking. The beam swept right to my feet. I wanted to drop the feathers and run for it, but I knew that would be a disaster. I dared not move. 'Call her in, Bernard. We don't want her getting bitten. Foxes have rabies.'

Bernie guffawed his pompous, haughty laugh I had heard so often. 'Not rabies, Meg, there is no rabies in Britain, but mange, yes. Foxes do have mange. Come on, Bloddie, in you come, no hunting tonight.' Slowly the dog turned and ambled back across the lawn, stopping twice and glancing back, a growl still rumbling in its throat. The Forbeses' and their corgi disappeared inside. The door closed and the porch light went out. I breathed again.

Still trembling, I sneaked into the school clutching ten large feathers. I headed to the changing rooms where I knew no one would be at that time of night. Then I did the most unbelievably stupid thing. I crammed the feathers into my games locker. They were too long, so I had to bend them double, breaking at least two in the process. Then I rushed upstairs to the dorm. I had failed to notice that the locker door had a gap at the bottom and at least one feather poked out into full view.

Dylan was already in bed. 'Where have you been? I thought you said it was your bath night.'

'Oh, I made a mistake.'

'You look a bit flushed, have you been fighting again?'

'No, no. I've just been running about outside.'

'Ye-ah. That's likely!'

After breakfast we filed into chapel. At the end of the service Bernie mounted the five steps to the pulpit. 'Last night a boy entered my peacock hut and cut tail feathers from three of my birds. I know who that boy is and I give him until eleven o'clock break to come to my study and own up.' *He's bluffing*, I thought, as fear pummelled my bowels. But I didn't yet know that while we were in break-fast all the house matrons had been instructed to search all lockers. The feathers had been found.

On the way out of chapel, Dylan sidled up to me. 'You stupid ass! You're in for it now. What the hell did you do that for?'

'How do y' know it was me?'

'It was ruddy obvious, Liss. In late, red-faced, out of breath and all that about your bath night.' My heart turned to stone, breakfast curdling in the pit of my stomach. 'Sorry, Dyl.' And I was. Oh God, I was sorry!

'Are you going to own up? You'll get the cane, you know.'

'He doesn't know who it was, does he?'

'Yes, he does. They've found the feathers. Where did you hide them?'

'In my games locker.'

'You daft twit! That's the first place they'd look. You're rumbled. You'd better own up and get it over with.'

So I did.

Beetroot-faced and fuming like a firework, Bernie roared at me. 'I might have guessed it was you. How dare you interfere with my property? You've been nothing but trouble since you arrived here. *And* you broke Butterworth's pen on purpose. *And* you lied to me. *And* you ran to Mrs Warmley to get her to support your lies. I am giving you minus eight for lying and minus eight for damaging my birds. I have spoken to your housemaster and he agrees that you are to go home immediately and not to return until next term. But first you must take your punishment. Bend over the arm of that chair.'

I closed my eyes. It seemed to take forever, counting seconds like waiting for thunder after lightning. *I'll get six for sure*, I thought. I heard his sharp intake of breath behind me . . . then a whistling rush of air. ONE! An electric stab of pain surged through my buttocks. Swish! TWO . . . I bit my lip. Images flashed through: my mother in her hospital bed, Nellie at the Aga, Mrs Warmley . . . I bit my lip again, hard. Swish! THREE . . . There was the dead dog and my grandfather lowering himself into his kitchen chair . . . My head was swimming, eyes clenched as hard as I could. Swish! FOUR . . . the Dun Cow rib swinging on its rusty chains . . . Swish! FIVE . . . I could taste the blood in my mouth, fingernails clawed at the leather. Swish! SIX. *Thank God*, I thought, *it's over*. 'Stay where you are,' he barked. Swish! SEVEN . . . The world went red, yellow, orange, white . . . Swish! EIGHT . . . I was squirming with pain, choking, chest bursting, desperate not to cry out. *I WILL NOT CRY*, I said to myself over and over again. *I WILL NOT GIVE HIM THE PLEASURE OF SEEING ME CRY.* Swish! NINE . . . Swish! TEN. 'Now get out of my sight. Matron will tell you when you are to go home.'

I ran to the lavatories, downed my trousers and plunged my handkerchief into cold water to bathe my screaming, raging bottom. Then I saw that I had wet myself. I cried. I cried and cried, grateful there was no one there to see.

★   ★   ★

That night at lights out Matron came and sat on the edge of my bed, placing a hand lightly on my hip, an uncharacteristic intimacy she had never shown before. She gave me two aspirins and a sip of water. 'To help you sleep,' her words a gentle whisper. 'Your father will be here to collect you at eleven o'clock.'

Word had spread like wildfire. The other boys in the dorm begged me to show them my wounds, but I refused. Dylan whispered, 'Hard cheese, Liss.' In the morning I tried to get into the cold baths early, but a fizz of sensation had crowded the bathroom before I could get there. There was nothing for it. To a gasp of horror I dropped my towel and leapt into the bath. I ducked under, holding for a full ten seconds. The cold water was curiously friendly, both calming and soothing. When I surfaced and stood up, a rousing cheer engulfed me. I smiled a limp acknowledgement as someone handed me my towel. A senior boy called out: 'Bloody hell, Liss! Bernie's a beast.' Back to the dorm I walked tall, my head full of the triumphant, sinew-stiffening moment Horatius plunged headlong into the Tiber, *'And when above the surges / They saw his crest appear, / All Rome sent forth a rapturous cry, / And e'en the ranks of Tuscany / Could scarce forbear to cheer.'*

At ten to eleven my father arrived. 'Hullo, old boy. You all right?' His huge hand landed reassuringly on my shoulder. He didn't seem angry. The Menace appeared looking stern and ushered him straight to Bernie's study. I hovered in the corridor. Several minutes ticked past. I could hear raised voices. When he emerged, my father was red-faced and tight-lipped. 'Come on, old thing.' His moustache bristled with – not anger, but fury – exploding the space around him and shedding like a trail of jagged scales. His heels echoed sharply from the parquet floor as we strode out to the car. I followed in silence, inwardly dreading his rage. But he had not called me John.

We drove away in silence. Down the avenue of pines to the copse. I glanced up at Mrs Warmley's window as we passed Hampton House. She was standing in the casement with a white handkerchief held to her face. She raised her hand in a faltering wave, a tiny token gesture, but it shouted from the hilltops to me. I waved back as vigorously as I could.

A few miles down the road my father pulled into a layby and turned the engine off. 'You're not going back to that place,' he announced solemnly without looking at me. 'You shouldn't have done what you did, but that man's got it in for you and I'm not having that.' Then he lit his pipe, fired up the engine and we drove forty miles without another word. I lay on my side on the back seat because I was so sore.

When we arrived home, my mother was in tears. 'Oh Jay, what have you done?' She sobbed as she hugged me.

'He's cut a few feathers off a bloody peacock, that's all he's done.' Still fuming, my father stomped up and down the hall. 'A prank. A silly schoolboy prank, that's all. Not the bloody end of the world. You'd think he'd stolen the crown jewels from the fuss Forbes made. He's not going back to that place, I tell you. Certainly not.'

Slowly it dawned on me that my parents weren't angry with me at all, but whatever Bernie had said to my father had enraged him. The tirade wasn't over. 'Did you smash that boy's pen, John? Tell me straight.'

'No.' I looked him in the eye. 'No, I had nothing to do with it.'

'As I thought,' he snapped. And to my mother, 'Our boy's a prankster, maybe, and a blithering young fool, Helen, but he's not a malicious little brat – that's what Forbes called him. And he's certainly not a bloody liar. Forbes hasn't heard the last of this, I tell you, not by a long chalk.'

I began to feel good. I was home. The whole Easter holiday spread out before me and soon we would be off to the Manor House. That night my mother made me have a bath. She wanted to see for herself. I heard the sharp intake of breath when she saw the grid of welts across my backside, raised in angry bars like a washboard, already showing the dark magenta of beetroot. She left the bathroom quickly. 'Christopher, you *must* come and see,' her voice sharp and unfamiliar. She wasn't just angry, she was spitting, the deeply roused outrage of a mild and generous spirit who abhorred all forms of violence.

'No, Helen. I don't want to humiliate the boy any more. They're only bruises and they'll heal soon enough. He's been through an ordeal. The important thing is he's learnt a lesson. From now on, he'll know a bully when he sees one.'

'*Yla'an haramak! Ibn himar! Ornak sharmoota!* Mr Bernard bloody Forbes.' Her words fired like bullets, hard and fast. *Good old Mum*, I thought.

13

Summer and the Arabian Nights

Long holidays, two houses: the *where* and the *when* now so impossibly merged into one long synthesis of freedom and utter rapture that the *which* no longer seems relevant. Perhaps it was the contrast, the release from the caustic strictures of boarding school and the knowledge that I wouldn't be going back, at least not to that regime. Perhaps because my parents weren't angry with me. Perhaps just having my mother home again had so completely transformed my world that a sunlit childish elation had flown in like a dove descending and taken me over. I found myself smiling and laughing out loud at the slightest incitement.

Our mother was still severely limited in what she could do with us, so it was always a broken-winged happiness, subconsciously constrained and prevented from lifting off again by the unspoken current of anxiety that her condition trailed through all our lives. The only available remedy was escape.

Both at the Manor House and Bartonfield, during her long absences, freedom had become the accidental and uncharted norm. No one had supervised me except in the most cursory definition of the term. Nellie had never been officially charged with my care, it had just been allowed to happen. In the nine and a half short years of my life, despite her best attempts at picnics and other family outings, my mother had never been well enough to oversee my out-of-doors play and can only have had the scantiest notion of what I got up to, and the significant others – the nanny figures in our lives – had never been equal to the task. Early on I had learned how to escape.

At both houses it was easy to disappear. At the Manor House there were so many exits to the outside that I could select a different one for each escapade, and while Bartonfield only had three outside doors, those at the back and side were both out of sight of any other part of the house. And then there was the upstairs lavatory window.

Russell Brock and Paul Wood's exceptional skills had greatly improved my mother's quality of life and had deferred the threat of imminent heart failure – a temporary lifeline, no more than that. She would never escape the malevolent and persistent corrosion of her valves. To regulate her struggling heart she took *digitalis* and *digoxin* every day – both derivatives of the venerable foxglove – immediately panicking if she forgot. Once, seeing tears in her eyes, I asked her, 'Why do you need them?'

'Come here, Jay.' She held her arms out to me. 'Now, listen.' She pressed my head to the left side of her chest, my ear flat to her heart. What I heard was more of a rumble than a heartbeat. There were lumpy, muted thumps and soft, whooshing noises like the echoing rush of distant traffic. They came and went, punctuated by random alarming pauses. 'That's why,' she whispered. No metronomic rhythm at all. 'I need my pills to keep my clock ticking.' And then she laughed the nervous little laugh she always produced when she was trying to make the best of things.

At home there was a new routine; she was on strict orders to rest on her bed for an hour every afternoon to allow the cardiac muscles to relax and recover. With her bedroom door open to listen, we children were encouraged to do the same, to read on our beds – an intolerable imposition to me when excitement beckoned outside.

It was the perfect opportunity for escape. Carrying my shoes, as long as I kept hard to the wall, the floorboards were silent. The rest was easy. I could climb out of the lavatory window and down the waste pipe. I was free. Out, past the stables and garages with a row of pigeons shimmering on the ridge, past the plot where Mark Cuff weeded the leeks and cabbages in tidy rows, down the old cider track and through the gate to the towering elm tree, the sentinel that marked the gateway to adventure, the beginning of my wild world.

*   *   *

I would not wish to mislead you. Neither Bartonfield's enticing orchards and damp fields nor the Manor House gardens and the Manor Farm's chervil-scented meadows of my boyhood were, by any contorted definition of the term, anything remotely approaching wilderness. They were no more than the friendly but fading echo of a far older, richer world. They were the un-mechanised and un-chemicalised countryside of post-war England, land that had been farmed for a thousand years and more.

It was a farmland unrecognisable today, now a vanished and a vanquished world. A farmland of labourers walking or cycling to work to hand-milk cows into a bucket; milk delivered warm and frothy to the Manor House back door every morning in white enamel cans; of the jingling harness of working horses and their rickety carts; of herb-rich meadows of clover, buttercups, cowslips, corn marigolds and ox-eye daisies humming with bumble bees and the rasping serenade of grasshoppers; of wheat cut by a binder's rattling blades, sheaves hand-tied with a twist of straw and leaned against each other in stooks of three dotting the fields like fleur-de-lys on a golden counterpane. When dry, they were pitchforked onto a trailer and hauled off to the tractor-powered thresher beside the barn, where the men yelled to each other above its roaring, churning and flailing din as the grain was beaten free. Bronze arms pitchforked the straw away into a stack while the chaff flew through a chute to a dusty heap.

It was the farmland of cockerels crowing at dawn and hens scratch-pecking through every yard and ditch; of haystacks in the corner of every field; of uncountable hordes of rats and mice; of dense thorn hedgerows skilfully laid by hand; of ducks dabbling messily on stagnant ponds and a brood of barn owls wheezing in every barn. Worked by farmers who paid country lads thruppence a rabbit to go ferreting and long-netting round the fields, it was the farmland of hay meadows and hedges brimming with cow parsley, meadowsweet, crimson poppies and ragged robin, loud with industrious bees and the omnipresent erratic flitterings of myriad butterflies. It was also the nocturnal farmland of bats in roofs and church belfries, of rabbit warrens on every bank, of foxes and badgers, of deer tiptoeing out of the woods at dusk, and a dawning world of hedgehogs and hares, otters and water voles in streams, of weasels and stoats, and chirruping hosts of farmland birds – linnets, corn buntings, turtle doves, goldfinches and yellowhammers flittering like blown sunshine through the fields and along luxuriant hedgerows bright with crab apples, sloes, hips and haws, where every autumn hosts of thrushes, redwings and fieldfares gorged like avian locusts – a thronging, simmering diversity almost unimaginable in today's machine- and chemical-purged agri-deserts.

To a country boy this tapestry of colour, movement and mystery was an irresistible draw, a treasure trove wholly unimagined, each discovery bursting unforgettably into my consciousness: every newt a nugget of gold, every wren's nest a gem, every slow worm a bracelet of silver. To a nine-year-old, a muddy ditch became a great wetland. A tangled hawthorn thicket with a magpie's nest embodied all the thrill of the wild wood. It was a countryside that never ended: always another lane, another haystack, another copse, pond, spinney, thicket and rambling, unkempt hedgerow to probe and crawl through, always a far-off woodland to discover, another stream, river, reed bed and marsh to explore. The cold ingenuity of insects to fathom. They became the private and deeply personal wildernesses of my dreams.

Out there those dreams came alive. I was discovering a countryside of thrilling and boundless adventure. I wandered and watched and listened, pried and prodded my way into its limitless undertakings. On cardboard wings woodpigeons clattered off their twiggy nests in the gnarled forks of ancient cider apple trees, easy to climb to, where two fat squabs squatted like overfed miniature dinosaurs. When a sparrow-hawk coasted over the orchards, trailing a tension of fear through the songbirds around me, I watched with awe and shared the sparkle of its urgent electricity while overhead buzzards inscribed their sky-wide circles above the woods. Rabbits scuttled for their burrows and I ran to plunge my arm in after them to see if I could catch one. I never could; the burrows were always too deep, but the thrill that one day I might be lucky never waned. I knelt on the piled diggings of badger setts to breathe in the musky aroma of freshly dug earth and a redolent animal presence. It was a natural history naturally gleaned. I had no concept of it at the time, but I was subconsciously building knowledge and understanding. It was an apprenticeship, time being served and the accumulation of experience I would call upon for the rest of my life.

*   *   *

One summer my wanderings took me a few miles along a tributary of the River Parrett near the sleepy village of Kingsbury Episcopi, where I habitually went to explore the muddy wonderland of the riverbank. Wind-rippled, light-flung, cursed by the heron's rough crake, I knew it as the land's secret edge. Water voles plopped into the slow stream and moorhens scuttled into the reeds fluting alarm, leaving a pointillist trail across the weed-stippled surface.

There I met a tramp known locally as 'Old Much', after the ancient abbey at Muchelney, one of the lowest flood-prone hollows of the Somerset Levels. He over-wintered in a hay barn beside the abbey, where I had first bumped into him while searching for barn owls. I believe his real name was Dan Tucker, but he was Old Much to just about everyone and always would be. All summer he lived out, moving from farm to farm, building crude shelters from the bent branches of osier willows that sprouted energetically along the wet ditches.

Old Much looked as rough as guts – but that was misleading. Where you could see skin through thickets of grizzled beard and scarecrow hair, it had the complexion of old chamois leather dotted with black blotches, but that hid a gnarled, intense handsomeness that would have been frightening if his eyes had not shone with friendliness and a smile of impish excitement revealing a row of surprisingly intact, tobacco-stained teeth. He wore a greasy old trilby with jay's wing feathers of startling blue tucked in the band. In his stained khaki greatcoat, tied with a plait of twine around his waist, and hobnailed boots beneath heavy serge trousers, he reeked like an old goat, smoking in a broken pipe such tobacco as he could get, made to go further with dried old man's beard from the hedges, rubbed together between grimy palms.

Old Much had lived off the land for decades, troubling no one. The local farmers who perhaps knew of his time in the trenches tolerated – no, I think better than that – freely accepted him as part of their landscape. It was said that he was a shell-shock case from the First World War, which would place him in his mid-fifties when I knew him – and anyway, people had concluded over many years that he was entirely harmless. He possessed curiously extravagant manners, always lifting his hat to women he passed on the roads and bowing when he thanked folk for their frequent kindnesses. Whatever trauma he had suffered had left him with an uncontrollable stammer, which would have been alarming enough had it not been for his openness toward everyone he met. It certainly never hindered his ability to find food and look after himself.

Mark Cuff told me that many villagers gave Old Much cast-off clothes, eggs, vegetables and even occasionally tobacco, but that he would never enter a house, almost as if that might somehow compromise his dedication to the wildness of his beloved hedgerows. If my parents had discovered that I kept such company, they would have been aghast and banned it immediately, but he only rarely came to Martock, so there was little fear of them ever finding out. At his own level I believe he lived contentedly and well. He would appear from the hedge as I cycled the country back lanes or down by the river where I went fishing for perch. I can hear his cheery greeting now, "Ullo J-J-J-J-Jack, b-b-b-boy. W-w-w-w-w-w-what's up with 'ee t-t-t-t-t'day?'

It was Old Much who introduced me to the sly trick of patiently observing woodpigeons' nests until the twin squabs were nearly big enough to fly. At this crucial point he would climb the tree and tie the hapless squabs' legs to their twiggy nest with a short length of twine. The doting parent birds would continue to feed their chicks indefinitely – until, that is, a few weeks later he returned to harvest them for his supper. By then they would be as fat as a Christmas goose, larger than the adult pigeons, and, with wings that had never flown, their plum-coloured breasts would be the most succulent morsels you could ever hope to sink your teeth into. In the summer months he often had ten pigeons' nests on the go at once – twenty suppers to be char-grilled on a stick held over his fire.

This was by no means his only ploy. In the embers he baked hedgehogs in a ball of clay, the spines sticking to the shell when he cracked it open. He told me that young grey squirrels filched from the drey were sweet when boiled with a potato; he showed me how to make a sort of chewy damper from the soft, tart pith hollowed from kale stems grown for cattle feed; he 'borrowed' mallard, teal, pheasant and partridge eggs from nests – never more than two – so that the birds kept on laying week after week. Most nights he milked a cow in the field and drank it hot from the udder; and he fermented his own rough cider in spring-clip-stoppered lemonade bottles thrust into the heat of a haystack. He taught me to snare rabbits and how to tie a bag net under a field gate and then frighten a hare into it. He never asked for anything except once quite early on, as I was departing, 'Y' c-c-c-couldn't find me a b-b-b-b-box o' m-m-m-m-matches, could 'ee, Jack?' After that I always took him matches.

But my favourite exploit on which I joined him on several

moonlit nights was eeling in wet meadows between the river
and a series of ponds which used to abound in that soggy
corner of Somerset. 'You w-w-w-wanna c-c-c-come e-e-e-
eelin' t'night, J-J-J-Jack, boy?' In certain seasons, when heavy
dew soaks you to the knees, eels leave the rivers and rhynes
(drainage ditches) and snake their way overland through the
long grass to these ponds. Old Much seemed to know it all.
He would sit on a hessian sack beside a pond and listen
intently, holding a slender, forked hazel stick at the ready.
The eels came in clots of three and four together, olive
green, slimy and sometimes over a foot long. ''Ere's a g-g-g-
g-good 'un,' he would cry, leaping up and pinning it to the
grass with the fork and then stabbing another sharp twig
down its mouth and out at the gills. When he had three or
four squirming in his sack, he would call it a day. 'D-d-d-
don't want to spoil it, now, do us?' Old Much knew nothing
of conservation, but he'd worked it out for himself. 'Y' take
t-t-t-too much an' you c-c-c-can't come b-b-b-back for more.'

*　　*　　*

That summer my parents tried to get me into another prep
school. It seemed hopeless. Private schools were bursting at
the seams; the de-mob baby boom had seen to that. One
morning my father announced that I would have to go to
the village school in Martock. I liked that idea. It was close,
a short walking distance from Bartonfield, and I would no
longer have to board. It sounded pretty good to me. Before
the end of the holidays, he added, 'You will have to go and
meet Mr Barron, the headmaster.'

'As long as he's not like Mr Forbes,' was my curtly muttered
retort.

The Hampton Down imbroglio had not entirely died. One

day my parents drove me to Bristol 'To see a doctor.' Confused, I thought that it was for my mother. It wasn't. 'He's a special doctor for youngsters like you,' my father said, explaining nothing.

'I don't need a doctor, do I?'

'Don't worry,' my mother smiled at me. 'He only wants to talk to you.'

The brass plate read 'Dr Fordham', buttressed by a string of incomprehensible initials. He was a child psychologist with rooms in Clifton overlooking the famous Brunel suspension bridge. He was jolly and slightly portly, wearing a three-piece Harris tweed suit in a hairy windowpane check, the sporty effect topped with a bow tie. A gold watch chain undulated between the pockets of his waistcoat. A wide smile rippled across his ruddy complexion and wobbled his double chins when he laughed. The waiting room had a gas fire and I remember finding a copy of a *Beano Annual* while my parents went in with him. 'Won't be long,' he said breezily.

When it was my turn, they left the room. I sat on an upright chair with a shiny leather seat. 'You've got nothing to worry about, but I need to ask you some questions,' he beamed at me reassuringly. 'Now I hear you've been in quite a bit of trouble at school. Can you tell me about that?' He listened intently and scribbled notes at his desk. 'And you're sure you had nothing to do with breaking Butterfield's fountain pen?'

'Yes,' I answered flatly. 'Quite sure.' Doing my best to swallow my surging indignation. How many times and how many people did I have to tell before they believed me? 'And he was Butterworth not Butterfield,' I added sourly.

'Ah yes.' He scribbled some more. When we got to Bernie's caning, he asked me: 'How many strokes did you get?'

'Ten.'

'Are you sure it was ten?'

'Yes,' I said. 'I counted them.'

'Are you quite sure it was ten? You're not exaggerating, are you?'

I glowered at him. *What a stupid question*, I thought. 'I can count,' I replied sullenly.

Then he changed tack. 'Now this was about two and a half weeks ago, I think your father said?'

'Yes.'

'Have you still got marks on your bottom?'

'I think so.'

'I'd like to see, if you don't mind.' I stood up and undid my short trousers. He came round from his desk and stood behind me. He lowered the top of my underpants. 'Hmmm. I see.' He went back to his desk. He pulled a gold watch out of his waistcoat pocket and glanced at it. 'Now you didn't like Mr Forbes, did you?'

'No. I hated him and he hated me.'

'What makes you think he hated you?'

Another silly question. I thought hard for several seconds. 'Mrs Warmley told me . . .' His eyebrows shot up above the gold rims of his glasses. 'And she said he was a bully.'

'Oh, did she?' He scribbled furiously, nodding, 'Did she now?'

When he called my parents in, my mother came straight to me and put her arm round me. 'All right?' she whispered, as she pressed my head to her cheek. There was a brief discussion. I was asked to leave the room. The door stayed open. I heard Dr Fordham tell them there was a corporal punishment convention of a maximum of six strokes. Then I heard the words 'unnecessary violence'. *I could have told you that*, I thought.

My father had loosed off an angry letter to the chairman of the Hampton House governors demanding a written justification for Bernie's breach of the convention and a return of the term's fees. A skirmish of threats and counter threats ensued, salvoes of solicitors' letters and harshly spoken telephone calls. A number of parents had been shocked by the way I had been caned and had threatened to withdraw their boys from the school. One of these, a Mr Peter Pargeter, was a local solicitor who offered to act for my father free of charge. His wet and apparently delicate son, Jeremy, with far too thin a neck and a runny nose, had been in the maths class with Butterworth and me, but between sniffs he had been decent enough to say he didn't think I had anything to do with it. He was withdrawn from the school that summer.

Mrs Warmley had also spoken up for me, convinced that I had nothing to do with the destruction of Butterworth's pen. She had told my parents Bernie 'had it in for me' and she had threatened to lodge a formal complaint to some overarching independent schools' authority. In the end, faced with legal action, more boys being withdrawn and the threat of bad publicity, Bernie caved in and wrote a letter of apology to my parents, fees repaid in full. My father was tickled pink. He bought me a sheath knife with a gleaming stainless steel blade in a leather sheath. Superseding my grandfather's clasp knife, it shot to the top of the list – the best present I had ever been given.

Off we all went to the Manor House. Proudly, I showed Nellie my new knife. 'Ooh, that's a beauty, just what I wants for cuttin' cabbages,' she teased, feigning to take it away.

'Oh no you don't,' I countered, pulling at her arm.

She handed it back. 'Now you just be careful what you gets up to, young Jack, or you'll be for it!'

I laughed loudly as I ran off. It seemed to me that I had been 'for it' far too much lately. I still didn't do irony, and besides, nothing mattered any more. I was away from Hampton House, away from boarding, away from the dystopian world of pompous Bernie and his swishing, stinging cane. My all-forgiving mother was back, issuing love and grace in equal measure. Nellie was there, right there, the same as always, laughing, teasing, adding succour to the generous, all-redeeming boundaries of my universe. There would be Aga toast and honey for tea and my grandfather would come in from his glasshouses and lower his great length into the big carver at the end of the table and ask, 'What you bin up to, boy?'

* * *

What I got up to was not intended to be trouble, but often seemed to court it. The law of unintended consequences chose to settle its unfair mantle upon me most of the time. So it was with the Arabian swords.

Rigid convention unchanged from Victorian days required that at bedtime, bathed, teeth-cleaned, hair brushed and in our pyjamas, dressing gowns and slippers, we were taken to the smoking room to say goodnight to the old boy (born in 1873, he was an immutable Victorian). It was a solemn affair. Nellie would knock on the door before entering, ushering us in in silence.

That room was a museum of intrigue and fascination for a child, and as I had been told repeatedly throughout my childhood, strictly out of bounds. It served as his study and estate office, where he sat at a huge roll-top desk beside the French windows leading out onto a wisteria entwined verandah with steps down onto the smoking-room lawn.

Sometimes he would be there, working at his papers, writing letters in his looping copper-plate hand, sometimes sitting in his vast wing chair beside the coal fire, almost always smoking one of his block Meerschaum pipes that sat in a rack beside him. A cigar humidor stood in the corner. The whole room reeked like a 1930s gents' Piccadilly club.

We were allowed to sit on the red leather-topped fender for a few minutes only. A brief exchange followed: 'Well, have you had a nice day?' 'Yes, thank you, Grandpa.' 'Have you caught any nice butterflies today?' – my latest passion. 'Yes, Grandpa, I got a red admiral and a green hairstreak.' 'Did you now? Well done, where did you get those?' 'The red admiral on the plum trees on the tennis court wall, and the hairstreak in brambles in the School Lane hedge.' 'Well done, dear boy, well done.' Then on tiptoe we would kiss him on his bald head as he leaned forward and patted us fondly on the shoulder. 'Goodnight, Grandpa.' And that was that. We would be ushered out.

Every time we performed this ritual, I spotted some other item of burning fascination. There was the long ivory spiral of a narwhale tusk propped in a corner. A stuffed hairy wild boar piglet was wedged behind the spindle bars of an ornately carved sideboard among rows of leather-bound books and a rank of very ancient pewter plates. Fallow deer antlers topped the bookcase. To one side an old English double-hammer shotgun with brown Damascus barrels straddled the wall. I tiptoed round a world globe on a side table, longing to spin it, and eyed with wonder a ticking barograph with its rotating trace of gentian violet. Little clusters of miniature portraits and silhouettes of family long dead studded another wall. On his desk I spied a long ivory letter opener with a huge curved whale's tooth mounted in silver for the handle, and the faded skin of an African spotted cat, perhaps an ocelot, flopped sensuously over the back of a chair.

I longed to examine these treasures, but dared not. We had been given strict instructions never to enter the smoking room unless taken there with an adult, and never to touch anything. My curiosity grew tendrils like a beanstalk. I had to be dragged out, longingly staring back over my shoulder at some new enticement I had only just spotted. But above all, trumping all other items, were the two curved Arabian swords, crossed like an insignia, hanging high up on the wall.

Always encouraging my reading, my mother had given me a children's version of *The Arabian Nights*. I knew Aladdin and Sinbad the Sailor intimately and had been utterly gripped by Ali Baba and the Forty Thieves. Those two swords must surely have belonged to a Persian king and were probably the very ones used to execute the virgin brides in the story of *Scheherazade*, the Grand Vizier's daughter. They had scuffed leather sheaths and silver hilts, woven handgrips with golden braid and fur tassels. 'Do you think Grandpa would let me see the swords?' I asked Nellie.

'Ooh, I don't know about things like that, you'd better ask your dad.' But I didn't. I knew he would say NO.

I lay in bed and wondered. I dreamed of climbing up and lifting one down. I dreamed of drawing it slowly out of its sheath, clasping the braided grip and flashing the blade through the air in a great sweep like Bernie's cane. Then I dreamed of slicing off his head like the Shah's hapless brides . . .

The sun awoke me, impaling my window with savage halberds of daffodil light. Motes of dust danced in its dazzling shafts. Rooks were cawing and racketing in a sky raked by the vast old beeches and oaks in the churchyard. The Bowler

in the hall struck with its ponderous booming chime. One
. . . two . . . three . . . four . . . five o'clock. I blinked into
not just awake but as wide awake and eager as the sun itself.
Then I remembered the swords. Would I ever get to touch
the swords? The church clock clanged five falsetto bells and
the feral pigeons on the tower clattered away in alarm.

No one gets up at five o'clock, I thought. *Not even Nellie.* I
dressed quickly. Out into the corridor on tiptoe and silently
on down into the hall. The Bowler ticked portentously. I
heaved open the heavy swing door into the servants' quarters, grimy green baize on both sides, and closed it quietly
behind me. I ran down the corridor to the game larder, past
the rows of black riding boots and jackets, and turned out
into the stable yard through the back door.

Outside I sauntered, adventure bubbling excitedly in my
chest. Up through the tall, boarded gate into the gardens
and past the smoking-room lawn. The French windows onto
the verandah were never locked. *I could just take a quick look
at those swords. No one will know.* The doors clicked open and
the stern embrace of stale tobacco flooded over me.

A bergère and a table piled with books and copies of *Punch*
and *Country Life* stood immediately underneath the swords.
Up onto the bergère and I could touch the tip of the sheaths.
Up onto the table and I could reach the hilts. Carefully and
slowly I lifted one off its hooks. Heavier than I expected, it
took all my strength to draw the blade from the sheath –
long, curved, with a vicious point and an edge like broken
glass. It was magnificent. I wanted to swing it like the Persian
executioner, but there wasn't room. I moved out onto the
verandah with its rows of terracotta pots of rambling geraniums and its wisteria twisting and winding vine-like up
through the wrought iron work. Still no room to swing it
properly.

Down the steps onto the smoking-room lawn. I was in full view of the bedrooms high above, so I ran fast and silently out onto the Broadwalk. I ran and ran, determined not to stop until I was well away from the house. At last a good barrier of laurel shrubbery protected me. I relaxed and swung the sword. Wheesh! Wheesh! The blade sang and flashed through the bright morning air. Wheesh! and off came the tops of a dozen stinging nettles. Swish again and a whole throng of thistle heads leapt into the air, scattering dew like penny brilliants. This was fun.

At the end of the Broadwalk, now well away from the house, I climbed the post and rail fence into the paddock adjoining the farm. Wheesh! A forest of tall cow parsley collapsed into the grass. Just then I heard the triumphant crowing of a cockerel pricking the dawn from the farmyard. I wandered over to see. There he stood, as proud as a weather vane, strutting and crowing his morning machismo. He was majestic. Bright scarlet crest wattles and glowing, golden mantle, resplendent green tail feathers curving out behind him in an extravagant arc. *Ha!* I thought. *It's a villain in disguise.* I ran at the cockerel, flailing the blade in front of me like a Cossack with a sabre. The bird ran flapping and squawking in alarm. 'Stop and fight!' I yelled. It ran on. I gave chase, still flailing the sword wildly from side to side. Suddenly it changed direction, swerving hard to my right – too late to stop the swing of the heavy blade. Whump! and off came the cockerel's head, clean at the neck.

I stood and stared in disbelief. The bird's body was flapping about on the ground, legs still running, pedalling air, blood gushing out of its neck and pooling thickly in the dust. The head lay three feet away, beak agape, astonished eye staring at me from the dirt. *Oh cripes!* I thought. *What have I done?*

It has taken me sixty years to confess to this lurid, accidental crime. I never breathed a word to a soul, not even to Nellie. Howson, the intemperate Manor Farm tenant, the man who had shot his own dog, complained angrily that a fox had taken his prize bird. He accused my uncle Aubrey of harbouring the fox in the Manor grounds – a charge we all knew to be more than likely. I sat at the tea table and listened to the discussion between my grandfather, uncle and my father, longing to join in but gagged by guilt. What seemed so unfair, and still rankles today, is that I did not mean to harm the bird at all.

A prankster, my father had called me. That had seemed almost complimentary at the time, far better than anything Bernie had said. Now it rang a little hollow. This escapade had not been intended as a prank, and chasing the wretched bird was certainly unpremeditated. No, as usual, I was behaving wildly, caught in the wrong place at the wrong time when the witless cockerel made its fatal sidestep – in that split second its error became my crime, guilt greatly magnified by the self-imposed silence of fear. The capricious law of unintended consequences had visited itself upon me once again.

I hid the cockerel and its head in the thickest patch of stinging nettles I could find and I scrubbed the blood into the dirt with my feet. Then I ran back to the house, stopping only to wipe the blade clean on the dewy lawn. A few minutes later the sword was back in its sheath on the wall. I scuttled indoors and leapt up the stairs two at a time. As I climbed back into bed the Bowler struck six.

A few days later I crept over the fence to see if the cockerel was still there – the criminal drawn back to the scene of the crime. Nothing. I searched and searched. No sign of the body or the head, not a feather. Only a smear of blood on the nettle stems and a few gobs of clotted blood on the bare ground at their roots. I laughed and laughed, skipping and dancing all the way back to the house. The fox had got it after all.

14

'All my holy mountain'

'In the beginning was the Word, and the Word was with God, and the Word was God.' It couldn't have been clearer. *'All things were made by him; and without him was not any thing made that was made.'* So that was that. No room for doubt and even less for argument in the two boarding schools that had so far been responsible for shaping my mind.

I can't remember at what age religion first appeared as a classroom subject. I'm sure it would have been at Hampton Down and it was probably called Scripture. From the very beginning it was made clear to us all that the whole educational ethos was founded upon and revolved around a GOD, usually, but confusingly by no means always, called Jesus Christ. Even more bewilderingly we were told that this God was plural, the 'Godhead, three in one', the Father, the Son and the Holy Ghost, the last of these a particularly appealing notion to a seven-year-old, and someone I longed to meet. I visualised the Ghost as an angelic-looking older boy, perhaps a teenager, with wings and a halo, whom, if I was very lucky, I might glimpse flitting mysteriously in and out of churches and chapels with the unquestioned ability to be everywhere at once.

Slowly and irrevocably, such imaginings led us dumb and blindfolded into the mystical, and at that point in our slug-like progress toward the unimagined sunlit heights of awareness, the mysteriously undefined concept of spirituality. We were simply required to believe what we were told, a part of the pattern of life. I don't think any of us ever questioned it or, more significantly, understood it.

At Hampton House we had been made to say our prayers at bedtime. When I wasn't praying for the downfall of Twig, I prayed to go home. From a mishearing of 'Hallowed be thy name', Betty prayed fervently to Harold. Such were the religious boundaries of my known world. I don't ever recall praying for my mother to get better because I had never fully accepted that she might not. And although on Sundays the whole family dutifully attended church across the lane from the Manor House, waiting for the saddling bell and entering last to take our places in the family pew we had occupied for centuries, I had never really associated this conformist ritual with either the God we had been taught about or religion in general. It was just something we did, one more unchallenged ingredient tipped into life's preordained recipe. Nor was I in the slightest aware that any of my family might have adhered to a faith. It was simply never mentioned.

At Hampton Down we attended chapel every morning and twice on Sundays. Bernie never missed a chance to bray about the school's long-standing Christian foundation. Missionaries came from countries I'd never heard of and preached to us about the evils and the ignorance of the heathen and of savages apparently living their entire lives in the pitch darkness of unenlightened purdah. Moral rectitude was ladled out in bucketsful, pious, self-serving and imperious. The underlying message was always the same – our God was not just the good God, the great God and the right God, but he was also the only God, despite occasionally being plural. It was a given, brooking no dissent and stifling all debate. This rigid diktat was further endorsed by frequent sprinklings of the word 'gospel', which, it was militarily drilled into us, meant 'the absolute truth of God's word'. I would go on believing that for years. When much later I discovered that it meant nothing of the sort – that its proper translation was simply 'good news' – I felt duped.

The inevitable consequence of this indoctrination from such an early age was that we didn't just believe it, we never dreamed of either questioning it or exploring any alternative view – a point which now seems to me to deny the very basis of education and the development of critical faculty. The fact is that by the age of nine I not only believed that the Bible was God's word, I liked it too.

By some curious genetic alchemy I had inherited a precocious awareness of metre and cadence. Combinations of words fell naturally into rhythms – rhythms that either sounded right or they jarred. Wholly untaught and certainly not influenced by either of my parents, it was the first teetering step toward a lifelong love of poetry, which, I quickly discovered, I found easy to learn by heart. Sixty years later I can still reel off the long, rhythmic verses of Macaulay's *Horatius at the Bridge*, of Coleridge's *The Rime of the Ancient Mariner* and Yeats's 'The Lake Isle of Innisfree', as well as yards of Shakespeare's iambic pentameter, all downed at school like cod liver oil and sticky and delicious malt extract that we were given every day, taken and absorbed without question. It would be some time before anyone recognised this affinity for poetry and even longer before I realised that not everyone shared it, but one unsolicited event brought it sharply to my attention for the first time.

We were versed in the King James Authorised Version of both the Holy Bible and the Book of Common Prayer – the seventeenth-century literary masterpieces that were still in universal use throughout the Church of England. Although the original muscular translation from Latin and Greek had been tweaked many times over the centuries, and canonical pedants had quibbled endlessly over tiny details, the overall literary brilliance of that translation was never challenged. It was what the portmanteau term 'Scripture' meant to us all – weighty, leather-bound family Bibles at the Manor House, even larger ones on school chapel and church lecterns, red prayer books, psalters and navy blue hymnals, 'Ancient and Modern'. The whole religious experience seemed to me to resonate around the sonorous, immutable solidity of an unquestionable presence, the unfathomable truths of which lay hidden between the covers of those ancient and venerable tomes.

Mr George Barron, the Martock village schoolmaster, had asked to interview me before I attended the school at the end of the summer holidays. Holding his huge hand, my father trailed me through the village, past the imposing and dignified thirteenth-century church, to meet Mr and Mrs Barron one August afternoon. They lived in a new house in the grounds of the large Georgian vicarage with their only daughter, Susan, who was almost exactly my age. Hair brushed and shoes polished, I wore my now redundant Hampton Down uniform. Smiling broadly, Mr Barron answered the door. 'Hullo, John. You look very smart.'

This new headmaster displayed none of the pomp and disciplinarian aura that had surrounded Bernie. It would be several weeks before I began properly to comprehend the oceanic difference between the grand, inflated authority of the British private school system and the practical, undis-tilled, rough-and-ready approach delivered by rural village primary schools of the day.

Mr Barron had a round face and the dark hair and swarthy

complexion of the Ordovician Celts. In his forties, he was quietly but clearly spoken, with carefully enunciated words charged with a gentle and friendly authority. Mrs Barron gave me a Wagon Wheel, a large chocolate biscuit with a squishy jam and marshmallow filling. The interview turned out to be little more than a friendly chat. Mr Barron asked me what subjects I enjoyed most. Without thinking, I said, 'Shooting.'

'Humph. I'm afraid you won't be doing that at Martock,' was his mildly amused response. Hampton Down had had its own indoor small-bore range where we lay in pairs on gym mats with an instructor between us and fired open-sighted .22 rifles at targets twenty-five yards away. I had emerged as a good shot and I was proud of it. 'Mr Barron means classroom subjects' – a reproving frown from my father.

'Oh, English,' I added quickly. 'I like English best.'

On the way out, I heard Mr Barron confide, 'Better not to wear his old school uniform.' When I turned to shake his hand, I noticed a movement on the stairs. Their dark-haired daughter Susan was eyeing me suspiciously through the banisters.

Since we were near the vicarage my father took me to meet the Reverend Lionel Walsh, a tall, imposing man of natural dignity, balding with ruddy cheeks and a ringing laugh, who had been a loyal friend to my mother throughout her illness. The vicarage stood in grounds of fine mature trees and neatly mown lawns. Mr Walsh ushered us into a formal study, with a noted absence of chocolate biscuits.

The introduction only lasted a few minutes, but the vicar instructed me to return a few nights later for some private religious tuition to prepare me for the new school. 'Be sure to bring your Bible.' *Why do I need special religious instruction for this new school?* I worried on the way home. It built on anxieties already implanted by my mother, who had proffered mysteriously, 'You'll find this little school very different.'

'How will it be different?' I had quizzed from the fog of innocence.

She backed off, almost as though she didn't want to pursue it. 'You'll see.' Then, as an afterthought, 'It is very small.'

Two evenings later I returned to the vicarage, clutching an old black leather Bible. Mr Walsh took me into a large, sparsely furnished dining room where we sat at the table. To my surprise he took the Bible from me and turned quickly to Isaiah, Chapter XI. 'I'd like you to read this chapter down to verse nine, please. Nice and loud.' I took a deep breath and pitched in. *'There shall come forth a rod out of the stem of Jesse, and a Branch shall grow out of his roots . . .'* – I don't think I understood a word, but it wasn't difficult to read – *'. . . for the earth shall be full of the knowledge of the LORD, as the waters cover the sea.'*

'Well! Well!' He was nodding and smiling expansively. 'Have you read those verses before?'

'No, sir.'

'Have you ever read a lesson in church?'

'No, sir.'

'Would you care to? We have a harvest festival next month. I'm looking for someone young to read that passage.'

I was surprised, but the compliment had scored. My cheeks glowed. This vicar seemed nice, not a bit like pompous Bernie or sour old Reverend Ferguson at the Manor House church, who always glowered and made me feel guilty for no reason at all. Besides, I loved the music of those words, and all the animals: *'. . . and the wolf also shall dwell with the lamb, and the leopard shall lie down with the kid; and the calf and the young lion and the fatling together . . . and the cow and the bear shall feed . . . and the lion shall eat straw like the ox'*. But most of all I loved the sound of it: the rolling metre; the sonorous, tonal modulation of its phrases; its commanding cadences that drew me further and further into the swirling authority of its language from so long ago, carrying with it a certainty infused with a strange and beguiling awe. 'Yes, sir,' I said, without another thought. 'Yes, I would.'

That day stands out because in some strange way I had suddenly become an immeasurable fraction more aware both of myself and of the written word. It was a dawning, not of any great revelation – far from it – and precious little to do with religion, but it was a tiny incremental step away from the existential mindlessness and childish impenetrability of my own being. Until that moment my world had been largely defined by the likes, dislikes, rules, decisions and edicts of others without reference either to what I might have thought or wished. This decision was different, not earth-shatteringly different, nor would it change much, but it was mine and mine alone – and perhaps, just perhaps, it was the beginning of the discovery of *ME*.

Looking back now, I thank that kind vicar for giving me the chance to read the lesson, for believing in me and giving me something to lift me away from the fear and the hurt of beatings, of Hampton Down, and from the nagging dread of my mother's illness, and from constantly being in trouble. On my way home I entered that splendid medieval church with brighter eyes and a new spring in my step, determined to do my best.

It was cool inside and my footsteps echoed from the flagged floor. The massive oak door clunked shut behind me. Parallel arcades of tall, pointed arches framed the nave on both sides, embracing an empty silence. From high windows the dying sun slid golden stripes across the carved pews. An ornately patterned and heavily sculpted timber ceiling of dark oak bore down from high above. *Would I like to walk up this aisle to the great carved eagle lectern with most of the village faithful staring at me? Could I make my voice heard?* I walked forward to the chancel steps, footsteps echoing in the loaded silence. A wave of self-belief flooded in. The vicar had asked me to read a lesson. *ME.*

The lectern was only a few feet away. I stepped up and looked out between the spread wings of the great bird, its rapacious hooked beak and hooded eye half turned toward me, as though it didn't quite trust what I was up to. I imagined all the villagers sitting there, Mr and Mrs Browne from the ironmongers, Mrs Walsh, Mark and Dizzy Cuff, Mother, Father and Mary too. Perhaps Mr and Mrs Barron would be there with their daughter, Susan. Then in the loudest voice I could manage without shouting, I pealed out the only Isaiah lines I could remember '. . . *and the weaned child shall put his hand on the cockatrice' den. They shall not hurt nor destroy in all my holy mountain.*'

Out from the shadows of a side aisle came an old man wearing a flowing black gown. He limped and was stooped with age. "Ullo, young 'un.' He smiled and nodded. 'You readin' Sunday? I'm Mr Morley, the verger. Give you a fright, did I?'

'No, no,' I said, blushing horribly. 'Mr Walsh asked me to read later on, for the harvest festival.'

That night I lay awake. I read and re-read the Isaiah passage. I hadn't a clue what a cockatrice was, or an asp, and I had no idea why the lion should eat straw like the ox, but I loved the undulating landscape of its images, every rolling syllable. '*He shall smite the earth with the rod of his*

mouth, and with the breath of his lips shall he slay the wicked.'
God had spoken. I loved it all.

★ ★ ★

That summer holidays we spent at the Manor House, where, unforgettably, I would witness an event of biblical dimensions, the chilling ramifications of which would mark a shift in the way I thought about animals and stay with me for life. I have already said that haystacks, sometimes the size of cottages, were a common feature of farm life in those days. Often they were of hay, a store for winter feed for cattle, sheep and horses, and others were skilfully constructed corn-stacks of harvested sheaves – wheat, barley or oats – waiting to be brought in to the thresher. A bulging larder of ripe grain-filled ears, a cereal bonanza for rats and mice.

At kitchen tea one afternoon Nellie told my grandfather that a call had gone out from the Manor Farm for local boys to attend the dismantling of a large wheat-stack the following morning. 'You'll want to go, young Jack,' she said, making it sound as though it was something not to be missed. 'Would that be all right, sir?' to my grandfather.

'Have you ever seen a stack taken down?' He turned to me, peering over his half-moons.

'No,' I replied hesitantly, not understanding the significance of the event. 'Then you must go.' He was smiling and I thanked him warmly; any excuse to join in with things on the farm always excited me. The conversation ended.

After tea I asked Nellie what it was about.

'Rats,' she said. 'Ooh! I does hate rats.'

'What do you mean, rats?'

'You'll see. Mind you gets there early.' I didn't know what I felt about rats, but the prospect of finding out was an anticipation that bubbled and fizzed within my chest all night long. I couldn't wait.

When I arrived at the large stack in the corner of one of the Longbottom fields, the intemperate Manor Farm tenant, Howson, was there with his red David Brown tractor and a large trailer with outward angled hayracks at either end. Two of his men, George and Sid, armed with fierce-looking, two-pronged pitchforks, were standing on the trailer and two more men, whose names I didn't know, also with pitchforks, had climbed a ladder onto the top of the stack and were unpicking the straw thatch, the waterproof protection for the sheaves beneath. The stack was already surrounded by a gaggle of village boys and men, more arriving all the time, walking and running in, tipping their bicycles onto the hedge and hurrying to join the crowd. The air was loud with their shouts and a general buzz of excitement arose, engulfing us all. Everyone seemed to be armed with stout sticks.

Once the thatch was thrown aside, the two men on top began to fork the sheaves, sending them flying through the air down to George and Sid, who deftly caught them on their pitchforks and, with a flick of practised wrists, tossed them into place on the trailer. There must have been twenty onlookers by then, forming themselves into a tight cordon around the stack and the trailer, more arriving all the time. I still had no idea what was about to happen.

When the first layer of sheaves had been thrown, a few mice appeared, darted haphazardly to the edge of the stack and leapt to the ground, scuttling away into the hedge and vanishing. One or two youths swung at them half-heartedly as they passed. Then a rat. A shout went up – 'Hoy!' – and men were pointing. The rat hit the ground running and tried to nip past the hobnailed boots of the cordon. A club swung. A hefty swipe felled it with one blow. 'Hoy!' again, and 'Hoy! Look there, and over there!' Suddenly there were rats bursting out in all directions at once. The scene became a hubbub of excited shouts, wildly swinging clubs and sticks, and rats flying in all directions. 'Gor! There's a big 'un!' and 'Nice one, Dick! That got the bugger.' 'There! Bert, there!' Another two rats were smartly felled.

The two men up top never wavered. Their pitchforks stabbed and swung with an easy, unchanging rhythm. George and Sid calmly caught sheaf after flying sheaf, never missing, as the stack on the trailer grew and grew. It was a seamless, ageless ballet, performed with a sensuous and fluid grace, never hurrying, never changing pace, two sheaves flying through the air at once, the pitchforks immediately swinging back to raise another two in a mesmerising tandem of synchronised and apparently effortless skill.

The rats kept coming, mice darting helter-skelter among them. I was speechless at the sheer numbers. Hundreds of rodents, large and small, perhaps thousands. As each sheaf was lifted, a rat, sometimes two or three, huge ones almost the size of rabbits, middling ones and hordes of youngsters not much bigger than hamsters, seemed to be lurking beneath. They bolted in all directions, swarming so fast and so thick that many escaped untouched. And still they came.

This was the awesome horde of Samuel the Prophet, visited upon us by the wrath of God. It was a plague, a swarm, a multitude, a host, or a living, surging scourge unlike anything I had witnessed before. It belonged with Moses' plagues of locusts I had read about in Exodus, and the plagues of blood, flies, frogs and lice, the plague of rats and mice that 'marred the land of the Philistines'.

When the trailer was fully loaded, the ballet ceased. The tractor and trailer departed and the men climbed down. The farmer's wife arrived with flasks of steaming tea and home-made drop scones, sweets and lemonade for the boys. The men sagged to the stubble and leant against the stack. Boys ran round collecting up dead rats and piling them into a bloody heap. A shout would go up, 'That 'un's still alive, look!' and a cudgel would thwack to finish it off.

''Ow many's that, Marty?' someone called out.

''Bout four hundred 'n odd,' came the reply.

When the tractor returned, the whole riotous affray started all over again. A man walked over to me. 'You ain't got a stick, sonny. 'Ere, take this 'un.' He handed me a weighty blackthorn stick with a lumpy end. I thanked him and swung the cudgel. It felt good. A few minutes later they came again. A big rat, fully twelve inches from nose to tip of tail, came bounding straight at me. 'Get 'im!' someone shouted. Instinctively I swung. The rat flew into the air and fell a yard away. I turned it over with my foot. It was twitching, but blood was oozing from its mouth and ears. 'Look out!' the shout came again and another big rat dashed between my legs so that I had to swivel and swing at the same time, catching it behind me. It fell dead too, its back broken and its skull crushed. Then another and two more together. Clubs and sticks were flailing in all directions. The horde was dispersing thicker and faster than ever. Many more were escaping through the cordon because they came in twos and threes, too fast to catch. Some I had to stamp on because I had no time to swing the club.

The nearer the bottom of the stack the men got, the more rats there were. Many had migrated down their tunnels within the sheaves hoping to escape that way rather than breaking cover. At the end, as the last three feet of the stack was whisked up onto the trailer, those remnant hordes finally broke free. It was bedlam. Hundreds of mice and rats burst out together in a swarming, pulsating, leaping, squirming and bounding carpet of grey fur and hairless tails spreading across the trampled and bloodied stubbles at our feet.

Men and boys, some as young as ten, everyone charged with adrenaline, fired with blood lust, with the craving elation of mob sport, were shouting, laughing and yelling as they stamped and swung in a medieval orgy of death and destruction. I was swept up in it, consumed by the same ghastly waves of urgent and jubilant slaughter that surrounded me. We were rat mad, rat obsessed, rat frenzied, rat drunk, rat crazed. I killed and killed. I stamped on heads, guts burst open, entrails squirted out, the air pierced with the shrieks of dying rats.

I don't know how many I killed that day, maybe only twenty or thirty. At the end I was trembling. Some strange and chilling power had rushed in and taken me over, swept me out of my carefree boyhood and into some terrifying, uncontrollable animal impulse. I had become a predator beyond restraint and sanity, a killer overwhelmed with a deviant sadism justified by the enticement of the mob and the universal hatred of rats. It was a feeling I would not forget and which, when some hours later it had subsided, emerged in a confusion of guilt and remorse. It seemed to eclipse everything I had learned and felt about animals until that moment and it cowered uncomfortably in my heart. That night I lay in bed, still tight-chested at the events of the day, but the words I could not dispel, the words ringing in my head and which would not go away, were not mine. They were Isaiah's – *they shall not hurt nor destroy in all my holy mountain*.

★   ★   ★

We returned to Martock as the long summer holidays drew to a close. The new school loomed. On that first morning my father walked me to the school building opposite the church. It felt strange going to school without a uniform. Boys and girls were walking in from all directions. Up above, on an ornately carved stone shield on the peaked gable above the entrance, were the words:

Glory to God in the Highest
MARTOCK
NATIONAL SCHOOL HOUSE
ERECTED BY
PUBLIC & PRIVATE
CONTRIBUTIONS
AD 1846
Jesus said suffer little
children to come unto me

'You have to find Miss Gibbs and report to her,' he announced. Then 'Off you go.' He stood and watched me disappear through the green arched doorway.

The building divided into two high-ceilinged classrooms at the front, and a smaller one behind. Mr Barron had the seniors on the left and Miss Gibbs's class on the right, and a Mrs Hillsden had the youngest children at the rear. A timber and glass partition separated Miss Gibbs's class from Mr Barron's, the glass panels too high for us to see through. Light streamed in through high arched windows, wilted and dying wild flowers in jam jars on the sills. There was a walled playground at the back with lean-to corrugated iron lavatories, boys one end, girls the other, a thin wooden partition between them, where small holes had been bored for prying eyes. Each classroom had rows of desks and hard wooden benches, largely unchanged for the 109 years since it was built.

Most children had gone straight through to the playground. Their shrieking and racketing outside shredded the air. A hand bell jangled angrily. They filed back in, pushing and shoving, moving to their designated desks in a ragged babble of broad Somerset voices. Miss Lily Gibbs stood at her own desk at the front. She was short, perhaps fifty, well-padded and greying, her hair pinned back, glasses sliding down her nose. She had a kindly face that reminded me of Nellie, but with a strong jaw, and sagging skin only loosely draped over the skull beneath. Then a roll-call.

Names I had never heard before, but which would become indelibly familiar as I began to engage with Martock village life: Tucker, Hebditch, Brooks, Chant, Gould, Cornelius, Yandle, Florey, Sparrow, Morey, Palmer, Paull . . . many of whom are still deeply embedded within the district sixty years later. These were the children of farmers and farm labourers, shopkeepers, glove makers, a tent manufacturer, a maker of hen houses, timber mill workers and road menders, postmen . . . all the local industries and regular services of rural life, including the schoolmaster's black-haired daughter Susan, who studiously avoided my eyes as she stalked to her desk. Two immediate differences from Hampton Down struck me that first day: no semblance of uniformity – children wore anything, ranging widely from boys in scruffy shorts and jeans to tidy skirts and blouses for the girls – and the habitual use of Christian names, something it took me a while to adjust to.

Miss Gibbs puffed out her cheeks and spoke slowly. She introduced me as the only new boy in her class. Twenty pairs of eyes drilled into the back of my head. Boys and girls. GIRLS. I had never been to school with girls before.

Despite having a sister, I didn't know anything about girls. Mary, older by two years, had also been sent away to boarding school. We had grown up on gradually but persistently divergent tracks. In the holidays she did her things with her friends, while I did mine, usually on my own. I don't think either of us knew it at the time, but when at six I was sent way to Hampton House, our lives had begun to move apart, almost never fully intersecting again. It was just the way things were. Suddenly there were girls all round me. Little girls from the age of six, girls my age, and girls quite a bit older, girls in huddles whispering conspiratorially, girls crying, sulking, giggling, bossing and screaming at the tops of their thin, penny-whistle voices. Whether I liked it or not I was going to have to get to know girls.

15

An innocence exposed

It was different. Oh yes, *different*, capital 'D' Different. So different that through those first weeks in Miss Gibbs's class I sat in bewildered silence, unable to take it all in. Different dress, different voices, different rules, sounds, smells, facilities, lessons, totally different behaviour and codes of discipline, and, I would not properly grasp until years later, utterly different pupil, parent and teacher expectations. Each day I ran all the way home to tell my mother about it.

Lessons were straightforward but never memorable or stimulating, teaching the barest necessities for rural life. Reading and writing were easy, although some children struggled agonisingly. We did no French or Latin, but I have a dim recollection of some geography about paddy fields in China. Maths was called Arithmetic and was adding, subtracting, dividing and tedious multiplication tables we had to learn by heart and then stand up and recite to the whole class in a sing-songy voice.

The principal teaching aid was a blackboard, while we wrote with pencils in exercise books with plain manila covers, the tart savoury of chewed wood and lead habitually on our tongues. I don't remember possessing a textbook of any kind. Some children who seemed to find the whole educational process a mystery – not to say a waste of time – were well behind, still grappling with the basics of reading and writing at ten and eleven years old. I overheard Miss Gibbs tell Mr Barron that my reading was advanced, which gave me a funny inner buzz.

Books were an escape from which I could garner self-confidence and serenity, and, I now realise, a shield against the chill winds of fear that had exposed my nakedness at Hampton Down and made me shiver with perpetual apprehension. I was allowed to read on my own while she battled with those less proficient. They were given chalk and slates and told to copy what she had written on the blackboard. Then she walked round with a damp cloth, rubbing out their ill-attended endeavours while the mists of education swirled past, high over their heads. We heard the same entreaty issuing over and over again: 'No, Mervin, that's no good, try again and pay attention this time.' Mervin, we all knew, could not have cared less.

For my birthday I had just been given Robert Ballantyne's *The Dog Crusoe and His Master*, a rip-roaring tale of the prairies, of settling the Wild West, of Redskins and the redoubtable courage and loyalty of Crusoe. I loved that book with an intensity of emotion that brought me to tears over and over again, embodying a passion for freedom and wildness already deeply anchored within my psyche. I longed for those sessions when I could transport myself away from the stuffy classroom to thrilling, far-off plains and Red Indian tepees, to stalking deer in the woods and facing down towering, snarling grisly bears. Later, at home in the long summer evenings, I could escape into the humid Somerset orchards and fields in search of those same adventures. Grisly bears there may not have been, but it didn't matter. There were rabbits, hares and grey squirrels to stalk and dark thickets to explore, where imaginary Indians might easily be lurking. Primed with such fizzing expectations, my heart would leap when the occasional cock pheasant burst from beneath my feet with all the shock and alarm of a wolf breaking from its lair.

After a few weeks I had fallen in with a friend of about my age, Charlie Morley, a quick-witted lad with an easy laugh, who, unfathomably, was being raised by his grandparents. I asked him one day where his mother and father were. 'Dunno,' he said and ran off. I never asked again. When eventually he took me back to his dark sixteenth-century cottage home, grace and favour quarters in a medieval almshouse of low-ceilinged, shadowy rooms, I realised that his grandfather was the verger, the old man with a limp I had met inside the church. Their kitchen was an outhouse under a corrugated iron roof across a narrow flagstone passage open to the sky, where his grandmother lurked like a malevolent spider, ready to pounce. She was a small, hunched woman in her late sixties with frightening pebble glasses beneath a tangle of silver hair, who swore volubly and reeked of stewed cabbage. If Charlie was late home, she shot out of that cave-like kitchen, cursed him roundly and whipped him across the back of his bare legs with a hazel switch.

One morning on the way to school I passed their house. Charlie ran out waving his arms excitedly. 'Come and see yere,' he called, rushing along the pavement to the iron railings in front of the village library. He stopped at a place where the arrow-headed top of one railing was missing – bright new metal gleamed where it had just been hacksawed off. 'It were ol' Mrs Crawley last evenin',' he recounted breathlessly. 'She were drunk again and come off 'er bike right yere.' He fingered the fresh cut. 'Went right through 'er cheek and into 'er mouth, it did, so's they 'ad to cut it off with 'er still on it. Stuck like a lolly on a stick, she were.'

'Is she dead?' I quizzed, captivated by this rural drama.

'Nope. She's in 'ospital down Yeovil. They said she didn't feel a thing she were so drunk.'

Just then old Mrs Morley came panting out onto the pavement waving her hazel switch. 'What you boys on about, gossipin' all bleedin' day? Get on down to school or I'll want to know why.' We ran the last hundred yards, shirt-tails to the wind.

In truth, the most startling difference was that I had never witnessed real poverty before. There were children who came in rags, not just hand-me-downs but threadbare garments, pullovers with elbows out, and torn, stained trousers. Some had no socks, pale ankles protruding from ill-fitting shoes with worn-out soles. Shoes without laces lashed loosely with string; sometimes odd shoes, one brown, one black; one a boot, the other a shoe. But above all, some from the very poorest homes, or no homes at all, the unkempt kids of travelling people, stank with a rich and rodent odour like a hamster's nest. Davy Briggs, who could neither read or write, nor had any desire to, came from the roadside encampment at the crossroads up at the top of Bower Hinton. His father wore a greasy cap at a rakish angle and delivered Davy to school perched on the bare boards of a trailer drawn by a large skewbald horse with feathered hooves. Davy had a turned-up nose so that you could peer right into his nostrils. The older children named him 'Piggy' and made snorting noises whenever he walked by.

We called them Gypsies, and their presence was a characterful signature of rural life of the '50s. My father condemned them as poachers and thieves who would filch anything they could get their hands on: pheasants, chickens, pigeons, dogs, horses, sheep out of the fields; any farm tools left lying about would fall to their roving, predatory eyes.

Their ageing womenfolk, swarthy and often toothless, wrapped in crochet shawls and floral headscarves, big golden hoops punched through sagging ear lobes, sold wicker baskets and white split-ash clothes pegs door to door, calling everyone 'dearie'. 'Pegs t'day, dearie? A penny ha'p'ny each, only a bob for twelve, dearie.' But my father's censure faltered over the bold equestrian skills of their men and boys. Horsemanship lay close to his heart; when the summer fairs came round, he couldn't conceal his admiration for their fearless displays of roping and breaking wild ponies from Exmoor.

Many of their children never came to school at all, but those that did, mostly boys, arrived in a redolent breeze of warm bodies and wood smoke, of chickens, dead mice and unaired emotions, the sort of sweet and creaturely smells you might find lingering in an old farm byre. At first I found them repugnant and pulled away, not knowing what to say or think. But as the weeks drifted by, those bucolic essences, their dirty fingernails, thick greasy hair and stale sweat ceased to offend me and I began to accept their scent as a primeval animal pungency not unlike that emanating from fox earths or badgers' setts, familiar and somehow complementing the wilder cloisters of the woods and fields.

In marked contrast the well-scrubbed children of relatively well-to-do families dressed tidily and took their studies seriously. Mr Barron's daughter, the dark-haired, slight, imp-faced Susan, was one of those. Always immaculately turned out in a smart frock with white ankle socks and polished shoes, she was the first Martock child I had seen when I was summoned to her parents' house with my father, peering warily at me through the bannisters. I thought she was aloof and I think she must have looked on me as a curiosity, perhaps coloured by something her father had said after that first interview. Did she know I had been expelled from Hampton Down? Did she know why? Later both my sister and I came to know her better, appearing together in a fancy-dress pageant at the church fête on the vicarage lawn. She was bright-eyed, intelligent and fun in a tom-boyish sort of way, always a ready laugh with the flush of Somerset meadows colouring her vowels; but just as I would be pigeon-holed by many of the children because of my unfamiliar voice and mysterious background, I was never able to see her as anything but the schoolmaster's daughter, always wary that she might tell her father what I was up to.

In the playground I was ragged about my accent. 'What you doin' yere? You'm a college kid, bain't you?' Or 'Where you bin to? Oi ain't never seen the likes of you round yere afore.' It dawned quickly that speech was the key to conformity. Mimicry came easily; in just a few weeks I could imitate the fruity Somerset patois with its rolling Zs as in 'Zomerzet', its gratuitous Rs tipped in when 'grass' became 'grarse', and the total abandonment of Hs as in 'Look at 'arry, 'e's a lazy sod, 'e is.' And 'thic' for 'that', as in 'Give thic ball yere, will 'ee?' When asked 'Where do you live?', you didn't say 'I live in Martock.' You said, 'Oi stay down Mardick.' Before long I was fluent; a home voice and a school voice, the one barely intelligible to the other. Swearing was surprisingly mild, with 'sod' being the commonest insult. 'You daft sod!' or ''E's a silly sod, 'e is.' But in anger it was often piqued by stronger spices – 'Oi told 'im to bugger orf an' mind 'is own soddin' business.'

One afternoon a barn owl flew low over the playground. 'Look at thic fuckin' owl,' Davy Briggs called out. I'd often seen barn owls but I imagined 'fuckin' owl' was the local name. It seemed to slip off the rural tongue with a glassy resonance. As I walked home I met the vicar outside the church.

'Hullo, John. How are you getting on at school?' He smiled broadly.

'Very well, thank you, vicar.'

'What sort of things do you enjoy most?'

'This afternoon a fuckin' owl flew across the playground.'

Instantly his face clouded.

'Go home and wash your mouth out with soap and water,' he insisted, banishing me down the road. I wondered what on earth I had said. My mother looked shocked when I told her, but later I heard her chuckle as she recounted it to my father.

What I was up to was, on the face of it, the most innocent of pursuits that a country boy could indulge. I was escaping. Escaping into the woods and fields of a self-perpetuating, effervescent adventure. I was living two worlds, a world of conformity, the rigour of school, striving to fit in and the dull routines of the learning process, and another world altogether, as much in my head as in reality, as I disappeared off into the imagined wildernesses of the countryside. The misery of homesickness and Twig at Hampton House; my mother's unexplained absences; bullying Bernie at Hampton Down; the freedom of the Manor House, delicious and heady, and the hundreds of hours of solitary exploration during those formative years had armed me with a sturdy carapace of independence and self-determination. At that moment in my young life I had no need of friends.

Innocent, that is, until I set eyes on Noreen Ashby. Are boys of ten supposed to be acutely gender aware? I certainly hadn't been until that exquisitely feminine thunderbolt speared into me. With the notable exception of Twig, whom Betty and I had viewed as an unpleasant affliction unworthy of any gender, all the women in my short life had been benign mother figures – Nellie, Mrs Warmley, the sympathetic matron at Hampton Down, my own mother, of course, even Mrs Barnwell, Sally Franklin and the bird-like Dizzy Cuff had shown me affection and warmth. In their various roles I had loved them all for their compassion and manifold kindnesses, much as a dog dotes on its master who feeds it. Theirs was an open, unqualified brand of love, pure, nourishing and unquestioning, like the Mississippi, rolling on 'full flood, inexorable, irresistible, benignant'.

Late summer and a stuffy classroom. An enervating airlessness hung thick and heavy as syrup. After lunch we tumbled back in from the playground. In a conspiratorial gaggle, girls tittered as they took their seats. Mickey Florey from the old forge cottages at the back of North Street had picked a fight with me – a sort of pecking-order skirmish, more bluster than anger, his only weapon in a struggle to assert himself over this bumptious, uninvited incomer. I'd stood my ground. When the bell rang my hair was ruffled, blood from my nose smeared my sleeve and my hands were dirtied. He'd torn my shirt, but I had pushed him over, downed him, and that was good enough for me.

Miss Gibbs called me to the front of the class. 'You've been fighting, haven't you?' she snapped. Her grey hair framed a brow doubly creased with the force of interrogation.

'Sort of, miss. Sorry, miss.'

'Fighting in the playground is strictly forbidden.'

'Yes, miss.'

'Who were you fighting with?' Her hooded eyes glared. The class fell silent.

'It wasn't really fighting, miss, just ragging.'

'I asked you who with?' Her voice was honed to a sabre edge.

'Just some of the boys, miss. We were just fooling . . .'

'I want to know who you were fighting with. If you don't tell me, I shall send you through to Mr Barron.'

I said nothing. To this day, I don't really know why. It certainly wasn't through any love of Mickey Florey – I thought he was plucky, but I also knew he was what my father called a lout. But the rough and tumble of boarding school had taught me jungle lore. Survival was bigger than just winning a fight. I had somehow osmosed a knave's honour. The prospect of being labelled a sneak swirled in front of me like an autumn fog. *No*, I thought, *No, No, No*. I stayed silent and looked at the floor.

'Are you going to defy me?' Her face reddened, the colour diffusing down her neck in a tidal rash.

'Yes, miss.' I dropped my voice. 'Sorry, miss.'

A knife-edge moment. I stared at her button-over shoes, black and scuffed, and gritted my teeth. I had no idea that I was calling her bluff and I would not have known to call it that, but it would be a valuable lesson that grafted itself onto life's budding stem that day. One I would never forget. 'Go and sit down.' She spat out the words. 'I'll think what to do with you later.' But she never did. She was unsure of her ground and I had sensed the chink in her mail. Perhaps it hadn't been a proper fight after all. Without a name she was stymied.

The sun ripped through autumn's yellow fingers in dazzling bites of late September heat. At the end of lessons we all shuffled out, squinting, into the street. A tap on the shoulder. I spun round, thinking it was Charlie. I found myself staring into the wide, dark eyes of a girl. Noreen Ashby. I barely knew her – had never spoken to her before.

'Well done,' she said.

I was speechless – had no idea what she meant. 'What for?' was all I could manage.

'For not telling on Mickey, silly.' A smile spread across her rosy lips and danced in her brown, laughing eyes. My lungs emptied, the sky fell in, time crashed to the dusty pavement at my feet.

'Thanks,' I spluttered, pinned wordless and lost to a suddenly gyrating universe. When eventually I broke free, I raced all the way home.

I ran straight to the loft to sit with the dulcet certainty of my pigeons. The males were billing and cooing, bobbing, bowing and pirouetting to their virginal white hens, coy and demure. But the metaphor was utterly lost on me. I was yet to understand, and would not properly grasp for several years to come, that what had happened to me that afternoon could be anything to do with biology, with mating, with the continuing propagation of our species.

Looking back, it was a bizarrely contradictory juxtaposition. I was a country boy, always watching, always learning. I knew and probably understood more about sex – especially bird sex – than any other pupil of my age in that school – every precise detail, from the parent birds' courtship to the chicks' fledging and maiden flights. And not just birds. By the age of ten I had witnessed snorting stallions with elephantine hose-like erections rearing onto their mares; I had marvelled at the glistening pink billiard cues of lumbering Hereford bulls stabbing into the Manor Farm cows; I'd watched rams pounding the rumps of their ewes; every morning rampant cockerels trampled their hens into the dirt. I had seen farm dogs tail to tail in a tied coital clinch, and I had captured toads gripped together, males riding the females in raw amplexus. I had watched engrossed as Bernie's peacocks fanned and vibrated their absurdly extravagant tails at their dowdy little peahens before crushing them underfoot like so many grapes. But human beings? Parents? School teachers? Girls? No. Never. Not in my wildest imaginings. The sex taboo was unbroken, as thick and *intacta* as the Virgin Queen's hymen.

The word had never been mentioned in our family and the same was true of the other boys at Hampton Down – probably of most children of our pre-sexual revolution epoch. We were all cocooned in the same impenetrable warp of innocence, an innocence unimaginable today in our world of multimedia information overload. To us 1950s boys, parental sex was not just myth; it didn't exist and never had. Inconceivable. Unimaginable. Unfathomable. Not just improbable – impossible. Far less had we ever dreamed of Mrs Warmley baring her nether regions to a man, or Bernie prancing around a bedroom with an erection. Yet despite this blackout of unknowledge, in the dorm after lights out we had explored its mythology of denial in exaggerated and creative detail.

Many of us had sisters. We were well aware of the physiological differences between boys and girls, men and women. But we had never made the connection. Not for a fleeting, flickering moment. Even Bramley, a quiet and serious Hampton House boy whose mother had recently presented him with a baby sister, was unable to add more than that it had been in her tummy and she went to hospital to have it.

'Where did it come from?' we asked, agog at this hot, topical intelligence. There was a long silence. 'How did it get out?' we pressed.

He looked nonplussed and confused. It was no good. 'The nurses took it out,' was all we got.

We were primitives staring in fearful disbelief before a full solar eclipse. We knew there was something out there, some vague, intriguing, hovering adult mystery, arcane and untouchable, but we had not the slightest idea what it could be.

Wild theories had been aired by Hampton Down boys who had tried to assert themselves by claiming superior knowledge – fragments of truth cobbled into absurdities: that your belly-button was somehow where it all took place; that women had to hand their eggs in to a doctor for hatching; that parents could dictate sons or daughters in advance, like choosing apples or pears; that God, the church font and saying your prayers somehow had something to do with it. In the end, the unanimously agreed and entirely satisfactory conclusion was that to have babies women went and spoke to a special nurse who arranged it all for them. Nor had love anything to do with any of it. The *love* word had never once emerged from the swirling fog of our long, inventive discussions.

Love existed in an entirely separate compartment, as distinct as whisky from water. To me *love* was warmth, security, home. Love was Nellie, Mrs Warmley, my mother's perfume. Love was a hug, my own bed, toast and honey at the Manor House. Love was happiness and unfettered freedom, running wild. It was watching the pigeons lay eggs. I knew perfectly well what love was and where it belonged. I had read it in the Bible – the love of God and the God of love – plain for the world to see. All the rest, all that romance stuff, the sugary sweetheart hoo-ha, all that poetry and song, was make believe, a boring game adults played – so much froth.

If that was the case, what in the name of God's breakfast was happening to me? That night I sweated; I tossed and turned. I got up and drank cold water, tried to read a book. Nothing helped. No matter how hard I tried to dispel her from my thoughts every few seconds my mind boomeranged back to Noreen Ashby and the irresistible vortex of that hollowing out, excoriating smile. In the morning I was trembling. I couldn't eat. All the way to school I ached in the pit of my stomach. I thought I must be ill.

I had often listened to my mother's gramophone record of Richard Tauber singing the songs of Old Vienna, 'Girls were made to love and kiss . . .', words that had been utterly meaningless and which I had dismissed as so much theatrical hogwash. But as I dragged my raincoat along the Martock pavement that morning those lyrics now came flooding back to me with a fresh and deeply unsettling bite: 'I *have suffered* in love's great deeps, I know the passion that never sleeps, I know *the longing* and wronging of hearts . . .' *Oh Cripes! Is that it? Am I in love? Is this hopeless, nagging confusion what all the fuss is about?* The thought horrified me, but I couldn't shake it off. It refused to go away.

My sister had been given a shiny red yo-yo for her birthday. That night I crept into her room and stole it. I wrapped it in tissue paper and took it to school the following morning. I wrote 'from John' on the paper and left it on Noreen's desk. The bell rang. She filed in with the other girls and sat down. I glanced across. She opened it, looked up, smiled. There it was again, that pulverising, liquidising smile. I felt sick. My palms went clammy. Nausea washed over me and I felt myself wilting like a frosted bud. If she'd said drink poison, I'd have gladly done it, right then.

I don't remember Noreen as exceptionally beautiful. She had long, dark hair braided into two fat, glossy plaits down her back. She was slender and willowy with that fleeting, nymph-like quality some girls possess before the helter-skelter of puberty kicks in. If she had budding breasts, I wasn't aware of it. Her eyes were as wide and dark as an antelope's, as wide with innocence as with allure, and her cheeks shone with the softly muted glow of a white peach. Nor do I believe that what had happened to me had solely resulted from her physical appeal, although I'm sure it helped. And it was entirely unintentional, I'm convinced of that. She was just being nice to me, laced perhaps with an intuitive female magnetism of which she was probably not yet fully aware. No, I think I was simply overwhelmed by a chemically induced crush to end all crushes, perhaps as much to do with my own pre-pubescent transmutation as her own.

But for me, for as long as it lasted – perhaps two or three weeks at most – it burned as an incomprehensible and inextinguishable longing, a flame that seared through all my days and all my nights and which, at its peak, brought me over and over again to the edge of tears. 'What *is* the matter with Jay?' I heard my mother ask. 'He's been moping for days.' I ran and hid in my room. I knew they wouldn't understand, and anyway, what could I possibly say?

It was an emotional fixation of such intensity that I would not experience again until I was twenty-one. It was such that never, in all the ensuing decades, and through all the convoluted turmoil of the real mating game, have I for one moment forgotten Noreen Ashby. Nor ever will. She has never made it into the present. She is still there, forever fixed at her Martock school desk with the sun slicing through the high windows, shedding shoals of glitter from her ebony hair, motes dancing in its beams. Peacock butterflies fluttered hopelessly against the glass and from across the road the mellow chime of the church clock hallowed that fateful, rosebud hour. Noreen remains for me an ageless goddess of deliciously unsullied, uncontrived and flawless femininity. Yes – perhaps *pure* is the right word after all.

Where are you now, Noreen Ashby? Who are you, sixty years on? On what foreign strand have life's rough old seas pitched your slender barque? Did you safely steer through fate's most treacherous rocks? Did your anchors hold? Have you reached the harbour of your dreams? And did you ever comprehend that in the fierce sunlight of that dusty village street your smile had spun a carefree ten-year-old boy into a whirlpool of blinding confusion from which life would never be the same again – that you had inadvertently delivered a clearing blow to the gut?

Was it pheromones? Perhaps. Although I'm unsure that many girls start pulsating their chemical bio-conductivity as early as eleven. But also I believe I was exceptionally vulnerable because I had never engaged with girls before at any level. Boys' boarding schools were just that: an unnaturally enforced segregation so that when at last we began to split the pupal case, to emerge blinking from that imposed institutional isolation, most of us would flounder helplessly before the sexual tsunami that would eventually swamp us all.

I still had no idea what it was about. In an anguished vacuum of ignorance a child loves for the first time without bias, without suspense, regret or hope. It was like a sunrise: pure, transfixing and beguiling. Yet the notion of conjugation, of any physical contact or taking Noreen to bed, even of kissing her mouth to mouth, was unthinkable and would, had I been able to imagine it, have been utterly abhorrent to me. I had not made the connection. Pigeons were pigeons. I was different. It would be a long time before I would chip through the protective shell of innocence to reveal the true animal beneath. And that would be somewhere else altogether.

16

Hill Brow

Another year, another school. My father had finally secured a place for me in a prep school to the north of the Somerset Levels, at Brent Knoll, that spectacular hump that looms out of the flatlands as though God has tipped it out of a pudding basin. Called Hill Brow School, and closed down long ago, it was based at Somerset Court, a modest eighteenth-century country house, which, in a former existence had achieved infamy as one of 'the hanging judge', Judge Jeffreys', courts in the aftermath of the 1685 Monmouth Rebellion.

My sojourn at Martock village school came to an abrupt end after only three terms, just as I was becoming properly Somersetised. My heart sank. I was adjusting well. I had learned to mimic the farm boys' hedgerow and haystack patter; Mickey Florey had taught me to make the bully-boys think twice by lashing out with my fists and then a sharp kick to the shins so that I could hold my own in the playground; I'd become used to wearing open-necked shirts, pullovers and old clothes; I'd mastered the trick of wolf whistling through my teeth, and to spit and curse with the best of them, and, once I'd recovered from my bewildering *engouement* for Noreen Ashby, I really rather liked having girls around all the time. Most of all I loved the unshackled freedom of afternoons, evenings and weekends at home on my own. I loved my pigeons. It had never dawned on me that none of those things were what either of my parents expected of their son.

As the day neared my spirit plunged and a vacuum of dread engulfed me. I pleaded to stay at Martock. The misery of Hampton Down had never gone away. The prospect of returning to a disciplinarian regime like Bernie's hollowed me out. I fell asleep struggling to hold off tears. But my father's reasoning was not just conventional class and educational prejudice, although I'm in no doubt they were visible seasoning within the cocktail. No, the founding motive was a much deeper cause for concern. The spectre of the Dun Cow rib was closing in again. We had all noticed that my mother's breathlessness had returned, her fingers were blue and her afternoon rests had grown progressively longer. I had watched her toiling upstairs, having to stop twice, chest heaving to get her wind. I had read the pain on my father's face and her gritty fortitude manifest in the thin line of her blue, pursed lips. Russell Brock and Paul Wood's notes had proved accurate. Now, looking back, they seem chillingly prescient. By 1955, her aortic valve was leaking badly.

Our move to Martock had provided my mother with a new doctor in the village's small rural practice. John Parker, of blessed memory. John Howard Knight Parker, to award him the full recognition he unquestionably deserves, had been an instant hit. Classically handsome in an un-rugged way, more suave country than slick urbane, he wore a ready smile with a habitual chuckle, always with a deeply engaging natural modesty. Years later my mother would tell me that John was 'the kindest, gentlest, most understanding and the most rigorously honest GP' she would ever have. 'He told me that my heart was failing again and that without further intervention I would die – that I had no choice. He also said that I would never find a more skilled or courageous team than Brock and Wood.' It was John Parker who persuaded her to return to the Brompton sooner rather than later. She dreaded the whole idea but he insisted. 'Don't let it get so bad that you have to be wheeled there on a trolley, only to find it's too late.' Then he offered to go to London with her.

What my parents did not know was that in 1945–6, as a young registrar, John Parker had worked under the cele-brated surgeon Professor Sir Arthur Rendle Short, FRCS, at Southmead Hospital in Bristol, who in turn was a former colleague, close associate and friend of Russell Brock.

When Paul Wood was appointed the first director of the newly formed Institute of Cardiology in 1947, he turned his attention to the highly controversial and experimental proce-dure of cardiac catheterisation – the improbable idea of inserting a fine wire into the femoral artery in the groin and gently pushing it all the way up the body, past the lungs, round and down into the beating heart. Then inserting a catheter tube over it and withdrawing the wire. This delicate procedure, still an essential part of heart diagnosis today, was in its absolute infancy.

Just as the establishment dinosaurs had argued that the heart could never be opened by surgery, now they argued that the catheter would cause clotting and strokes or that the risk of damaging the arteries was too great. The brilliant and incisive Paul Wood took no notice. Backed by Russell Brock, he was convinced that catheterisation would prove an essential diagnostic tool, hugely helping the surgeon to know what to expect. Wood performed the first one on 6 April 1948. In their chapter on catheterisation in *British Cardiology in the 20th Century* (2000), medical historians Malcolm Towers and Simon Davies would write: 'Wood's integration of careful (patient) history taking, the precise assessment of physical signs at the bedside with the newer knowledge from . . . catheterisation was one of the most exciting developments in the whole of medicine.'

Only now do I realise how very lucky my mother was to have landed in the hands of Russell Brock and Paul Wood. While heart surgery was still embryonic and experimental when she so badly needed help, their brilliance and their redoubtable collaboration had saved her life in 1953 and prolonged it again in 1957. In an essay on Valvular Disease, Emeritus Professor of Clinical Cardiology at Imperial College Celia Oakley wrote: 'Paul Wood's clarity of thought and incisiveness of speech were riveting . . . His teaching further increased understanding of . . . heart disease, obtained through catheterization . . . (and) the foundations of accurate diagnosis had been laid.'

In the nine years up to 1957 catheter diagnosis technology had been greatly improved, now permitting doctors to take X-rays inside the heart, to take blood and tissue samples, to administer drugs and even perform minor corrective surgery, all without having to break into the chest and open the beating heart. During those early years word had gone out to doctors throughout Britain to identify patients who were unlikely to survive more than six months without heart surgery and to recommend them for experimental catheterisation.

My mother's case history was well known to Brock and Wood. The assiduous John Parker had seen their observations in her notes. With characteristic foresight he contacted Paul Wood to see if she was a suitable case for catheterisation. The response was an immediate and enthusiastic 'Yes, please.' This made my mother a 'special patient' to Parker, who, despite having studied surgery and qualified as an obstetrician, had ultimately opted for general practice in a sleepy Somerset village, far removed from the cutting edge of medical science and its hierarchy of the day.

Once more we were told nothing. Again my father was chewing his nails to the quick. With typically practical decisiveness he had concluded that having children at home was too much. Mary was banished first, sent away to board at a prep school in Dorset. Our brief, flickering childhood of living at home with our mother was effectively over. I was ten and Mary was twelve.

*   *   *

I entered Hill Brow for the Lent term in 1957, a very small school of only sixty boys. There were no 'houses' and we were all lumped together, divided only by forms: juniors, middles and seniors by day and similarly in dormitories at night. Discipline was much gentler but also much more tightly observed than Hampton Down, far less opportunity for challenging the bounds. There were no cold baths and no penal scoring system that had so consistently marked me down. Instead, the school operated an inflexible system of almost permanent supervision by a small team of masters.

We were never left unmonitored and our every move was managed and recorded, even going to the lavatory, sent there after breakfast, then ticked off on a list, a process I found deeply intrusive and disturbing. My bodily functions had never been regimented before and I found it impossible to perform to a pre-ordained routine. To add to this indignity, the lavatory doors had no locks and the only paper provided was thin and shiny 'Bronco – medicated with Izal germicide'. The wide gaps above and below the partitions so you could see the next door boy's feet and trousers I found to be a denial of privacy so distasteful that I declined to perform for nearly three weeks. When at last my alimentary system could contain the pressure no longer, and gripped by excruciating bowel cramps, I crept out of the dormitory at night to an upstairs lavatory we were not supposed to use, where I erupted painfully and with such copiously extruded amplitude that the entire sewage system choked and had to be cleared by a plumber.

I now see Hill Brow as a happy little school of entirely benevolent intentions only vaguely fulfilled by a small team of largely unqualified, and mostly ex-forces teachers. The headmaster was a Cambridge arts graduate, but he was also the only teacher with university education or any formal credentials. John Matthews, known as 'Mathey', was a large, treble-chinned man in his fifties with owl-like horn-rimmed glasses and an air of stately self-importance further endorsed by his maroon Daimler Consort that swept him sedately to and from the front door. If he ever taught me anything memorable, it has long since evaporated, but I do retain the abiding image of him sitting at his study desk in a pale grey double-breasted suit with a filter-tipped Benson & Hedges cigarette permanently attached to his lips, which jiggled up and down as he spoke with a muted chin-wobbling stammer at the beginning of every sentence, cigarette ash cascading down his lapels, and regularly thereafter. That stammer fascinated me, emerging as multiple barely audible Ms, before locating the desired consonant. 'M-m-m-m-Good morning, John.' He and his wife, Gerry, a skinny but kindly Scot with a tobacco-induced hoarseness to her Morningside accent, both chain-smoked, as did almost all the teaching staff, including sometimes during lessons.

Major Rory Newbery, 'Newbug', smoked unfiltered Player's Navy Cut. His fingers and bristly military moustache were permanently stained bright nicotine orange, as visible as henna on a Polynesian tribal warrior. I think he rather revelled in presenting himself as a bumbling English eccentric, which he undoubtedly was, but a fool he was certainly not. As second master he was omnipresent, quietly and unobtrusively helping to hold the school together.

The master we all respected most was James Serjeant, universally known as 'Sargie'. He was a tall, stern-faced bachelor in middle age with a prominent brow and dark, swept back hair with a glossy application of Brylcreem. He taught me maths, but probably other subjects too. He was a generous-spirited man of skyscraper principles, reputed to have been in the Military Police during the war, but who was afflicted by regular attacks of apoplexy when boys were rude or disorderly. At heart he was a thoroughly decent, gentle fellow and I don't believe there was a shred of malice in his heart.

My favourite was Bill Mayo, or 'Maybags', ex-Merchant Navy, tall, red-haired and as obviously Irish as a shamrock. He wore alternating green and brown corduroy jackets, taught geography and Latin, and smoked a pipe with a straight stem. He had travelled widely in his seafaring career and regularly injected personal vignettes of Hong Kong, Peking, Brisbane, New York . . . all of which I loved. He cut a swashbuckling figure as he roared helmetless to and from Brent Knoll village on a noisy 500cc Norton motorbike, pipe protruding from his gritted teeth and red hair streaming in the wind.

The suitably black-haired matron was Miss Hamilton, who never looked you in the eye when speaking to you. When we angered her, which we achieved often and for sport, she revealed her displeasure by stomping off into her bedroom and slamming the door, a reaction that simply encouraged us to do it more. In a stiffly starched white tunic hauled in with a broad navy blue belt, at surgery after breakfast she dispensed iodine for cuts and grazes, kaolin poultices for boils, calamine lotion for rashes, Californian syrup of figs for constipation and two aspirin for everything else.

The whole team would nowadays be deemed comically eccentric and their irrepressible tobacco addictions beyond the pale. Yet for all their peccadillos they were thoroughly worthy people, dedicated to their educational cause with genuine, if unpredictable, professionalism. Without them ever guessing it, their peculiar amalgam of abilities and idiosyncrasies were in themselves a profitable baptism for later life.

*   *   *

In May that year John Parker escorted my mother to London for a consultation with Paul Wood. Her condition was dire, worse than even John Parker had realised. Dr Wood recommended immediate catheterisation. Then the trail goes cool. We know that she remained in the Brompton for five weeks; we know that Dr Wood's catheter procedure was deemed a great success. What we don't know is precisely what he did.

The catheter had crossed my mother's aortic valve – that much is certain – and we also deduce that it must have temporarily improved the malfunction. We also know that Donald Ross, a brilliant young surgeon from the cardiac unit at Guy's Hospital, who would go on to achieve fame by performing the world's second and successful heart transplant in 1968 (the first was by his friend and colleague Christiaan Barnard at Groote Schuur Hospital in Cape Town in December 1967, but the recipient only survived for eighteen days), expressed special interest in my mother's case and came to see her at Russell Brock and Paul Wood's behest. There was talk of replacing her aortic valve with a plastic ball valve, but Paul Wood dismissed that idea as too risky. She was too weak. Because of the strong possibility of heart failure, he decided not to recommend immediate further surgery. Instead my mother underwent a protracted period of medication under Paul Wood's personal supervision. His view, confirmed by Russell Brock, remained that she would eventually have to have her aortic valve replaced, but he wanted it to be deferred for as long as possible.

Reading the copious notes and researching the late 1950s and '60s history of cardiology, it's clear that Wood and Brock (by then Sir Russell, soon to be Lord Brock of Wimbledon) were playing for time. In 1957 aortic valve replacement was still highly experimental and risky. Despite year on year advances, the technique was not reliably successful until 1960. Mother had already been one of their guinea pigs and got away with it – just. They were reluctant to make her one again. Paul Wood's almost superhuman diagnostic skills led him to believe that with care and medication to control heart strain, she would survive long enough for aortic surgery to be a much safer bet. Once again his cautious, methodical skill had saved my mother's life.

★   ★   ★

I was summoned to the headmaster's study one morning after breakfast. Both Mr and Mrs Matthews were there. 'M-m-m-m-Don't worry, John, you're not in any trouble,' was Mathey's greeting. 'Your m-m-m-m-father is coming to collect you and take you up to London to see your mother.' A huge wave of relief flooded over me. I knew what to expect and it had all turned out to be OK. 'She might have to have another operation,' was the only other insight they could offer. That was all right too. I had absolutely no concept that once again she was teetering at death's door.

This time she was in a small ward with only one other bed, occupied by a Mrs Maydwell who had a blue rinse hair perm and wore glasses with matching blue frames. She was a highly-strung woman who jabbered compulsively and nervously at both my father and me to a point that became an irritating intrusion. That evening in the hotel he told me that Dr Wood had asked whether they could move Mrs Maydwell in with my mother because 'She's got the heebie-jeebies about her operation and we urgently need her to calm down.'

'How would moving her in with Mummy help?'

There was a long silence before my father spoke. 'John, your mother is a very remarkable person. She is very brave and very strong, even though she has had to put up with such a lot of pain. The doctors know that, and they think that Mummy will be a great help to Mrs Maydwell, who has to have a big operation on her heart very soon.'

'Oh,' I said. 'I see.' But I didn't. I didn't care about the heebie-jeebie woman. I just wanted my mother home again.

Years later I discovered in her private correspondence that she was also shoring up my father.

Being a burden and worry to you has always been a hard cross for me to carry. Thank you for being so marvellous all these difficult years. Take good care of yourself; don't sit alone feeling jolly sorry for yourself. Remember, smile and the world smiles with you – weep and you weep alone. When one sees the human suffering on all sides – a poor old soul here aged fifty dying from Parkinson's disease – ours is not the worst of fate which life hands out. So have courage by continuing

> *to encourage and support me and I can face up to whatever*
> *is necessary.*

Some time later Paul Wood wrote to my mother personally to thank her. 'It is largely due to your great fortitude and kindness,' he wrote, 'that Mrs Maydwell has come through her ordeal so well. We could not have operated in the state of extreme anxiety she was in before we moved her in with you. I would even go so far as to say that she owes you her life.'

Every week my mother wrote to me from hospital on pre-stamped folded letter-cards with a glued edge. To open them you had to tear off the perimeter strip. Written in a mature, flowing hand, her letters were always loving and emotionally charged, written the way she spoke, but never – I'm sure intentionally – revealing anything significant about her condition.

> *I do hope you are being a good boy this term. Please try your*
> *best at lessons and have lots of fun, but try to stay out of*
> *trouble. I am being very well looked after and will be home*
> *again sometime soon. I am missing you all the time and I*
> *send you all my love, darling, as always.*

Hidden, tucked into a margin or sometimes even concealed within the date, always in tiny capital letters, was our private code, ILY, which she had faithfully maintained in every letter since Hampton House.

My father, ever the pragmatist with no capacity for elaboration, penned his brief, perfunctory and almost formulaic letters on Sundays, always on blue Basildon Bond formally headed writing paper. He could summon neither verbal nor written expression.

Dear John,
I hope you are well and playing lots of games. I am very busy
at work and away from home quite a lot. I am trying out a
new car called a Ford Zephyr. It is black. We have a new
Prime Minister called Mr Harold Macmillan. I am going to
see Grandpa on Thursday. Mary is getting very good at
netball. Mummy is doing well and sends her love.

Your ever-loving father.

★   ★   ★

The boys at Hill Brow were a game lot. Older than the usual
new boy intake, I entered the middle form and the middle
dormitory, quickly progressing to the seniors. In that first
dormitory a boy called Peter Gwyn was in the bed next to
mine. He was small in stature and powerfully muscled with
the barely contained energy of a wild animal ready to
pounce. His father was a local gentleman farmer and Master
of the Banwell Foxhounds, a country convention with which
I was entirely familiar from the sporting traditions of the
Manor House. Even at the age of eleven Peter was a bold
and fearless horseman, his life's passion and only topic of
conversation while the clouds of a broader education swirled
over his head.

The Somerset Levels are flat meadow wetlands drained
by deep ditches called rhynes (pronounced reens) at the field
margins. The Banwell hounds and its unruly gang of
mounted followers, mostly local farmers, stampeded harum-
scarum across these flatlands, their horses and ponies leaping
the rhynes with lunatic abandon. That Christmas holidays
my father drove me to Banwell to join the hunt. Together
Peter and I careered across field after field in some of the
wildest riding I have ever done. If your pony mis-timed the

leap and crashed into the stagnant rhyne, both the horse and rider would emerge drenched to the skin, spitting foul-smelling water, smothered in green duckweed, to scramble up the other side, remount and gallop off again without a thought. It was exhilarating beyond anything I had ever done before and I was determined that as soon as I was old enough I would own my own horses and become an ardent foxhunter. Peter's ambition was to be a jockey, a profession for which he was ideally built. He lit a flame with his infectious dedication to the equestrian life and it is partly because of him that I have owned, loved and ridden horses of my own for more than forty years.

My time at Hill Brow was not entirely trouble-free. There was one incident that brought me close to being expelled for a second time and, upon reflection now, perhaps should have done. On Sundays we were encouraged to engage in pastimes and hobbies. Mine was collecting stamps. For a recent birthday my father had bought me the heavy, red-bound Stanley Gibbons catalogue, the indispensable bible for all serious philatelists.

One Sunday afternoon I sat down at a table beside the stove in the main classroom to sort out a large envelope of stamps my mother had sent me. Among them I hurried to find her coded inscription, always tucked in, a tiny cut square of plain blue writing paper the size of a stamp upon which she had drawn a smiling woman's face and underneath were the initials I always searched for – ILY. These cyphers were fiercely important to me. They were tiny cherished signals from the most important person in my young life.

Carefully I spread the stamps out, sorting them into countries and checking them against the catalogue. Soon the table was entirely covered, literally hundreds of them in little, carefully organised groups. Then, with delicate stamp hinges and special tweezers, I began painstakingly to stick them, one by one, into the large album given me for my birthday, carefully positioning my mother's little blue square on the title page. I was totally and happily absorbed, just getting on with what we were supposed to be doing. Major Newbery was on duty, overseeing our activities in two adjoining rooms. A plume of cigarette smoke followed him as he wandered between the rooms, offering words of encouragement here and there.

A boy of roughly my age – Duncan Wells is as good a pseudonym as any – wandered up to the table. 'Stamps is a girl's hobby,' he pronounced with a sneer.

'Clear off!' I sniped back, scarcely bothering to look up. I was just attaching a hinge to the back of the blue square. He stood there for a moment in silence. Then, without any warning or provocation, he bent forward and blew noisily at the stamps laid out in front of me. They scattered before his spitefully gusted wind. He laughed loudly and blew some more, chasing them off the table and onto the floor. My mother's square flew with the rest. It was too much. A white heat surged into my brain.

I leapt up and grabbed him by the throat. He fell over backwards and the back of his head crashed against the sharp edge of a cast-iron surround to the stove. Rage utterly consumed me, blinding me to what was happening. I banged his head continuously against the metal edge, over and over again with all my might. A prefect ran to get Major Newbery, the whole room suddenly in uproar. Boys were shouting. Newbery dragged me off. Blood was gushing from the back of Wells' head.

There was a general mobbing kerfuffle as boys crowded round Wells, still lying on the floor, Newbery telling everyone to go to a desk and sit still, trying to calm everyone down. Blood was pooling across the floor and Wells was wailing loudly. Matron arrived and wrapped his head in a towel; he was led staggering away. Major Newbery then marched me off to the sick room, an upstairs room smelling of Dettol, with a single bed in it. The key turned in the lock. A few minutes later I looked out of the window just in time to see Wells being helped into the back of Mathey's Daimler. His whole head was swathed in bandages. The car crunched away down the gravel drive and disappeared.

I don't know how long I stayed in that locked room – perhaps three hours, maybe four. But eventually the key turned and Mrs Matthews came in with a glass of orange cordial. Oddly, she didn't look angry and she spoke softly. 'You shouldn't have done what you did, John. The head-master has taken Duncan to the hospital in Taunton to get his head stitched up. He will want to see you as soon as he comes back.' Then she left. Another hour passed before I heard the Daimler return. This time it was Major Newbery who came to the door. 'Come along,' he said, 'the head wants you in his study.' *Oh God*, I thought. *I'm for it now*. Up loomed the image of Bernie and his stinging cane. It all seemed so horribly familiar; I was convinced I was about to be caned and then expelled.

I was completely wrong; my fear and misgivings were so entirely misplaced that confusion swamped me. Mathey was standing behind his large leather-topped desk, cigarette dangling, hands behind his back, Mrs Matthews perched on the arm of a sofa in the window. He spoke first. 'M-m-m-m-Major Newbery has told me exactly what happened and m-m-m-I've just spoken to three boys who were very near where you were doing your stamps. I believe Duncan's actions were entirely m-m-m-unprovoked. Is that correct, John?'

'Yessir.' I tried not to sound surprised.

'M-m-m-I shall be talking to him when he comes back from hospital. But you must understand that I cannot have that sort of extreme violence happening at Hill Brow. M-m-m-provoked or not, you should not have attacked Duncan like you did. I'm assuming that you didn't know he had hit his head on the fire surround. Am I right?'

I thought for a moment before answering. 'Yes, sir. Er – I mean no, sir. I didn't know about the metal.'

'M-m-m-but you did carry on banging his head?'

'Yes, sir.'

'Why did you do that?'

I thought this was a silly question. I thought it was obvious, so after a pause I said, 'Because I was so angry, sir.'

'M-m-m-m-I didn't know you had a temper, John.' I was still puzzled by the tone of this interrogation. He sounded calm, reasonable, even placatory – yes, he was being nice.

'Sorry, sir. I was just very angry.'

'But you still wanted to hurt him.'

I looked down at the carpet. Its swirling floral pattern of gold and green seemed to reflect the emotions swirling in my head. *Should I own up to that?* I wondered. *Is this a trick to get me to admit that I wanted to kill him?* But things didn't add up. No one seemed angry with me. My heart was still pounding, my head still fizzing with the electric discharge of things I didn't understand, but something in his tone was calming me down and I began to breathe more easily. I glanced at Mrs Matthews and then at Major Newbery. There were no red faces, no snarling voices, nothing like Bernie at all. 'Yes, sir.'

'Hmmm. I see.' He walked to his desk and drew another cigarette from its box, lighting it from the tail end of the old one, which he stubbed out in a glass ashtray while he thought.

'Sorry, sir.'

'M-m-m-yes, John, I expect you are. So am I. I shall now have to decide what to say to Mr and Mrs Wells when I tell them that their son is in m-m-m-hospital with seven stitches in his head.'

'Is he going to die?'

'Humph!' Mathey almost laughed. 'No, he's not, luckily for us all. Just a nasty m-m-m-cut. Oh, and by the way, John. Major Newbery has seen that all your stamps are carefully put away for you.'

Then his wife spoke for the first time. 'Is your mother still in hospital, John?' Her voice was soft and conciliatory, almost affectionate.

'Yes, Mrs Matthews, she is.'

'I hope she's getting better.' I had no idea whether she was or she wasn't, and it was puzzling that Mrs Matthews seemed to care. Very slowly I began to understand that both the Matthewses were on my side, that perhaps they had even understood why I attacked Wells. She turned to her husband, 'I think it's very important John's mother doesn't get to hear of this. We don't want to cause her any worry.'

Mathey thought for a moment, glancing first to me then back to his wife as though he didn't quite know what to say. 'M-m-m-m-yes, dear, quite right. Yes, I agree.'

Good old Mum, I thought.

17

'Upon thy belly shalt thou go'

An avenue of magnificent English elms lined the Hill Brow drive, now all so grievously beetle-purged from the Somerset landscape. I can see myself looking up into those lofty, cloud-raking trees while rooks circled and cawed against an ocean of high, softly winnowing cumulus. I ran there every day. Their constant rough music was to me a joyous symphony, transporting me straight back to where I really wanted to be, to the Manor House and its own rookery, embraced by the glorious, cloud-raking beeches of the grave-yard.

I was twelve years old and in my last year at prep school. For the moment life's barometer was set fair. My mother was home again – not well, of course, but the crisis of her leaking aorta had been temporarily averted. Every week the loyal and diligent John Parker came to Bartonfield to adjust her medication and listen intently to her lumpy, dysrhythmic heartbeat. She looked forward to these visits, often told me that it wasn't just that Dr Parker was a very good doctor and a friend, but that he inspired her with self-belief that she would be OK – that she would somehow scrape through. On rare occasions I would be allowed into her bedroom to sit on the end of her bed during these chatty consultations. I remember it as though it were yesterday: the sternly studied concentration on Dr Parker's face, eyes tight shut, as he slid his stethoscope across her chest . . . side . . . back. Then he would smile broadly. 'Still ticking,' and she would laugh, the sunlight of everlasting hope dancing in her luminous grey-green eyes.

I was no longer afraid or homesick. I had become comfortable with the familial ambiance of little Hill Brow School in the way that one enjoys a sloppy old pair of shoes. I had made friends: Roger Potter, Ian Cocks, Peter Bennett, Peter Gwyn, David McCaig, Goofy Isaacs . . . and, perhaps for the first time in my rather Byzantine school career, I'd begun to fit in, to lose myself in the conventional potage of uniformed boys around me. Yet one frustration continued to haunt me – no one else showed much inclination for or interest in nature.

Very slowly a truth was dawning: that my years of unsupervised wanderings had thrust me into natural history in a way that was unusual – not the way that most boys grew up. Either by circumstance or parental intent, none of my Hill Brow contemporaries had experienced those freedoms or influences that had tipped me firmly into nature's grip.

Those rows of wonder-filled fusty old books in the Manor House library, the manuals on moths and butterflies full of delicate paintings and line drawings compiled by passionate amateur naturalists; the endless tomes on hunting, shooting and fishing written by gentry for gentry; the venerable bird books; guides to moths and butterflies and the uncounted volumes on gardening, trees, wild flowers, and even on fungi and injurious pests, had found their willing mark. Whether by inquisitive intent or simply because they were there, their splendid, heartening enlightenment and boundless intrigue had seeped in through the receptive pores of my boyhood.

Day after day, week after week, holidays after holidays, those cloth-bound books with embossed board covers and such enticing titles had sent me out in search of wildlife. One of my favourites was *The Feathered Tribes of the British Islands* (1834) by Robert Mudie – it took me years to work out that the 'screech owl' was the same as the barn owl, that the 'fern owl' (nightjar) wasn't an owl at all, and that the 'greater pettichaps' was a garden warbler – with its artificially posed, hand-painted illustrations and its exciting uncut pages that I had to slice carefully open with my knife, revealing images and written secrets that had never before seen the light of day.

It never occurred to me that because so many of the books were so old they might be out of date, or even incorrect in their findings or speculations. To me they were *the* authority, and one I never thought to challenge any more than you would question a dictionary. By the simple virtue of being on the printed page and being on the Manor House shelves I believed every word. Only years later did I realise that some of the volumes I loved most had been presents to my great-grandfather, Arthur (1813–1910), or to my grandfather, born in 1873, when he was a boy, and therefore reflected the country values of their time. Knowing their birds and plants, and building collections of birds' eggs, had been the way they were expected to spend their childhood. That I was now accidentally mirroring those same values had never crossed my mind.

There was also the much friendlier *Familiar Wild Birds* (1883) by W. Swaysland, in four volumes, in the popular Cassells series, and their companion *Familiar Wild Flowers* (1890) by F. Edward Hulme, in nine delicately illustrated volumes. And one of my favourites, to which I turned every Easter holidays, *British Birds' Eggs and Nests Popularly Described* (1898) by the Revd Canon Atkinson, who loomed large and benignly dotty in my schoolboy imagination. I saw him in his dog collar and grey shirt, long grey mackintosh, lace-up black boots and leather gaiters to the knee buckled onto baggy black trousers. As I explored the wildest reaches of the Manor House grounds it seemed entirely possible that I might bump into him out there with wire-framed pebble glasses on his nose, little black binoculars round his neck, notebook in hand, creeping round the hedgerows, peering into thickets, parting branches and exploring nooks and crannies in his never-ending forages for nests. It was a possibility beyond parody and one whose latter-day stereotype I would encounter countless times in the years to come.

As the outside world opened up to me, so I began to search out and build collections of my own. Moths with names as vivid as their exquisite colours and riotous patterns: the Elephant Hawkmoth in startling pink and cinnamon; the migratory Death's Head Hawkmoth with a white human skull leering from its back; the opulent shimmer of the Golden Spangle; the Emperor, with four glaring eyes on its pink and orange wings; The Snout, with a ludicrous Cyrano de Bergerac nose; the spectacularly pointillist day-flying Scarlet Tiger; the heather-feeding True Lover's Knot wrapped in umber brocade; the Feathered Gothic, with its intricate cathedral tracery; and the Leopard Moth in the glowing white fur and stippled black spots of a snow leopard.

Clutching my treasured guide, *The Butterflies of the British Isles* (1918) by Richard South – 'with accurately coloured figures of every species and many varieties, also drawings of egg, caterpillar, chrysalis and food plant' – I forayed out to find and capture: Painted Lady, Speckled Wood, Grayling, Green Hairstreak, Brimstone, Orange Tip, Clouded Yellow, Peacock, Small Tortoiseshell, Common Blue and Red Admiral. Page upon page of delights that were rarely difficult to locate in those treasure-filled days of lark trilling meadows, rampant hedgerows and bright, sparkling streams. I loved stalking them through the heady herb-scented pastures, adored seeing them jump and blow away with the wind.

And then there were the adrenaline-pumping encounters with scurrying, leaping, burrowing, snuffling, tiptoeing, plodding, wriggling, flittering, squirming, swimming, dipping and diving antics of bats and badgers, voles and squirrels, rabbits and rats, hares and dormice, weasels and stoats, deer and otters, foxes, frogs and toads, newts and slow worms, lizards and grass snakes, mice and moles. Oh! The rapture the first time I found a nest of harvest mice, no bigger than my fist, woven into the long, golden stalks of wheat. I ran all the way back to tell Nellie.

The birds were my constants, always coming and going, honouring and saluting the seasons, often taken for granted, expected, unconsciously loved and an endless source of wonder. The moorhens on the orchard pond; the swallows skimming in and out of the stables' rafters; the rooks' nests clotting the tops of the oaks and beeches in the graveyard; the starlings bursting from the missing tile in the apple store roof; the long-tailed tits in their domed nest in a prickly *Berberis* thicket, tail protruding from the hole like a teaspoon in a jam pot. It never occurred to me that they might not always be there. They were 'a tremor at the edge of vision', as John Alec Baker would so electrically describe them in his unforgettable elegy to the peregrine falcon. Despite the constant killing, our English countryside of the 1950s was rich and I did not know it. To me it was the endlessly engaging projection of those old books, a gloriously illustrated album to be opened, absorbed and into which I could utterly lose myself, a found fulfilment all my own.

The mistake I made was the naive assumption that other

boys and girls shared the same opportunities, enthusiasms and interests. They didn't. But long ago at the Manor House, oblivious that Robert Mudie had published it 120 years before, when William IV was on the throne and in the year of four Prime Ministers – Earl Grey, Lord Melbourne, the Duke of Wellington and Robert Peel – I had taken completely to heart the injunction in his 1834 preface: 'to entice my fellow Britons of all ages . . . into the fields, that they may know and feel the extent of delightful knowledge . . . to say nothing of well-sinewed limbs . . . met there . . . in abundance by all who will but take the trouble of seeing with their own eyes and hearing with their own ears'. Hear! Hear! Robert Mudie. Every word absorbed by me in 1954 with Elizabeth II only just crowned and the eighty-year-old Sir Winston Churchill in No. 10.

In 1834, most people, it seems, had not been listening. The great flywheel of the Industrial Revolution was spinning like a top and country people in droves were abandoning the land for work in the cities. A hundred and twenty years later, in what was rapidly becoming an urban and suburban-based, although still industrial, post-war British society, wealth creation had taken over as life's principal cultural goal, totally supplanting the rural idyll. Even if it had been explained to me, I would not have understood that like a failing marriage, nature and the people of Britain were losing touch with each other and drifting apart, the gulf deepening and widening with each successive generation.

To my dismay I discovered that I was on my own. Neither at Hampton Down, at Martock nor at Hill Brow was there a nature club or even a master or mistress any more than passingly interested in wildlife. I drew a blank. The other boys had virtually no knowledge of natural history, knew nothing of birds or mammals beyond an obvious few, knew the names of only the commonest butterflies, no moths, no wild flowers or even the trees. 'He's a nature freak,' they laughed.

Bleak moments stand out. I remember a humble woodlouse, lost and helpless, ditheringly multi-legging it across a boy's desk. 'Ugh!' he cried out and pulled back.

'What's the matter?' I asked. 'It's only a woodlouse.'

'It might sting,' was his stridently ignorant reproof as he flattened it with a book.

One day after games I was strolling back to the school from the cricket pitch with a gang of boys and a young master called Mr Kennedy, when a grass snake slithered from the verge and began to wind quickly across the track in front of us. Before I had even seen it Mr Kennedy had shouted 'Keep back!' and had beaten the snake to death with a cricket bat. I was shocked. I picked up its limp, broken body and curled it in my cupped hands. 'Drop it this instant!' Kennedy barked at me. 'It could still bite.'

'It's a grass snake, sir,' I answered flatly. 'It's harmless.'

'Oh,' he said. 'How was I to know that? It could have been an adder.' I wanted to say, *So what if it was? You didn't have to kill it. It was trying to get away from us.* But I didn't.

That was the first time I'd held a grass snake, or, for that matter, a British snake of any kind, except shiny slow worms, which are not snakes, but legless lizards. But I had seen adders and grass snakes coiled in the spring sunshine and watched in awe as they silently flowed away into the undergrowth. Even in its broken stillness this grass snake possessed a stark, functional perfection that both embraced and surpassed beauty. That the life had been so abruptly and so unnecessarily hammered out of it only seconds before filled me with a silently simmering resentment. The more I looked at it, the more I felt embittered. The other boys crowded round. 'How d'y know it's a grass snake?' 'Are you sure it can't bite?' 'Ueere, it's slimy!'

'It's not slimy, you idiot! That's blood because it's been squashed. Snakes aren't slimy, they're dry and silky.' Instinctively I was defending the loss of this lissome young life. 'It's beautiful,' and then I added, 'It was much more beautiful a moment ago, when it was alive and doing nobody any harm.'

Mr Kennedy reacted angrily. 'Oh, do shut up! It's only a ruddy snake.' He stomped off, leaving me holding the snake, with one or two boys still lingering, intrigued as much by the taut exchange as by the dead snake itself.

It was beautiful and I was not ready to abandon it. About sixteen inches long, it was a young male grass snake. Most of its length was a slender mosaic of dull olive green scales with a hint of lemon, broken by black bars and flecks on its flanks and belly, tapering to a finely pointed tail. Separating its flat, spear-shaped head from the body was a broad stripe of bright citrine yellow fringed by black. The same yellow flowed down its face to its jaw and circled its lidless eyes of fiercely staring jet. Underneath, its scales broadened across the whole of its width. Its spine was crushed in several places, but its head remained intact, both glossy eyes too fresh to have dulled. I held its little face up to mine and wondered what it was like to be a snake. I remembered what Bernie had made us learn by heart: *'thou* art *cursed above all cattle, and above every beast of the field; upon thy belly shalt thou go, and dust shalt thou eat all the days of thy life'*. The resounding, echoing, damning directive from Genesis he had spouted at us over and over again came flooding back to me: *'And let man have dominion over . . . every creeping thing that creepeth upon the earth.'* The devil incarnate.

Nature conservation was in its infancy. As a prep school

boy I don't think I had even heard of it. But I knew in the deepest marrow of my bones that, metaphor or no metaphor, the Bible was wrong. The first flickerings of a challenge to such a cogently endorsed diktat were beginning to form not just in my head, but in my heart. Of course, in the 1950s I had no idea that humankind was hell bent upon wreaking environmental havoc across the globe, but scientists have now determined that 1955 stands as the date when negative human influence could be detected in every habitat and ecosystem on earth. We had certainly taken that edict to heart. Dear God, we had. And *dominion*? We were well on our way to achieving full marks for that. A long time later, in adulthood, I would arrive at the life-long conviction that mankind's God-directed habit of blaming wild creatures for problems largely of our own making was a fundamental philosophical error both of judgement and understanding. We have yet to learn how to live with other life forms on earth.

I can still picture that wrecked snake, the boys gathered round. The memory is sharp: the people, the pressing faces, the hot chemistry of discord swirling through the moment. Like bashing Wells' head on the metal fire surround, witnessing that snake bludgeoned to death was an indelible event, locked in for life, another rung on the ever-ascending ladder of awareness, not just of the natural world but of myself and my own emotions and those of the others around me. It was also the slow awakening of something new – of conviction.

I have revisited that day in my head and re-run the event a thousand times over the years and wondered why it should have mattered so much. It wasn't anything like an epiphany or even a watershed moment, and anyway, at twelve I was still far too naive and diffident to be able to exercise any sort of objective critical faculty. Much as the grass snake was beautiful, it had been the ignorance of the perpetrator far more than the death itself that had rankled. I've never forgotten it and never will, but two distinct hallmarks were indelibly tattooed into my expanding consciousness that day. The first was that it endorsed in the minds of my contemporaries that I felt differently about nature from them, and the second, that I was aware of a new sensation – that I was inadvertently assembling a reputation.

*   *   *

Behind the cricket pavilion in the south-west corner of the games field lay a stagnant rhyne. It was typical of the smaller man-dug rhynes, many of them very ancient, which drained that low-lying corner of Somerset. For most of the year these deep ditches remained static, a residuum reflecting the high water-table of that low-lying land, only filling and flowing outwards in the very wet months. As a consequence, these linear ponds were exceptionally rich wetland habitats. That particular rhyne was fringed with sedges and tall, whispering reeds, open water stippled bright green with duck-weed like a Seurat painting. I was well aware that both coot and moorhens were abundant in the rhynes and I could often hear them calling to each other from the dense perpendicular sanctuary of the reeds.

Cricket was lost on me. I found fielding yawningly boring and always asked to be posted out to the boundary, where I could watch birds in the hedges or red ants tirelessly processing in and out of their tunnels in the parched summer soil. Batting was not much better. I was placed well down the order, a tail-ender, which meant that I had tedious hours of sitting waiting in the pavilion, often never getting to bat at all. The rhyne was a far more interesting place to be, so

I would wander off behind the pavilion to explore its secret, wonder-packed *Wind-in-the-Willows* world of water voles plopping in and out of the stagnant water. More than once I got caught out when there was a sudden collapse of wickets and I heard frantic shouting, 'Lister! Where the hell are you? Come *ON*! You're in.' And I had to rush back and get padded up, lolloping out onto the pitch still struggling to do up buckles, arriving at the stumps breathless and sweating, only to be bowled out three balls later.

During one of these long waits I found a pair of coots building their nest mound of dead reeds, stems in a twiggy tangle and lancet brown leaves crudely woven into a bowl-shaped basket, about two feet above the water level. It was very close, so I could watch them to-ing and fro-ing as well as keeping half an eye on the batting order. As the weeks slid by I came to long for afternoons of cricket. When the incubating bird got off to feed and stretch its wings, on tiptoe I could just see in sufficiently to count the nine blue-green, black speckled eggs of her clutch. Incubation is twenty-one days. I kept count.

On day twenty-two there was a cricket match against a Taunton school. I prayed for us to win the toss and to bat first. I hit lucky. I wouldn't be needed for hours. I crept to the edge, slowly and carefully parting the reeds. There, to my utter delight, was a huddle of fluffy black chicks, newly hatched. I didn't know that they would be so beautiful, all together in an indistinguishable bundle except for their tiny red bald heads, absurdly fringed with ragged yellow down. One was still struggling out of its shell, wet and bedraggled as it pulsed and wriggled free. One egg remained, addled or the chick dead in the shell. An adult coot stood on the rim of the nest glowing with pride and energy.

Suddenly it cried out in alarm, answered by its partner in

the reeds, their sharp klaxon calls rending the sultry summer air. The adult vanished off the nest but stayed close by, calling anxiously, but not in my view. Then with a slow, sinuous ripple, the surface duckweed wavered and parted. The water seemed to cleave itself apart right to the edge of the soggy mound of the nest.

At first I thought it must be a fish, but a second later a flat, angled, weed spotted head emerged at the nest rim and rose stick-like out of the water. I held my breath. Like an unstoppable wind-wave rippling through a hay field, a large, long grass snake wove its effortless way up the side of the mound and onto the top. Its long body flowed out behind it, tail still invisible in the water.

I was planted, fixed, as rigid as a graveyard angel, gripped by this latest, unexpected fling of nature's revelations. I had seen grass snakes before, but never one swimming like this, its shining wake stretching out behind it, and so very close. But I was slow. Oh! I was so very slow to understand what was happening, to take in what ageless elemental drama was unfolding only a few feet away. Snakes have to feed; they eat mice, frogs, newts, water voles, they devour whole nests of rats, but it had never occurred to me that I might witness the removal of an entire clutch of coots. I wanted to cry out, but no sound came; I was speechless with disbelief, with horror, with fascination, with helplessness. But with awe, too. An uncertain rain-washed acceptance slowly overcame me. This was nature, the nature I had come to love – vital, wild, random, remorseless. All I could do was watch.

With a quick, sharp lunge the snake's jaws gaped and engulfed the first chick, head first. I saw the tiny backward-pointing teeth descend and a muscular convulsion flow down the snake's body as the chick disappeared from view. Then a sharp jerk forward and a second chick was grabbed by a stubby wing. Its little red head disappeared into the gaping maw, tiny pink feet paddling air. Then a third, and a fourth, and a fifth.

The parent coots were still squawking frantically from inside the reeds. One bird broke out and scuttled across the surface, slicing the duckweed into a long stripe of black water. It vanished but its anguished cries continued. The snake now slid further up the nest. I could see the bulge of chicks behind its head gradually lumping backwards as the powerful contractions hauled and flexed. The jaws stretched again. The white interior of its gullet flashed as a sixth chick was grabbed. I heard its thin, faint cry as it disappeared and the jaws lunged once again – the seventh. All that was left was the chick so recently hatched, still too weak and wobbly to stand, a life barely begun, beside the solitary addled egg.

The snake seemed to know there was no hurry. It jaws closed and its tongue, black and bifid, flicked in and out several times before it slowly eased forward until its nose was up against the last helplessly wobbling chick. Almost in slow motion the lower jaw dropped away, the pallid throat yawned and the chick's head was grabbed. The reptile's head rose and fell in what passes for a swallow in a snake, a peristaltic muscular ripple, before it turned and slid silently down the side of the nest and into the water. As it swam away, gliding right past me, head just above the surface, I could see the weed coiling and waving to the sinuous weave of its long body. The weed-clogged wimples of its wake made it look far larger than it really was, spinning the weed dots into tiny whorls and eddies as it flowed, unhurried, away across the rhyne to disappear into the reeds on the other side. I stared blankly at where it had vanished and then back at the nest, empty but for its lonely addled egg.

There are moments and incidents that engrave themselves

permanently into memory. They become way markers on the blundering journey to comprehension. I was shocked, but only mildly. Predation was no new revelation, far from it; I had witnessed nature's harsh old laws many times at many levels and seen the evidence: badgers ripping hedge-hogs open and leaving only the spiny skin; sparrowhawks plucking chaffinches alive; I'd heard the piercing screams of a young leveret being mauled and dragged off by a stoat. But it was the unexpectedness of the snake event, and its totality, every last chick so efficiently gobbled, and the speed. The whole drama barely took two minutes.

But there was another dimension, too: the unpredictable, complicated, loaded, helplessly subjective one of human emotion. I had watched the coots build their reedy nest, counted the glowing eggs of the completed clutch, ticked off the days, been there for the moment of final hatching. They were mine. I ran out that day uplifted by the loaded bounty of expectation. I had hoped to see the chicks out on the water, riding on their parents' backs, snatching insects from the weedy surface. But instead I had to stand and watch their summary destruction. I told some of my friends and they laughed. 'So what?' one said.

The following week in Mr Kennedy's English lesson, in preparation for the Common Entrance exam we would all have to pass if we were to be accepted by a public school, we were required to write an essay on something recent of our own choosing, like the cricket match or being taken out to Sunday lunch or . . . it didn't matter what. Carefully and faithfully, I wrote the doleful tale of the coot chicks' demise.

The last lesson before lunch, a subject reserved by Mathey himself, was Divinity. Both he and his wife were dedicated Christians who took their religious responsibilities very seri-ously. His subject that morning was human frailty, and in particular that of Judas's betrayal and Peter's denial in the Garden of Gethsemane in the run-up to Jesus's trial. Mathey had made us explore the narratives in all four gospels of the New Testament. I loved the resonant solemnity of Jesus's prediction to Peter in St Matthew, Chapter 26: '*Verily I say unto thee, That this night, before the cock crow, thou shalt deny me thrice.*'

'M-m-m-it's an important lesson, boys. M-m-m-all about TRUST and m-m-m-BELIEF.' His multiple wobbling chins seemed to trebly labour the point.

To my surprise, later that afternoon I was called into his study. Mathey sat at his desk, cigarette dangling, my essay open in front of him and Mr Kennedy standing with his back to the window. I wondered what I had done wrong. 'M-m-m-m-Mr Kennedy has shown me your composition, m-m-m-John. It's very good. M-m-m-it reads very well. M-m-m-you obviously have some promise in m-m-m-English. Do you enjoy it?'

'Yessir, I do.'

'M-m-m-good. I'm pleased to hear that. M-m-m-but I'm afraid he has had to fail you this time because the m-m-m-composition had to be on a recent m-m-m-event, not a made-up story about snakes.'

'It wasn't made up, sir. It was true. It happened during the cricket match.'

He was shaking his head as well as stammering. 'M-m-m-now come along, John. I don't think so. M-m-m-I think you have a very active imagination. I don't think we have bird-eating snakes in our games field and, anyway, you can't have been watching snakes and paying attention to the cricket match, now, can you? In your m-m-m-Common Entrance exam you must be truthful or you will fail that too.'

Mr Kennedy joined in. 'That's right. There are so many things you could have written about, John. And I am bound to ask whether you made up that story just because I killed a snake last week. Were you trying to make a point?'

'No, sir, I wasn't. And it was true, every word, I promise.' Mathey and Mr Kennedy looked at each other and then back at me. I saw Mr Kennedy raise his eyebrows. Both of them looked smug, their expressions gripped by that nameless schoolmasterly certainty that, whatever argument is presented, they are bound to be right. Mathey began again.

'M-m-m-there's a place for fiction, John, and perhaps one day you will be able to write what you like, but for m-m-m-now and for you to m-m-m-pass your exam we need the m-m-m-truth. You'll have to write another composition instead of m-m-m-games this afternoon and hand it in to Mr Kennedy by suppertime. M-m-m-m-do you understand?'

'Yessir,' I muttered darkly and turned to go.

Then he added, 'And, John, no more m-m-m-imaginary snakes, please.'

As I closed the study door carefully behind me I thought to myself, *Hmmm, so much for trust and belief.*

18

Dark shadows, bright horizons

As I was about to ascend to public school, grim news came from the Manor House. My grandfather, then aged eighty-four, had been up to his usual horticultural activities in the gardens. He had long harboured an obsessive loathing of what he called 'Bloody dockweeds!' – the common perennial garden weed properly named Broad-Leaved Dock, *Rumex obtusifolius*, with a deep tap root, the plant whose leaves produce a milky liquid containing astringent tannins and oxalic acids, very effective for curing stinging nettle rash. I knew it intimately. For a country boy in those days of short trousers it was impossible to avoid getting your legs stung. I was always rushing to find dock leaves and clamping them to my calves and shins.

Early one afternoon, angered by a large specimen flourishing under a hydrangea, he bore down upon it with a sharp garden fork. He stabbed viciously at its deep root. His great height was already beginning to cause him balance problems and by then he was habitually walking with a stick. He wobbled, missing the dock and spearing his own left foot. Two prongs tore through the soft tissue at the base of his toes. He yelled with pain and yanked the fork out again.

He hobbled off to his armchair in the smoking-room and rang the bell for Nellie. For ease and comfort in his old age he had taken to wearing black lace-up boots of soft canvas.

The left one had immediately filled with blood. Nellie came and administered a large whisky. She tried to unlace the boot, but it hurt too much and he told her to leave it alone. She had no idea how serious the wound was. The old boy was in no mood to be humoured, so she left. 'Just you ring if you needs me and I'll bring you a nice cuppa tea.'

He always was independent of spirit and autocratic. He had never suffered fools. All his life he had been an author-itative figure, enhanced by his great height and having been a Deputy Lieutenant and JP for Warwickshire for decades. It was widely rumoured that when presiding on the bench petty criminals pleaded guilty at the sight of him. Since my grandmother's death he had become even more dogmatic, shutting himself off from a world he felt he no longer belonged to and entombing his opinions in solitude. No one challenged his authority. The old man had a long-standing dislike of doctors, calling them 'damned quacks'.

Nellie was devoted to him; the household had been her entire life and she cheerfully cared for his every need. As they had aged together he and the Manor House had become her whole existence, a symbiosis based upon mutual respect and dependency that had morphed into a genuine but unspoken affection. She tried many times to persuade him to let her see the wound. 'Hadn't we better take the boot off and take a look, sir?' she pestered cautiously. 'I think I'd better call the doctor.' But he wouldn't hear of it. It hurt too much. He wanted it left alone. He wanted to be left alone. Wringing her hands on her pinny, Nellie retreated.

The next morning she was disturbed to find that he had spent the night in his armchair, foot up on a stool, the boot still on. She telephoned my father. By the time he arrived the following day the entire boot was firmly cemented in place with congealed blood. After a long argument he persuaded the old man to be helped upstairs and to soak the boot off in a warm bath. In the end he had to cut the boot away with sharp scissors. He revealed a horrid mess – black swollen toes and a strong smell of rotting flesh, foetid and foul. Gangrene.

In hospital the doctors took one look and announced that he would have to lose his left leg above the knee. It was amputated a few hours later. To a proud, elderly man who had been physically fit and active all his life, it was a devastating blow. With so many levels, steps and stairs, the Manor House was wholly unsuitable for a one-legged octogenarian. He had to stay in hospital while my father organised moving a bed to the large drawing room and fitting it out with a commode and all the necessary aids that an exceptionally tall invalid might need. When a few weeks later I was taken to see him, I rushed to the servants' hall to make sure the Dun Cow rib was still in place. It was and I heaved a huge sigh of relief.

Until that moment I don't believe I had ever given a thought to my grandfather's death, or that the Manor House might not always be there at the heart of my family. Together with my mother they were the rocks around which my whole existence had revolved. I had yet to learn that the world constantly moves on, that change is life's inescapable yoke. When I travelled with my father to see him a few weeks later, I was shocked. He had aged visibly; the trauma of amputation and the total loss of mobility had taken a heavy toll – at his age an artificial leg was out of the question – but instead of shrinking with age, the lack of exercise had expanded him dramatically.

His days consisted of the slow and laboured process of getting dressed with the help of a full-time male nurse, teased gently into a bold windowpane-checked tweed suit with shirt and silk tie, empty trouser leg neatly folded under his stump, silk handkerchief overflowing extravagantly from his breast pocket. Then to be wheeled across the room to his huge winged armchair, where he would spend the rest of the day listening to the Home Service and reading the *Daily Telegraph*.

On fine days, with a wide, pancake-like Edwardian tweed cap on his bald head, his nurse would wheel him out into the garden in his specially enlarged wheelchair, ivory-handled fly-whisk in hand like an African potentate, and up the flagged paths to his glass-houses so that he could direct my uncle Aubrey to tend to his prize blooms. At the sight of his flowers he would perk up, mutter, 'Delphiniums very fine,' and then move on to the next house. But at other times he became very morose. More than once I overheard him say to my father, 'I wish I was dead.'

When I reported this to Nellie she looked shocked for a moment, recovered herself and tried to reassure me. 'Now, don't you fuss so, young Jack. I'll look after 'im proper. Just you see.' But she was wringing her hands in her pinny again and a waver had crept into her voice. An inevitability was slowly dawning: that my treasured wilderness, my world of joy and discovery, my universe of freedom and escape, and what for my entire life had been my Shangri-La, might now be time-limited. Then Nellie made it far worse. 'When your grandpa passes on, I 'spect your mum and dad'll be moving in, shan't they?'

Nellie had never properly comprehended the extent of my mother's incapacity. She hadn't understood that my mother would never get better and was far too infirm to manage a large, rambling country house. It had not entered her head that the family might be forced to sell up. Nor mine.

*   *   *

By 1959 my grandfather's amputation was not all that was going wrong. Ten years after the nationalisation of the coal industry it had proved impossible for our cousin, Sir Kenelm, to hold the Yorkshire estates together. In an attempt to duck the socialist government's swinging capital taxes – death duties claiming an excoriating 80 per cent – he had removed to Ireland, to an estate at Mullingar, where, as a failing old man he had neglected to make any sensible provision for succession. When he eventually died, and although my grandfather succeeded to the baronetcy, what was left of the Yorkshire estates had to be sold up to pay the duty. So collapsed my family's presence in the West Riding of Yorkshire, a proud presence that had run continuously from father to son, ducking and weaving through the jungle of outrageous political fortune – and surviving – for more than 700 years. Now my grandfather was head of the family and the little Manor House estate was all that was left.

Adding to this overarching family *dénouement*, my unsupervised upbringing and chaotic educational career had, as Mathey had predicted, produced dismal results in the Common Entrance examination. The post-war baby boom had filled most English public schools to capacity. As they came under pressure for places, so they raised the entrance pass mark from an achievable 70 per cent to as high in some schools as 85 per cent. At birth I had been entered for my father's old school – my parents' intended and expected school of choice. They had never dreamed that I might fail to get in and they had never considered anywhere else. My dismal score of 64.3 per cent now ruled that out, as well as all the other favoured possibilities. In desperation, my father tried to get me into Allhallows, an ancient but little-known public school perched on the Devon–Dorset clifftop between Lyme Regis and Seaton, whose entrance requirement was a modest 65 per cent. Even they were distinctly sniffy. It would all depend, I was coldly informed by Mathey, upon an interview.

I remember the July day, the scudding sun-bright clouds, the first glimpse of the sea, Lyme Bay a brilliant lapis lazuli with cloud shadows as dark as great whales surging purposefully through on a brisk breeze. I loved the rattling drag and crash of the waves on the shingle beach. Lunch in awkward silence at the Bay Hotel in Lyme Regis, the smell of my father's pipe and stewed cabbage in the dining room, taking my mother's arm as she teetered unsteadily back to the car. 'Now do your best, darling,' she whispered. 'Remember to say please and thank you for everything.' Politeness and good manners were her default tonic for all ills. I remember the ten-minute drive to the imposing school gates, the long curving driveway until the vast central building loomed into view with its black-and-white mock-Tudor porch suspended above twin arches on massive Doric columns and its high, pitched-roofed tower offset to one side – the whole edifice a faintly ludicrous Victorian schloss built with Empire firmly in mind.

We were met by a tall, good-looking school prefect in a flowing black academic gown. He had immaculately groomed hair and an aquiline nose. He was studiously polite to my parents, loftily welcoming to me. Aged seventeen he already possessed the confidence and presence of a leader of men. His name was Roger Wheeler, shortly to embark on a career that would see him achieve General Sir Roger Wheeler, GCB, CBE, Chief of General Staff of the British Army, 1997-2000.

Parents in first. Wheeler escorted them up the wide Italian marble staircase to the headmaster's study. I sat in a waiting room and watched in expanding horror as boys in grey herringbone tweed suits and jackets, as tall as full-grown men and with gruff voices, strode past the window. I was not at all sure I wanted to attend this frightening school. My parents came back from the headmaster. 'He's serious but charming' was my mother's reassuring verdict. Wheeler whisked me away. Up to the first floor where, to my speechless astonishment, I found a vast array of stuffed birds in massive floor-to-ceiling glass cases running the full length of a long, wide corridor. 'Wait here.' He disappeared along a passage.

I walked to the nearest case, where seabirds of every description – puffins, auks, shags and cormorants, gulls and terns, gannets, shearwaters and petrels – were displayed on artificial rocks and cliffs against a dioramic background of blue sea and sky. It stretched away down the corridor, further than I dared go. I could see great eagles, hawks, falcons, herons, cranes . . . they went on and on. I had never seen anything like it, even in the natural history museums I had visited in my short, sheltered life. Suddenly I liked this school.

Wheeler came back. 'You can come now.' Gown billowing out behind him, he strode down a dim passage and knocked boldly on the headmaster's study door. As I entered he whispered, 'Good luck.'

I wasn't expecting two men. The headmaster, Victor Archibald Lord Hill, inevitably known to the world as Val Hill, was wearing a hairy Harris tweed suit of startling burnt sienna. He was sitting in a captain's chair behind a large leather-topped desk with an embossed border. Up loomed the horrible image of Bernie and his study. This was bigger and grander, with more soft furnishings and big windows looking out over gardens and a terrace toward fields and the distant sea, but the image persisted. I wondered how many boys had been caned in this room. He stood up and smiled.

He was a big man, with wavy black hair carefully groomed and a slow, deliberate manner of speech. 'Come along in and take a seat.'

With his back to the fireplace, the man I later discovered to be the deputy head, Horace Lee, came forward and shook my hand. Then blank. I remember nothing more of the formal bit of the interview. All I could think of were the birds in the corridor. They had knocked me off balance, taken me completely by surprise. I'm sure I said all the predictable things: 'Yes, sir' and 'No, I don't think so, sir'; 'I like cricket [a lie] and rugger [I'd never played it] and hockey [true] and English is my favourite subject [nearly true].' And then, after ten gruelling minutes of what felt like floundering helplessly in deep water, buffeted by waves and dragged by currents, came the sudden, unpredicted, merciful wave that dumped me safely onto a bright, sunlit strand. 'And do you have any hobbies?' Mr Hill asked.

'Natural history, sir.'

'Oh. Natural history, eh? How nice. What sort of natural history interests you?'

'Everything really, sir. Birds, mammals, plants, insects. All that sort of thing, sir.'

'Really?' His eyebrows raised and he threw a glance at Mr Lee. I could see he was sceptical, an ill-concealed 'we'll soon see through this' lurked beneath his methodical delivery, then 'Tell us something you know about.'

I thought for a moment. Then from deep inside, from a living, singing core of confidence that had been silently fermenting within the hot canyons of my brain for more than ten years; from the hundreds of hours of wandering and watching in the wilds of the Manor House and the ditches, ponds and woods of Somerset; from the dozens of wet days in the school-room library poring through ancient tomes; from standing up to Bernie and the Menace over Butterworth's pen, and from defying Miss Gibbs at Martock, came a sudden surge of combative audacity. I took a deep breath. 'You can ask me anything you like, sir.'

Both men seemed taken aback and a glance flickered between them like a spark. 'All right,' said Mr Hill with a slow but not sinister smile. 'What sort of birds would you expect to find here at Allhallows?'

For a split second I hesitated. Was this a trick? Did he mean the birds in the corridor? I stood up and took a step towards the window that looked out over a formal terrace with woods and fields in the distance. I suddenly felt completely at home.

'There are rooks in those big pine trees, sir, and jackdaws with them, they flock together at this time of the year, and there's a blackbird on the lawn, and a song thrush over there.' Both men were now craning to see what I was pointing at. 'And those are woodpigeons flying over the field, and I can see a cock pheasant out there too, in the distance. There are house sparrows right beside us, sir, on the guttering just out there, and that's a pied wagtail on the balustrade. I expect it nests on the building somewhere. The nest is made of grass and it lays about five eggs of speckled grey. You can see it catching flies, that's why it has such a long . . .'

'Yes, yes, I see. You really do know your birds, don't you?' But it wasn't a question – it was an affirmation. His tone had shifted. I knew he was impressed, almost as though he was enjoying it.

'. . . a long tail for swerving suddenly, and of course near the sea there'll be lots of gulls.' I pressed on, determined to harness the moment. 'And I've seen the birds in the corridor, sir.'

'Oh, have you? Yes. They're rather wonderful, aren't they?

They were collected by Sir Henry Peek, the biscuit magnate who built this mansion in the last century. It was his passion. I believe every British bird is there.'

'Oh wow! Sir, they're amazing, like a museum.'

'Yes, John, they are, but you won't be coming to Allhallows to learn about birds. Your mark at Common Entrance was not very good. If we grant you a place, you will have to work hard to improve your academic standard.'

Mr Lee seemed to come to my rescue. 'He'll be good at biology, headmaster.' He had a whiney voice that seemed to emerge through his nostrils, but he was smiling. So was Mr Hill.

I knew I'd passed. Mr Hill pressed a buzzer and a secretary lady came to the door to take me back to my parents. Another black-gowned school prefect showed us round the school. When it was time to go, the headmaster, the man I would know for the next five years only as 'Boggo', and with whom, in time, I would forge a bond of mutual trust and respect, met us in the forecourt and shook hands warmly. My parents were nodding and smiling.

*   *   *

What I did not know until later, and what I am sure they had not properly appreciated, was that Allhallows sat on an 800-acre National Nature Reserve of international significance.

The Axmouth–Lyme Regis Landslip on the south Devon coast is one of the most remarkable geological phenomena in Britain. In his exhaustive tome *A Textbook of Geology*, published in 1882, that irrepressible Victorian Sir Archibald Geikie FRS records the Landslip:

> In the year 1839, after a season of wet weather, a mass
> of chalk . . . slipped over a bed of clay into the sea,
> leaving a rent three quarters of a mile long, 150 feet
> deep and 240 feet wide. The shifted mass, bearing with
> it houses, roads and fields was cracked, broken and
> tilted in various directions . . .

That Christmas Eve at around midnight a vast chunk of
clifftop farmland broke free and slid quietly and gently
towards the sea . . . A whole southern English estate had
effectively parted company with the world of agriculture
and human influence, and slipped away in the night to do
its own thing. It was a geological splinter group, a scion of
old England breaking free.

It became a great Victorian spectacle, drawing tourists
from all over Britain, and a mecca for fossil enthusiasts, who
crawled over the ammonite-studded lias beds and chipped
gleaming sharks' teeth out of virgin chalk terraces.

Slowly, as tourist interest in the land receded and it was
abandoned because of its inaccessibility, nature reasserted
its authority. Dominant ash woods began to cover the lost
fields and exposed rocks and soils. A riot of undergrowth
and wildlife invaded its cracks and fissures. It scrolled back
10,000 years, sloughing off the relics of human presence.
The cottages fell to rubble and disappeared beneath nettles
and fireweed. Bramble jungles closed over the farm tracks
and the fields sprouted unkempt crops of their own. It went
wild – for 120 years nature romped unimpeded across its
virgin terraces. It went gloriously, joyously, unstoppably
wild.

It was into this extraordinary Robinson Crusoe wilderness
that I strode, wide-eyed, flushed with excitement, in 1959.
In Elaine Franks' exquisitely illustrated sketchbook *The*

Undercliff (1989), a moving foreword by John Fowles precisely mirrors my own experience:

> on a fine summer's day the Undercliff is . . . a triumphant denial of contemporary reality, an apparently sub-tropical paradise . . . not a roof to be seen, not a road, not a sign of man. It looks almost as the world might have been if man had not evolved, so pure, so unspoilt, so untouched it is scarcely credible, so unaccustomed that at times its solitudes may feel faintly eerie.

In their beneficent wisdom my parents could not have chosen a school more appropriately suited to a child of the English backwoods. That they had no idea the Landslip existed, of its potential significance to their son, smacks of fate. What they could never have guessed, and almost certainly did not want, was that it would finally concrete in place a passion for nature that was already deep-rooted and vigorously sprouting. Sometimes these things just happen.

So I ascended, if that is the right word, to Allhallows for the beginning of the school year. To my utter delight I discovered that, at last, there was a natural history society I could join.

19

Rock of ages

After the very tightly monitored and regulated regime of Hill Brow, Allhallows presented itself as the sublime antithesis: a vast flint mansion perched among clifftop fields and wild woods overlooking Lyme Bay on the county boundary, Portland and the Golden Cap of Dorset in the rising east, the distant tors of Devon to the setting west. A littoral landscape where the sea and the land clashed with each other in never-ending turmoil, the seethe and drag of crashing waves framed our days. It was a dripping wonderland where sea mists rolled in as banks of dense, cloying cloud, regularly engulfing us all, and yet, for all its maritime dampness, it was a school freedom I had never experienced before.

It took a bit of getting used to, making Hill Brow look like a detention centre by comparison. I found myself searching for someone to ask if I could go here or there, if I could explore the extensive grounds, gardens and playing fields that surrounded the virtual village of flint-studded buildings and quadrangles that made up the school campus. Or whether I could cycle the half mile inland to the village of Rousdon and the general store called the 'Shrubs', where we bought ice cream and lollies, sweets and cream buns with money jingling in my trouser pocket, another complete novelty. Or whether I could take off on my ancient Raleigh

Lenton bicycle even further afield to the seaside resorts of Lyme Regis or Seaton, draughty and deserted in the winter gales, bright and bustling in the summer sun. The answer from older boys was always a shrug of the shoulders: 'Go where you like. Free time is free time. But just don't ever be late for lessons, prep or games, or, worst of all, for chapel or bed.'

Such liberty was exhilarating, a fresh breeze after a sultry day, almost as good as being at home, at Martock or the Manor House, not like school at all. Away was away and nobody, but nobody, seemed to care. Discipline was entirely delegated to prefects: 'school prefects' who strode about with the air of demigods in black gowns over their maroon waist-coated, grey herringbone tweed suits. They were senior boys of seventeen and eighteen, in their final sixth-form year. They ruled over the entire school, unlike the less exalted 'house prefects', also sixth-formers, whose jurisdiction was restricted solely to their own houses. Both ranks of prefect had the authority to administer corporal punishment – beatings with slipper or shoe; some with a sadistic streak even manufacturing stout wooden implements for the purpose. And they did – rites of passage for the prefect as much as for the unfortunate juniors upon whom they preyed. Catching us juniors talking after lights out was more about asserting power and providing sport for newly appointed house prefects than it was a justified corrective. I learned fast that one could be beaten for almost any misdemeanour, however accidental or trivial.

In that first term I quickly made friends, although as at Hill Brow I found no one in my house, Stanton, with whom I could share my passion for natural history. While this was disappointing, by the age of thirteen I had come to accept that I was different – and quite liked it. The other boys in the junior common room fell neatly into two groups: those who sought to be kind and generous-spirited toward new boys, and those who sneered and made us feel inferior to boost their own egos. Public school life was a jungle whose laws were rapidly and painfully absorbed. Hierarchy, I quickly realised, was everything. In a common room of their own, seniors studiously ignored us 'plebs' as though we were untouchables, beneath their dignity to acknowledge our existence unless it was to bark at us to perform some menial task.

House prefects enjoyed the privilege of shared studies with desks and armchairs, cookers and kettles, where they supplemented school food with toast and coffee, at weekends even cooking their own rudimentary meals on Baby Bellings. The aroma of burnt toast, Marmite and Welsh rarebit lingered permanently through their corridors. As juniors at the very bottom of this determinist pyramid, we were required to be domestic servants to our prefects, a universal and long-standing public school tradition known as 'fagging', so poignantly immortalised by Thomas Hughes in *Tom Brown's Schooldays*. If you were 'on studies', you had to get up early, polish the prefects' shoes, sweep their study floor, remove rubbish, do the washing up and generally tidy the room. If you forgot, you were beaten; if you were two minutes late, you were beaten; if you didn't do it thoroughly, you were beaten; beaten if you hadn't cleaned your own shoes or if you forgot to knock on the door. 'What is this?' I recall a prefect demanding as he pointed to a tiny scrap of paper on the study carpet. If you answered back, you were beaten for insubordination.

One boy in my house whose generosity shone out from day one was a year ahead of me. His name was Piers Youldon, in whose company life became at once more dangerous and more fun, and I am sorry that I have made no effort to keep in touch with him. I believe he went on to Sandhurst and a successful career as a regular soldier. It was Piers who said to me early on in that first term as we sauntered back to the common room one Sunday morning after chapel, 'I'm off down the cliffs. Wanna come?'

I had barely heard of the cliffs. I knew that they were there, that they were within school bounds, that there was a path beyond the tennis courts leading into dense, enticing woodland and, so I had gleaned, eventually on down to the school's private beach, but I knew nothing beyond that. Even if I had read of the remarkable geological incident known internationally as 'the Landslip', I had not understood what it was. 'Old clothes. Ten minutes or I'll go without you,' he said in his habitual, take-it-or-leave-it, no-nonsense manner.

I often think about that day. I don't believe there was any preparation. No plan, no explanation or indication of where we might go, what we might do or even when we might return. I was a new boy. New boys didn't challenge anything; you just accepted that was the way things were and went with the flow. Youldon was a year older, savvy, direct, decisive and, above all, genuine. It couldn't have been clearer: 'I'm going. You can come if you want to.' Just that. No detail, no stated purpose, no justification, nothing more or less. A spontaneous gesture of companionship, perhaps even of friendship, thrown out: to be rejected or grabbed at face value, no questions, no strings.

Off we went. I had no idea where we were going or what was coming next. Without any warning the reserved, apparently serious-minded Piers Youldon of the Junior Common Room transmogrified seamlessly and instantaneously into a wild animal. Once we had sauntered past the tennis courts and entered the woods, without a word he suddenly broke into a run. Not just a run – not a jog or a lope – he ran like a hunted stag. Full tilt. He was possessed. He shot off into the undergrowth ahead of me, vanishing from view. He leapt over fallen trees, skidded down muddy slopes, swung wildly Tarzan-like from creepers. 'Come on!' he yelled as I lagged behind, fearful of falling and hurting myself. I ran as fast as I dared, desperate to keep up, careering downhill, crashing through bushes, tripping over moss-covered boulders, slithering through muddy groves. Snagged by brambles, whiplashed by branches, I tore my shirt and grazed my knees.

After only a few minutes of this helter-skelter, lunatic assault on the cliffs we arrived breathless and panting at a derelict octagonal flint building called the Pumping Station. It had pumped millions of gallons of spring water up to the huge Victorian mansion that the school had taken over in the 1930s. Now it was an abandoned ruin, dank and smelly, the roof half off, windows smashed and its door hanging by a broken hinge. Its huge tanks still held water, overflowing and as clear as gin, but brimming with life: newts, tadpoles, dragonfly larvae, water snails and leeches, and to which I would return over and over again in the years to come.

The Pumping Station also stood at a crossroads, a parting of three ways. To the left and right a broad path led east to Lyme Regis, or west to Axmouth, both several miles away in either direction. Our path led on, steeply downhill to the school's beach.

'Have you been to the beach?' Piers asked when we had got our breath back.

'No.'

'Come on, then.' And we were off again. 'That's the proper path,' he yelled over his shoulder. 'I know a better way. Follow me.'

We veered off into the undergrowth again, ash fronds whipping my face as I plunged ever downwards, never knowing what was coming next, blindly following. Was this an initiation? Was he checking me out? Could I handle it, take the pace? Had I got what the older boys called 'spirit'? But I don't think so. It was what Youldon was like: straight, open or closed as a book, decent and kind. Running wild was his diversion, a private assertion of surefootedness, nerve and utter recklessness. It didn't have to have a purpose; it was a release, a fling; an extreme blossoming of youth's unthinking exuberance.

I continued to admire his no-nonsense approach to life throughout our years together at Allhallows. I began to understand that it was possible that it was also an escape, that his keenly honed personality had in part been forged by tragedy, like Gavin Maxwell's, and like my own constantly nagging spectre of the Dun Cow rib, the ever-hovering fear of losing my mother. A year later Piers and I were both sent to Northern Ireland to attend an army cadet force camp at Magilligan, on the northern shore of Lough Foyle, near Portrush, hosted by the Royal Ulster Rifles. As we crossed on the ferry from Heysham to Belfast through the warm summer night, I stood in silence with Piers at the ship's rail. The sea was dark and calm; the only sounds were the water rippling by and the dull throb of the ship's engines. Suddenly he spoke quietly. 'My father's out there.'

'What?' I said, failing to understand. 'Where?'

'He was drowned. Just here somewhere.' We stared out at the dark waves. 'The war was over, but his ship hit a German mine right here in the Irish Sea. Lost with all hands. He was coming home. They never found him.'

We made it to the beach that day, somehow, after crashing through what seemed like miles of entangling undergrowth, always plunging downhill, lurching over sudden unexpected mini-precipices of bare chalk, and glissading madly down wet and slimy blue lias banks or wading up to our shins through mud flows of porridge-like clay freshly squeezed out of the ever-shifting ground. The whole undercliff was as unstable as a recent earthquake epicentre, a constantly crumbling dynamic at the land's edge, where the heavy rain-laden chalk fractured and broke free, to lurch, buckle and collapse in huge ledges and terraces towards the sea, slipping and sliding on the greasy and impermeable clay far beneath.

At last we burst out onto the empty beach. The broad palate of Lyme Bay, a great arc of bright lapis lazuli, was spread before us on one of those flawless summer days that are such an inexplicable feature of childhood memory. Surf crashed onto steeply banked terraces in a slow, rolling and seething roar. The tang of salt keen in our mouths, we skimmed flat pebbles into the swell, dodged the rushing and sucking waves and fell breathless and panting onto the sun-warmed shingle banks. As we lay there a great surge of comprehension flooded over me as though I was awakening from a long sleep in a new country, and suddenly realising where I was.

All the fear and anxiety of being a new boy, all the worry about rules and regulations and petty traditions (such as juniors always having their tweed jackets done up on the middle button because to swagger about with your jacket undone was a closely guarded privilege of seniors and a misdemeanor for which you were certain to be beaten by a house prefect); fears about getting into trouble without knowing why; about being in the wrong place at the wrong time . . . All of those worries sloughed away from me in one sudden dawning that I could do this on my own, that the cliffs had no rules or prefects, that they were here and wild and unmanaged and as much mine as anyone else's. Still struggling to believe it, I think I stammered something like, 'Can we just go anywhere?'

'Yeah, course. Come on, let's go to the Slabs.' Piers leapt to his feet and we were off again, running the steep shingle contours, slipping and sliding as the pebbles gave way beneath us, falling and rolling in helpless laughter, leaping up and running on towards Axmouth in the west. It was a whole new dimension of freedom, something I had never experienced before, just as the novelist John Fowles would portray it: 'a triumphant denial of contemporary reality, an apparently sub-tropical paradise . . . not a roof to be seen, not a road, not a sign of man'.

The Slabs were just that. Vast slabs of flat, twenty-million-year-old Jurassic blue lias, a tough, compressed amalgam of limestone and mud, exposed at low tide, stretching far out into the bay. They covered many acres and had been polished smooth by centuries of wave action. As we meandered across them, fiddler crabs scuttled away and vanished into weedy cracks, and tiny gobies and blennies shot across shallow sun-warmed pools like computer cursors zooming around a screen. That afternoon the kingdom of the foreshore was all ours. I was excited and exhilarated; a hot fizz of elation coursed through my whole body, an intoxicating fix of sublime well-being.

There, in their uncounted thousands, were the massive spiral fossils of ammonites, antecedent cephalopod molluscs of the present day *Nautillus*, some of them measuring several feet across, dotted about like oversized Catherine wheels. I had never seen anything like it. They were a revelation. Awe and a flushed sense of discovery collided as we ran from whorl to whorl. We kicked off our shoes and paddled barefoot through the shallows of this tepid marine wonderland, shouting, 'Over here! This one's huge.' The gentle wavelets of the flooding tide lapped at our ankles, warmed by the sun-soaked lias beneath.

For me, it was a new sort of exploring. The cliffs were a frontier, a few hundred acres of real wilderness – such a rare phenomenon in Britain – where nature had grabbed the chance to pioneer a landscape handed back after thousands of years of human occupation. In just 120 years, with all the dazzling panache of true, uninterrupted biological succession, it had established a new woodland climax. Its bare rock terraces had witnessed the universal struggle for dominance from every tiny microscopic organism up to the glorious undulating canopy of the ash trees themselves. The sense of wildness was overwhelming, evoking an entirely new response, a comprehension of the wider world as lovingly invested in the immeasurable abstract as in the measurable reality, and which held within it something akin to rapture. I had never experienced true wilderness before and I wouldn't understand its real significance for many months, but slowly, very slowly, that reality would unfurl before my eyes.

We had seen a few gulls wheeling overhead and a roe deer had crashed away from us in alarm halfway down to the beach, but that was all in the way of animal life. I never managed to interest Piers in natural history, but I shall always remain grateful to him for that dramatic, unforgettable induction, that wild, abandoned baptism, not by fire but by sheer exhilarating, devil-may-care rejection of any sense of caution or self-preservation in a place that called for nothing less. In his company life at once became a thrilling and uplifting challenge. It opened my eyes and my mind to the endless possibilities presented by the luxuriant, living jungles of the Allhallows cliffs. It was as though that heightened freedom had shown me another view of the natural world, a view I would never forget. When, late that afternoon, we turned for home, toiling back uphill to the school, I fell silent and dragged my feet. I didn't want it to end. As Wordsworth had it: 'For I have learned / To look on nature, not as in the hour / Of thoughtless youth; but hearing oftentimes / The still, sad music of humanity.'

* * *

There was a school natural history society – at last – with all of eleven boys signed up, but eleven was perfectly good enough for me. It met on Wednesday evenings once a fortnight and had a field trip one or twice a term at most. For the rest, the members were left to their own devices and to foster their own interests. But there was one shining highlight, which, once I located it properly in my second term, became a driving force for the next five years.

The society was overseen by the director of biology, Tom Wallace, who was also a serious naturalist and an expert mycologist. I quickly discovered that he was a charismatic teacher who responded electrically to real enthusiasm in his students. He would become a mentor throughout my school days and a valued friend for the next thirty-five years, until his death in his nineties. While the general companionship of the natural history society was comforting, I lost no time in working out that direct contact with Mr Wallace was infinitely more rewarding.

One of his non-school responsibilities was to the Nature Conservancy, the government agency in charge of all National Nature Reserves. The Axmouth–Lyme Regis Undercliffs NNR was his personal bailiwick, where he was in charge of biological recording and general overseeing of the designated 800 acres between the clifftop and the sea, with a public footpath running the seven miles through the middle of it. By offering to help him with that task I could further my own interests at the same time as arriving at a special status with my mentor.

There was no end to his encouragement: preparing moth, butterfly and beetle collections; pressing wild flowers between sheets of blotting paper in his heavy cast-iron Victorian plant press; cleaning skulls and bones in vats of bleach; collecting fossils of ammonites and belemnites, sharks' teeth and *holaster* sea urchins; bird watching; identifying fungi; learning how to make proper biological observations and submitting records. That ongoing engagement with the statutory NNR became a constant, a dependable absolute that I came to rely on by day and night – a whole other reason for being at Allhallows.

If my father had known that the school was inadvertently directing me away from a more conventional education, I think he might have intervened. But he didn't. He knew very little. Such was his preoccupation with my mother's health and his dedication to his own business and family affairs that he saw little need to watch over his errant son's progress. Besides, natural history as a hobby had been an accepted norm for country boys for generations. He thought I would grow out of it. So did just about everyone else.

My father was also struggling with an extremely difficult decision. His father was dying. At eighty-eight my grandfather was bed-bound and wretched. He had openly declared that he'd had enough. We all knew it was coming. Whenever the phone rang my father jumped to get to it first. Every weekend he drove the 170 miles north to the Manor House. When home from school I went with him. To me it was much the same, the same freedom, the same fun and laughter in the kitchens, the same old Nellie. 'My, my, you have growed up, young Jack. Next thing I knows you'll be courtin'.' But there was also a hovering inevitability and the unspoken questions everyone was avoiding. Would we move there? Surely, we would. Surely the grip of centuries would bind us to it, come what may. I didn't dare ask. I couldn't imagine life without the house, the farm, the woods, the Longbottom meadows, Nellie's porridge on winter mornings and Aga toast for tea. And then it happened. A phone call to my housemaster. 'John, your grandfather has died. Your father is sending someone to collect you in the morning. You will need your Sunday suit.'

I was sixteen and over six feet tall. My voice had long since broken and I was shaving every day. The urgent current of adulthood was sparking through my veins. The drive back to Bartonfield was a desert of barren silence. Mother pale and drawn, Mary in tears. The next morning we all left for the Manor House.

Nellie met us at the front door. She was composed, but her eyes were red-rimmed. Sally Franklin told me she had been crying for three days. Nellie took my hand and led me straight into the drawing room, where the old man was laid out in his huge coffin. He was dressed in a pale blue satin suit with mother of pearl buttons. She leant forward and kissed him on the forehead. 'Don't he look peaceful?' she sighed. I had never seen a dead man before. In the dining room my father and uncle received a procession of tenants and villagers who had come to pay their respects. They came all day. In a heroic bid to overcome the sadness of the hour, he laughed and joked with farmers and workmen he'd known all his life, no hint of the long faces and sighs from the rest of us as he dished out glasses of port, Nellie bustling backwards and forwards with trays of scones loaded with jam. I sneaked off to check that the

Dun Cow rib was still in place. It was. A wave of relief flooded over me. For a ghastly moment, I had feared there was worse to come.

On the day of the funeral all morning the church bell tolled its doleful message across the village. The family assembled in our Sunday best and stood waiting in the hall until the vicar arrived in his vestments, billowing spinnaker-like in a bitter wind. My mother invisible behind a black veil. The pallbearers shouldered the old man out onto the gravel. He weighed nineteen stone and even with eight of them they struggled. We trailed along behind. When we passed through the white gates onto the lane I was astonished to see bouquets of flowers and wreaths lining the path all the way from the lych-gate through the graveyard to the church.

I had never seen it full before. More and more villagers were arriving all the time and the lines of flowers spread further down the lane. 'O God our help in ages past' and 'Rock of ages, cleft for me' lifted to the leaden February clouds, alarming the sparrows that hopped in and out through a broken pane in a high nave window.

Looking back all these years later, I am fully aware that what we were experiencing that day was a rural ritual that had remained largely unchanged since the Middle Ages. The funeral of the lord of the manor was one of the squirearchy of Old England's last hurrahs. It was a day out for everyone, young and old. There would be an extravagant tea in the village hall, beer and skittles in the evening. That the old boy was also a baronet simply added lustre to his name. Later my father told me that a thousand people had turned out that day.

★   ★   ★

When I returned to school a few days later, I was surprised to find that everyone knew. One of the masters had cut my grandfather's obituary from *The Times* and posted it on the school noticeboard. It was the first time in my life that I had felt self-conscious about my family. 'Hey, Liss. Is your dad a sir now?' I didn't know what to say. I was apparently interesting not just because I was a nature addict, which I was used to, but because I had now been re-labelled, shut in a locked box whether I liked it or not, and someone had thrown away the key. The world had shifted beneath my feet. Some things would never be the same again. It would take me many years to understand that people did not accept you for what you really were, but only for what you were perceived to be.

For the most part, after a few days my friends and the other boys in my house took little notice, which suited me fine. Slowly the mantle of amateur naturalist reasserted itself, and partly as a diversionary tactic I began to encourage it. From time to time boys and masters would bring me injured birds that had flown into windows or been hit by cars, or dazed hedgehogs in a box. I don't know why I was expected to be able to cope with these casualties, but my reputation somehow preceded me and I just got on with it.

One spring term a boy found a pair of newborn twin roe deer fawns in deep bracken down the cliffs. Instead of leaving them alone – which is what he should have done – he gathered them up in his arms and brought them back to school. They were exquisitely beautiful, golden fur with lines of white spots down their backs, long gangly legs, huge eyes and ears, and twitching liquorice noses. When I said, 'You idiot. The mother won't accept them back now they've been handled,' he was offended and dumped them on me so that I had to rear them myself and somehow try to return them to the wild.

I had never reared roe fawns before and I immediately got it wrong. One ailed and died within a few days, and I thought I was going to lose the other one too so I decided to try a crude post-mortem on the dead twin to see if I could find out why. I discovered that it was hideously consti-pated, its bowel distended and blocked solid in a long black line. On examining the back end of its living twin I acciden-tally stimulated a sudden outpouring of dung, also hard and clotted together, which didn't seem right. Then I remem-bered that I had watched a roe doe suckling its fawn in the woods at home and had observed that the doe nuzzled and licked the fawn's bottom as it suckled. *Perhaps that's what I have to do*, I thought. It worked. Every day, every time I bottle-fed the surviving fawn with a diluted cow's milk and glucose mix, I also gently massaged its back end with my fingers. The result was electrifying. Not only did it stimulate the bowel to work, but the fawn became energised and fed greedily.

The school possessed some semi-derelict farm buildings below the cricket pitches and we used them more or less as we pleased. Some became illicit smoking dens and I often saw furtive groups of boys sneaking in and out in the dusky evenings. The disused dairy made a perfect hideaway for my various animal charges. Over the years I raised orphaned badger cubs, roe fawns, tawny owlets, a brood of eleven mallard, grey squirrels, rabbits, and leverets and a fox cub, all hidden away in those old buildings. At three months old, I was able to release the well-grown roe fawn back into the wild ash woods of the cliffs. I don't know whether it survived, but I like to think that I had given it a chance.

★   ★   ★

And then there was Goat Island and the Chasm. After that very wet summer and autumn in 1839, the chalk cliff had fractured easily through the clifftop farm, skidded on the clay, and split away in a massive rift. A whole chunk of Devon farmland broke free and slid down towards the sea. It became known as Goat Island and the gap, three-quarters of a mile long, 150 feet deep and 240 feet wide, as the Chasm. This great gulf rendered the island inaccessible except with great difficulty, so it was abandoned to wild nature, which, with entirely predictable consequences, lost no time in taking it over.

Nature's default is woodland; someone once described it to me as 'God's best thought'. On alkaline rocks such as chalk and limestone, the common ash, *Fraxinus excelsior*, outcompetes other species and becomes the dominant tree. When I first fought my way through the bramble tangle of the Chasm and zigzagged up the steep escarpment onto Goat Island to set tentative foot on its thin woodland soils, I was immediately enthralled. The ash woods, 120 years old, were the wildest woods I had ever seen.

In the absence of grazing animals, no wild fires and without the interfering hand of man, the trees had germinated naturally from wind-scattered seed. They had surged upwards to the light, shading out competition so that each tree stood in its own private arena of influence, branches extended to their fullest reach and huge rounded crowns developing refined hemispheres of greenery. When seen from the clifftop above, they appeared like a gently undulating quilt of impenetrable jungle, appealing, enticing and beckoning. But from below, when I struggled in through the bramble tangle, it was impossible to tell where I was. It was a true wilderness, carrying with it all the heart-thumping uncertainty and excitement of a real frontier.

I quickly discovered that while the ash trees hogged most of the light, other shrubs and lesser trees also thrived in their own precise and particular niches. There were spindle trees, with their bright scarlet four-lobed fruits awarding a harlot's glamour to the shady depths, as well as handsome turkey oaks with glossy, deeply lobed leaves, scabby-skinned sycamores, soft-barked elders bearing clusters of fruit in the rich plum of venous blood, and the prickly evergreen canopy of holm oaks. Great banks of shiny hart's tongue fern lolled among bulging clumps of male fern, revelling in the humid shade of the woodland. The more delicate fronds of soft shield and broad buckler ferns crowded around the roots of ash trees and among mosses whose names and needs I would strive to learn in the years to come. But plants were not what really excited me in those formative years. It was wildlife that flooded and coloured my dreams, the animals and birds I had begun to understand at Martock and the Manor House. I knew they were there and I longed to find them for myself.

20

The Pheasantry badgers

When I went to Allhallows, I had never seen a living badger. Like everyone else in the West Country I had witnessed their corpses muddied and bloodied on roadsides. I had collected their skulls and bones, made plaster casts of their five-toed pads and found their deep, dank setts in the woods around my home. I'd driven Nellie and my mother to distraction by boiling up putrid heads on the Aga and filling their kitchens with foul-smelling steam.

I had even stumbled across a gang of farm labourers digging out badgers for sport. I had lingered to watch, shock and fascination clashing behind my eyes. A terrier was underground yelping frantically. Another strained at the end of its leash. Two men dug furiously, sandy earth flying. Two more stood by with shovels and thick hessian sacks. Large iron 'tongs' lay on the earth beside them. They dragged the terrier out by its stumpy tail. As he reached for the tongs one man turned to me and scowled. 'This 'int no place fer kids. You get on 'ome.' I walked slowly away, constantly looking back. 'On 'ome, I told 'ee,' he shouted, waving angrily.

I knew they were up to no good. As I left the wood I saw their bicycles against the hedge at a field gate, a motorbike and sidecar parked nearby. Overcome by the need to know, I stayed. A wartime pillbox stood a few yards from the junction of three lanes, a perfect hide. Half an hour dragged by. They came laughing and joking, two men carrying sacks bound at the neck with twine. The sacks bulged and bounced on the grass. One man dumped them with their tools into the sidecar. Another dragged the terriers away, still yapping hysterically as they rode off.

I ran into the kitchen and jabbered my breathless tale to Nellie. 'I think they had two badgers in those sacks. What were they going to do with them? Where were they going?'

'Ooh, now I think they men are cruel. They go baiting they poor beasts wi' dogs.'

'What for?'

'For bettin', young Jack. That's what for. It's a shame, I tell you. A right shame.'

Sally Franklin came in from the scullery, arms dripping with soapsuds. 'I 'eard what you seen, Jack. That'll be they Paget boys from over Dunchurch way. They're a bad lot, they are. My Tom says they do their baitin' in a barn late at night. There's plenty round 'ere go to their meetin's. 'Ee went along once. 'Orrible 'ee said it were. All blood and yellin'. 'Ee come away quick.'

This shocking revelation made me long to learn about badgers. At Allhallows that first term I asked Mr Wallace about badgers on the cliffs. 'It's excellent habitat,' he had replied, nodding enthusiastically. 'Badgers do well here.' I asked if anyone had ever studied them.

'No. No, I don't believe they have. It'd make a good project. Are you interested?' Just the answer I'd hoped for.

'YES SIR. Yes, please.'

'Then first you need to read Dr Ernest Neal's excellent monograph, *The Badger*. There's a copy in the biology lab.' That night in the dorm I read it under the blankets with a torch, hanging on every word.

Mustelidae. The weasel family. Otters, badgers, weasels, stoats, polecats and pine martens. *Meles meles*, the badger. The odd one out, the only one significantly different: un-weasel-like and the biggest and strongest member of the mustellid tribe in Britain, an omnivorous weasel-bear, a digging weasel-bear with a formidable bite. On witnessing the death of a sow badger, T.H. White had called them 'the last of the English bears . . . Her home was tidy, her habits industrious by night, her claws and forearms agriculturally strong.' I was on a mission, determined to find badgers of my own.

To the east of the Pumping Station, a deep gulley known as Charton Goyle separated the cliffs from the rough fields of Charton Farm. The land rose steeply to the crest of a bank crowned by a dark conifer plantation. I knew about badger paths, their habitual foraging routes from their setts night after night, some so well worn that you could mistake them for human trails. I searched for the giveaway signs: the path passing under a log or through a fence, black and grey hairs caught on wire, scrapes and snuffles in the grass where the badgers had grubbed out a beetle or an earthworm, or dug out a vole nest with their long, scouring claws.

I wandered through the farm fields following their paths back toward the cliffs. They led into the conifer plantation known as the Pheasantry. I could see the pad marks in the mud, counted the five claw indentations from the digging front feet – 'agriculturally strong'. And there they were. Badger setts. The triumph of ownership flooded in. My badger setts, mine. Huge mounds like mechanical earthworks, chalky clay heaped outside the entrances to a dozen or more dark burrows, spilling down the bank for many feet. 'Sometimes', Dr Neal had written, 'setts are hundreds of years old with dozens of entrances leading to a maze of tunnels deep underground.' I felt a huge buzz of pride.

As the weeks passed that summer term I located many more setts spread across the Landslip. I mapped them and showed them to Mr Wallace. He was impressed. 'Why don't you try some badger watching?'

'Would I be allowed to be out at night, sir?'

'Don't worry. Leave it to me.'

A few days later, between lessons, a maths master called Mr Barr stopped me in a corridor. 'So you want to go badger watching, do you?' It took me by surprise.

'Er, yes, sir.' I stammered. 'I do rather.'

'All right, boy. I'll take you.' I was astonished – the last thing I had expected. 'Do you know where to go?'

'Yessir. It's not very far, but we'd have to be out till quite late, sir. About ten o'clock.' He smiled genially, clearly amused by the whole idea. 'That's OK. I'll clear it with your housemaster. How about Saturday night?'

And so it happened. It was a flop – a monumental flop. Mr Leslie Barr, known to us in tasteless schoolboy parody as 'Larry' after a cartoon character called Larry the Lamb, was a distinctly un-lamblike, bluff, middle-aged widower with a military bearing and a bristly moustache whose alternative nocturnal forays I would get to know much better in the years ahead for another reason altogether. He was a kind and decent fellow, but with a famously short fuse, capable of exploding into a seething rant at a moment's notice. It was all bark. He bore neither malice nor grudges. If you had angered him, infringed one of his many fragile disciplinarian sensitivities and received the full fusillade of his rage, within minutes he seemed to have forgotten all about it and was genial all over again.

The evening came. He looked the part in a battle dress top with his trousers tucked into his socks and a pork pie hat on his head. He carried a shooting stick with a leather seat. The weather was set fair. Gnats danced in the cooling air. The sun had long slid below the western horizon, leaving a trail of fire-fringed clouds in its silent wake. We walked quietly down the path.

We settled in. I sat on a log and Larry perched himself on his shooting seat stuck firmly in the mud of the bank, about fifteen yards from the sett entrance. It had never occurred to me to brief him on what he could and couldn't do. Surely he would know, or perhaps Mr Wallace had instructed him? Maybe he'd been badger watching before. He would know that you had to sit still and be quiet, wouldn't he? I was wrong.

He fidgeted, shuffled his feet, swatted gnats, coughed loudly, blew his nose and then, as if to guarantee failure, he lit his pipe. A fog of yellow tobacco smoke hung in the static air. I longed to tell him to put it away and keep quiet, but didn't. I was too raw, too young, too naive, too polite, too diffident, too unsure of what a fourteen-year-old schoolboy could say to a master thirty years his senior. So we sat there for two and a half hours, Larry puffing away on his pipe and me cursing him to hell and damnation under my breath. No self-respecting badger would have come anywhere near us and, anyway, if any animals had approached our entrance they would have taken one sniff and headed back underground to an exit well out of sight many yards away. I was too shy even to say, 'Let's call it a day.'

'Well, that was a rum do!' he suddenly announced in his gruff military way. We trudged back in silence.

Yet Larry Barr had done me a huge favour. He had established a precedent and delivered mildly dotty respectability to a nocturnal activity that otherwise, and had it been proposed solely by me, would certainly have raised deeply sinister suspicions. Whether or not I sought permission to be out at night (which I bothered with less and less as the terms ticked by) really no longer mattered. If challenged, I had the perfect alibis. Entirely unwittingly, Larry Barr and Tom Wallace had legitimised both badger watching and my nocturnal wanderings.

Not long afterwards, I saw my first badger. In the years to come I would see dozens of them and would raise three orphaned cubs given to me by a local farmer at Dowlands on the Seaton side of the cliffs. I named them Shadrach (Shad), Meshach (Mes) and Abednego (Nego), rescued not quite from a fiery furnace but from the unpredictable and unstable geological forces of the cliffs. A group of setts had been ripped apart by a landslide and the unweaned cubs had somehow struggled to the surface unscathed. He never discovered what happened to the adults, perhaps buried alive. I raised those three cubs and delivered them back to the cliffs at seven months old, releasing them into some abandoned setts where I hoped they would survive. I think it's unlikely; badgers are very territorial and chase out intruders, often viciously. But back in 1960, in those days of far fewer options, it seemed to be the right thing to do.

What Shad, Mes and Nego did achieve was to cement my love of the Pheasantry badgers in particular and all mustelids, the whole weasel family, in general. I would come to know their individual stripy faces; I gave them names – Fluffy, Dozy, who emerged on summer evenings and went to sleep in the sun, a sow called Sneezy, and Battleface, covered in scars, Lousy, because he scratched so much, short-tempered Snappy . . . and so on. My field notebook quickly filled with sketches of their face patterns and scars. And inevitably, week by week they came to know me and my scent, eventually scarcely bothering to glance in my direction. Playful cubs ran over my feet. As if to claim me as part of her own territory, Sneezy even thoughtfully delivered a droplet of strong-smelling amber musk from her anal scent gland onto my boot, the ultimate badger accolade.

The cliffs and the Pheasantry badgers were, for the most part, a happy saga of natural history study laced with an adrenal frisson of nocturnal escapade. I was hooked, a badger junkie. I longed for dry summer evenings, thought about little else all afternoon. As soon as prep was over I was off and away, always alone, slipping quickly through the lengthening shadows of the trees, school and boring lessons and beastly, sadistic prefects shedding from my brain like thistledown, off into the beneficent sanctuary of the woods unseen, unheard and unmissed. Badger emergence was usually around eight and I would try to be back for lights out at nine-thirty. If I was late, I could wheel out my trump card – Mr Barr. It never failed.

*   *   *

Our dormitory of nearly twenty boys was at the top of a flight of wooden stairs on the third floor. Immediately opposite our door on the other side of the passage was the door to our house matron's room. She was a tall, well-configured but certainly not beautiful spinster in her late thirties called Miss Joan Metherell. She wore glasses with upturned wings and was bossy by nature, exactly what was needed to keep the domestic affairs of sixty rowdy teenagers in line. She darned our socks and tended to our laundry in austere sufferance.

In my second year we became aware of the clubby aroma of pipe tobacco lingering on our staircase. Masters never came near our end of the main building and we were unsure exactly who this unwelcome trespasser might be. One night I slipped out to visit my badgers, not watching but just in the wood with them, sharing it by association and enjoying the night sounds of tawny owls and barking foxes, and just occasionally stumbling across a badger snuffling towards me. It was a nocturnalism I was learning by rote, time well served, that would run deep and stay with me for life. That night I was out for about an hour and a half.

On my way in again, carrying my shoes for silence and halfway up the back stairs, I heard someone coming up behind me from below. I slipped into the shadows of a corridor and waited. It was Larry Barr. His tobacco aura followed him like a shadow. On the second landing he stopped, apparently to listen, only a few feet away from me. Then, moving furtively, he ascended the stairs again. I was intrigued, so at a safe distance I followed. The stairs spiralled upward in a tight circle. At the top he stopped to listen again before taking the last few steps to Joan Metherell's door. I heard a faint tap and the door opened. A slice of light cut across the landing and Larry Barr slid inside. The door closed. It was nearly eleven o'clock. *Hmmm,* I thought. *Interesting. Very interesting.*

I stood outside for a moment or two, just long enough to hear low music from a gramophone drown out any possibility of eavesdropping. I told the others, of course, hot with such splendidly salacious gossip. In no time we had branded Joan and Larry an item – this in an age of rigid propriety, when intimacy between adults was unspoken and extramarital sex was still severely frowned upon. To us it was a source of endless prurient speculation. We tied cotton threads across the top of the stairs and stuck thin slivers of Sellotape on Joan's door once Larry was inside so that we could see whether the seal was broken during the night. By these means we were able to chart the frequency of his clandestine visits. They were as regular as clockwork. Saturdays, Tuesdays and Thursdays. The possibility that three nights a week carnal knowledge might be acting out so close to our dormitory door drove us to delirious heights of pre-pubescent inventiveness.

I suspect that the reality was profoundly disappointing. It was a courtship, yes, without a doubt, but I think the over-powering shroud of propriety of the day and the dread of being caught in flagrante by us boys probably denied *la pénétration* on the premises. It pleases me to record that Larry and Joan would eventually marry and enjoy many decades of companionship, both living well into old age.

*   *   *

My badger-watching escapades were not always the idyllic pastoral preoccupation I have described. On my right arm I bear the scars of a savage badger bite. Returning one moonlit night from a successful visit to the Pheasantry, I was stopped in my tracks by an unfamiliar sound. It was a sound laden with distress, an ugly growling, whimpering punctuated with little yelps of pain. At first I thought it must be a dog, but then a rising tide of horror reared up within me. I knew what it was. Mr Wallace had told me that some locals in remote areas regularly snared badgers.

I ran to the hedge and broke through, snagging myself on thorns. The moon filtered through the trees as I ran along the edge of the wood, swinging my little torch from side to side. And there it was.

The undergrowth was flayed flat in all directions; the badger had its back to me in the centre of a ring of bare earth, a virtual crater, where the wretched animal was still digging frantically with its front feet. It was on a path. This was a badger out and about, on its rounds, heading along its habitual route.

A stout, many-stranded wire, as taught as a piano string, led from the badger's middle to a steel peg hammered deep into the ground. The unhappy animal had been there since the previous night, struggling in all directions, and had laid the ground waste with its desperate scrabbling. Finally it had resorted to what badgers do best, digging. It had dug and dug. Hopelessly and utterly in vain it had excavated a great pointless hollow of despair while the noose around its middle twisted ever tighter and tighter. It lay in its pit of exhaustion, still lamely digging with its front paws, suspended by the wire, scrabbling nowhere.

I ran to it. Blurry little eyes looked up at me from a striped face muddied with earth and saliva. Its gums and lip flanges were torn and bloodied from gnawing at the wire, at the roots, at stems and sticks, at the steel peg, at anything within its tethered reach. Its breath was shallow and laboured, a stentorian wheezing groan. The animal was beyond fear, crazed with the desperation of its plight through the long hours of torture. I had never seen a badger in a snare before and I was aghast. Common sense vanished. All I wanted was to set it free.

First I tugged at the peg. I tugged and heaved, but it was driven home with a sledgehammer. I grabbed the hawser around the peg and tried to bend it back and forth, but it was far stronger than my adolescent hands. I turned back to the badger. For the first time I saw that it was one of mine. It was the mature boar called Battleface; the scars on its nose and lower jaw gave him away.

The wire noose had drawn the badger's middle into a small circle a fraction of its normal girth, twisting round and round, tightening and tightening, the noose winding ever smaller so that the blood supply was cut off to its hind-quarters. The normally powerful back legs lay limp and useless. In that moment of naivety and swirling emotions it never occurred to me that the badger wouldn't understand that I was a friend. I knelt beside it. I ran my hands up the twisted wire to where it disappeared into the thick grey fur, feeling for a weakness where I could work on it.

In one sweeping lunge Battleface heaved up and round on its front feet and clenched its jaws fast onto my forearm. My yell echoed through the wood. But the badger did not let go. Badgers don't – that's what they're famous for. Their permanently articulated jaws deliver a terrible bite with a relentless grip. That's why badger baiting was and sadly still is seen by some criminal and mindless thugs to be a 'sport'. Battleface's teeth had stabbed through my jacket, pullover and my shirt. I felt the long, curved canines scrape past the bone as the bite closed on the muscle just below my elbow. The jaws clamped like a lock.

I cried out. But the badger held tight. I tried to stand up and pull away but it was too heavy and it hurt even more to pull. Fear flooded in. But I was also in luck. In its pain and exhausted desperation it turned to bite at the wire again. The release was wonderful, my own pain blanked by the rush of adrenaline, and unaware in the darkness of my own blood running freely down my arm. Now much more wary, I took off my jacket and smothered the wretched animal's head, quickly kneeling on it to pin it down so that I could work at the wire. Battleface had done most of the work. Those formidable jaws had almost chewed it through. With a dozen determined bends it snapped. A few seconds later I had unwound the last twisted strands and was able to pull the snare clear. I stood up and lifted the jacket off.

I have never forgotten the sight of that badger shuffling off into the wood. Its hindquarters were almost useless, dragged along by its powerful digging forelegs. I think it must have made it back to the setts where I suspect it died of internal organ damage deep underground. I'm sure the blood supply had been cut off too severely for too long. I never saw Battleface again, but to this day he lives on in the scars on my arm.

21

Ring of Bright Water

While I was still an impressionable fifteen-year-old helping out as assistant librarian at school, I noticed that Gavin Maxwell's global bestseller *Ring of Bright Water* was immediately taken out again after it was returned. It was a crystalline moment I have never forgotten: I was sitting on a bench seat in the sunny corner of the library reading the fashionable novel of the moment, Giuseppe di Lampedusa's *The Leopard*, and was happily engrossed in Sicily's dust, bed bugs, chapels and chandeliers.

The full extent of Maxwell's personal complications would only be exposed to the world at large in his lyrically poignant autobiographical account of the remote cottage hideaway Camusfeàrna and his pet otters. It was a book that would ensnare the public imagination for many different reasons and at many levels: its luminous descriptions of a landscape and an enchanting wildlife most people didn't know existed; its revealing honesty about Maxwell himself, about his esoteric upbringing and his feelings toward the otters; about the tragic circumstances of the death of his beloved otter, Mijbil; and the obscure, Robinson Crusoe lifestyle that was such an antithesis to the hum-drum, workaday existence of the vast majority of the post-war Western world. It would become a publishing phenomenon, selling well over two million copies, translated into nineteen languages and, to his intense chagrin, contorted into a very successful cuddly-animal-cum-romantic-tragedy feature film starring Virginia McKenna and Bill Travers.

That day in the library a sixth former came in to return Maxwell's book. But before I could sign it in for him another boy snatched it from me. 'I've been waiting for that.' In and out again, that fast. A third boy tried to claim that he had been waiting longer. A spat erupted in what was supposed to be the studious silence of the library. *Blimey!* I thought. *Perhaps I'd better read this book.* No chance. The list of others waiting was as long as a yardstick. I went to the master in charge of the library to ask if we could order another two hardback copies. As soon as they arrived, I grabbed one.

From the opening sentence on the first page I could see why it was in such demand. 'I sit in a pitch-pine panelled kitchen-living room, with an otter asleep upon its back among the cushions on the sofa, forepaws in the air, and with the expression of tightly shut concentration that very small babies wear in sleep.' An OTTER! I only knew otters from the snarling masks on their shields and their mounted pads and poles adorning the Manor House walls – hunted otters. I had seen otters' silver-capped webbed pads worn as badges on otter hunters' jackets. By the age of twelve, I had attended meets of the Culmstock and the Hawkstone Otterhounds, run the riverbanks in feverish excitement with the dozens of other country followers, watched the horn-blowing, staff-carrying huntsman in blue livery plunge into the icy stream with his hounds. I'd been there at the kill.

Throughout my childhood the English field-sports tradition, whether hunting, shooting or fishing, was never far away, an unavoidable cultural omnipresence, a constant theme permeating throughout leisure, language, social acceptability, literature, art, men and women's dress, jewellery and even interior decoration. The only otters of my acquaintance were revered for sport and hunted for pleasure. Dead otters. This one, Maxwell's Mijbil, brought back as a cub from the Tigris marshes, was not only alive but asleep on a sofa – on a *SOFA*. And, in common with just about everyone else from a rural background, by the age of fourteen I had read Henry Williamson's poignantly lyrical *Tarka the Otter* (1927) – another hunted otter, an otter gripped in the jaws of that grizzled old hound Deadlock, both drowning together in a gripping finale. It had never pierced my blinkered teenage imagination that an otter might be anything other than sporting quarry, certainly never crossed my mind that an otter might also be a pet.

Ring – as he always referred to it – was not Maxwell's first book, it was his fifth. While his previous books had been well received and moderately successful in general nonfiction terms, they had not been global or even national bestsellers. Until the publication of *Ring*, he was a well-respected travel writer, but not widely read. He can never have guessed that *Ring* would catapult him into preeminence, make him a household name and bring with it the unwelcome exposure to personal scrutiny he would come to resent so deeply. His literary agent, Peter Janson-Smith, once told me that Gavin had confided in him that he regretted having revealed so much of his inner self in the book. 'I knew . . . that *Mij* meant more to me than most human beings of my acquaintance, that I should miss his physical presence more than theirs, and I was not ashamed of it.'

In his friend and eventual biographer Douglas Botting's words, Gavin's upbringing of 'no father, and a suffocatingly adoring mother in whose bed he slept until he was eight' had made him 'a shy, fastidious, romantic and guilt-ridden young man' whose confused sexuality 'was virtually decided for him by the circumstances of his early childhood' and had rendered him incapable of forging a fulfilling relationship with another human being.

The world was very different in Maxwell's day. Gay rights did not exist and homosexuality would remain a criminal offence in the UK until after his death, and condemned by the church for much longer. A constant succession of animals, wild and tame, had formed a reassuring bulwark of security throughout his childhood. Hardly surprising that he would pour his emotional self into such an appealingly responsive animal as Mij, or that he would come to feel so keenly the outside world's intrusive scrutiny of that relationship, at the same time as knowing that he had been the unwitting author of his own exposure. Douglas Botting revealed to me that Gavin 'was never equipped to cope with himself, let alone with the unwelcome celebrity and fame dumped on him by *Ring*'. Fame weighed heavily. 'Oh Gawd!' Gavin would say, not always in jest. 'When's it all going to end?'

I would be as captivated by the book as everyone else and immediately fell under his beguiling spell. Not just about otters. Ever since those wide-eyed days of reading Charles St John and John Colquhoun I had harboured images of the Highlands of Scotland as a frontier of wildness that I wasn't at all sure still existed. Suddenly here was proof. Of the many differing enticements contained within *Ring*, and one that immediately fired my imagination, was his account of rescuing a wildcat kitten from the sea and keeping it in his Camusfeàrna bedroom until it could be shipped south to a zoo.

St John and Colquhoun had made me dream of seeing a Scottish wildcat, a species so conspicuously absent from my pastoral English boyhood. Colquhoun's words had branded themselves into my consciousness: 'When a schoolboy I remember how often the hen-roosts were plundered by . . . wild-cats, which nightly crept forth . . . and the superstitious awe with which I listened in the calm twilight of summer to the cry of the tiger-cat to its fellow.' I was a schoolboy and I longed to hear that too.

Confirmation in *Ring*'s pages that such a fabled creature still existed in the 1960s, eighty years after Colquhoun, and was apparently common on Maxwell's remote stretch of the west coast made me all the more determined to seek it out for myself. Early in the book, in a passage about the red deer stags that used to winter close to the Camusfeàrna house, in simple but electrifying prose he nonchalantly drops in that wildcats are there too: 'I would wake to see from the window a frieze of their antlers etching the near skyline, and they were in some way important to me, as were the big footprints of the wildcats in the soft sand at the burn's edge, the harsh cry of the ravens, and the round, shiny seals' heads in the bay below the house. These creatures were my neighbours.'

I wanted to see those big footprints for myself. I needed to hear Colquhoun's 'cry of the tiger-cat to its fellow in the calm twilight of summer'. And what did Maxwell mean, 'they were in some way important to me'? I pondered that line over and over again. Without understanding why, they were strangely important to me too.

At fifteen I felt that I was standing at the edge of awareness, not just an emergent pre-pubescent self-awareness but that something far bigger was unfolding, something urgent and personal and, yes, important – too important to ignore. If there was a revelation in that one sentence, it wasn't the stags or the ravens, the wildcat footprints or the shiny seals' heads, alluring though they all were to a budding naturalist.

No, it was that he was able to *feel* their importance. At that moment in my impressionable teenage existence I also wanted to be a neighbour to those creatures. For the first time in my life, I knew with a steely grip of certainty that discovering those things for myself was what I wanted almost more than anything else. It would remain a pipe dream for many years, but there was time, plenty of time. Eventually I would get there.

★   ★   ★

I've always been wary of destiny. As an appealing notion, even as a subjective rationalisation of past events, I can grant it credence, but not the other way around. To me destiny exists after the fact, not some fancifully orchestrated collision of circumstances brought about by metaphysical forces. I'm too pragmatic for that – a hammer and nails man. So it wasn't with any sense of destiny that I would meet and forge a brief but life-changing friendship with Gavin Maxwell – but it was perhaps serendipitous.

It would be many years before I visited his Highland home, properly called Sandaig, and by then I would be an adult and he would be a famous author and a household name.

By any measure Maxwell's childhood had been obscure and intentionally esoteric. His paternal grandfather was Sir Herbert Maxwell of Monreith, a Lowland Scottish grandee of ancient lineage. He was the Grand Old Man of Galloway, a seventeenth-century landed aristocrat, sometime Secretary of State for Scotland, a Lord of the Treasury, a painter, archaeologist, historian, naturalist, celebrated horticulturalist and prolific writer on country affairs. The aura of his presence dominated Gavin's childhood as an unassailably formidable model of the Anglo-Scottish Ascendency. As

Gavin would later write: 'he departed this life as a Knight of the Thistle, Privy Councillor, Fellow of the Royal Society and Lord Lieutenant of the County of Wigtownshire'.

Gavin's heritage was hugely important to him, not just defining who he was but also dictating what sort of a person he would turn out to be. The Maxwells had been at Monreith on the Wigtown coast since 1482, ruling lairds over the ancient royal Barony of Monreith granted by the Queen Anne charter of 1705. His father, Colonel Aymer Maxwell, was Sir Herbert's eldest son, heir to both the baronetcy and the family estates. In 1909 he had married Lady Mary Percy, the daughter of the 5th Duke of Northumberland and a celebrated society beauty. The Northumberland seats were the great medieval fortress of Alnwick Castle, surrounded by its vast estates, and Syon Park in London, as well as several other extravagant country and town houses up and down the nation, an aristocratic elite 'who held themselves in more than royal state and seclusion, moving with a medieval retinue of servants between their various castles and palaces' – another formidable family heritage, and one that would have a profound and lasting effect on all four children of the Maxwell marriage.

Together Gavin's parents designed and built the solid and bleakly romantic House of Elrig on the wild scrubland edge of the Galloway moors adjoining the Monreith estate, a country house and a setting ideally suited to an Emily Brontë or a Dickens novel. It was a mansion that matched the austere windswept quality of the surrounding landscape and the family tragedy that would almost immediately engulf it, changing everything. In October 1914, only three months into the Great War, Colonel Aymer Maxwell was killed in an artillery barrage at Antwerp, leaving Lady Mary with three children under four and Gavin, the final gift from her husband, barely three months old.

Recovering from this shattering blow, Lady Mary retreated to Elrig and, to all visible intents, shut herself off from the outside world, effectively abandoning her femininity, striding about the moors dressed in tweeds, brogues and thick hose, pursuing the qualifying sports of the landed, principally shooting and fishing. To compound this reclusive and obscure lifestyle, she filled the house with a procession of kind and generous but comically eccentric Percy maiden aunts. The obscurity of this upbringing, blended with the inherent desolation of the landscape, was almost certainly responsible for Gavin's consequential personality: 'an incurable romantic with more than a hint of melancholy'. In his autobiography of childhood, *The House of Elrig* (1965), Gavin describes the moorland view of heather and bracken from the windows of the house as 'the only landscape in which I ever felt completely at home'.

It was one of these aunts, Lady Muriel Percy, whose lifelong preoccupation with nature and exhaustive researches into the aquatic life of ponds and rock pools was to give the young Gavin such a profound grounding in natural history. She converted his father's unused gunroom into a nature laboratory full of aquaria. Frogs, tadpoles and gravel-shrouded caddis fly larvae mingled with sinister-looking dragonfly nymphs and the ferociously mandibled larvae of great diving beetles. Glass vivaria imprisoned slit-eyed toads, slow worms and lizards, while glazed cabinets displayed the various food plants of hatching butterfly eggs, caterpillars and pupae, eventually revealing the mysteries of complete metamorphosis and the slow, delicate wing-inflation of the exquisitely patterned imagoes of peacock, small tortoiseshell and red admirals. Rock-pooling forays to the nearby coast revealed the secrets of velvet swimming crabs, shrimps, tentacled sea anemones, little darting fish such as fin-waving blennies and rock gobies, tail-flicking shrimps and the occasional elongated pipefish.

But it was to the woods and fields, the heather moors and scrublands, and the dunes and low cliffs of the coast that for the first ten years of his life and for many school holidays thereafter Gavin ran with his butterfly net and his predatory eye for nests. His birds' eggs collection began in the nine acres around the house with meadow pipits, jackdaws, blackbirds and hedge sparrows and quickly blossomed into more adventurous expeditions to the nests of kestrels, curlew, lapwing, oystercatchers, black-headed gulls, herons, and the eider ducks he found nesting among the wrack and tangle of the beach's tideline. Almost by default, and certainly by undirected inclination, Gavin was training himself to be a highly competent field naturalist. He would write: 'I suppose I knew a lot about butterflies and moths. I . . . had collected all the species that were common at Elrig . . . I saw them in all their glory with the undimmed and finely focused eye of a six-year-old.'

Even today, a hundred years after it was built, Elrig stands stark and alone in its remote and unpopulated corner of rural Galloway. To Gavin and his siblings it was their 'Island Valley of Avalon'. It was where, in wholly unfettered freedom, they could explore the heather moors, the sweetly scented bog-myrtle flushes, the boomerang wind-shy woodlands and the sun yellow gorse- and broom-flowered scrublands of their childhood home. It was an altogether rarified existence, otherworldly, almost entirely cut off, both from people – except the deferential, liveried servants of the Elrig household – and, most significantly, from broader society's distantly fizzing reality.

Years later Gavin would tell me that virtually every night of his life, in those drowsy, half-sleep imaginings, he would find himself drifting back to Elrig and the moors, to the sound of the curlew's bubbling call, the drumming snipe, to bog myrtle's heady perfume and the rooks racketing in the long line of Scots pines below the house. He was only too well aware that this idyllic upbringing had been an unguarded preparation for a life in the real world. His mother encouraged his many pets – tawny owlets, a heron called Andrew, jackdaws, hedgehogs, woodpigeon squabs, among various others – and often their brief lives ended in tragedy, but 'through these extinctions we learned a little sympathy, a little understanding and a little compassion – things that could be . . . extended to other human beings in later life'. But the oversight the blinkered Lady Mary made was to comprehend that her children had known and cherished these animals and pets to the total exclusion of ordinary human beings in a crowded world, an exclusion that would shape the personalities and lives of all four of them, but particularly Gavin, and from which he would never fully escape.

As a boy growing up I was entirely unaware that a recent social connection to Gavin and his oldest brother, Sir Aymer, existed within my own family. When I went to Allhallows neither my parents nor I had ever heard of him until *Ring* was published in 1960. But years later Gavin would tell me that shooting partridges at Denby Grange, our family's Yorkshire seat, was an important part of his upbringing and that the Rabelaisian house parties thrown by our bachelor cousin Sir Kenelm had been 'huge fun'.

I didn't get access to Sir Kenelm's game books until some years after his death in 1962 and I'm not sure that my father knew of the Maxwell connection either. Even if he had he wouldn't have thought it remarkable or even worthy of mention. In those days between the wars, just as in the social milieu of his time, my grandfather had been invited to shoot on many family estates around the country, so, as grandchildren of the Duke of Northumberland, the Maxwell boys would have enjoyed the advantage of their much grander aristocratic heritage and the connections and social acceptability that inevitably preceded them. What it would mean to Gavin when eventually our paths did cross was that he would have immediately recognised my family name and would probably have turned to a reference book to check out my relationship to Sir Kenelm – whose mother was Lady Beatrice Pelham-Clinton, daughter of the Duke of Newcastle – a social parallel with which he would have immediately identified – in one of the several 'snobs' bibles' where Britain's ancient and noble families proudly logged their lineage and their achievements. As he revealed in *Ring*, describing himself in adolescence as 'an earnest member of the Celtic fringe, avid for tartan and twilight', and 'an arrant snob', Gavin remained acutely conscious of his family heritage throughout his life. 'To me the West Highlands were composed of deer forests and hereditary chieftains, and the sheep, the hikers and the Forestry Commission were regrettable interlopers upon the romantic life of the indigenous aristocracy.' In an idle conversation years later he observed to me, 'Dukes make a huge difference.' While that may have been true for him as a grandson of the Northumberland dynasty, what Lady Mary had failed to prepare him for was that as the youngest Maxwell son he would inherit no houses or estates and comparatively little money. Like many younger sons of the landed, Gavin grew up wholly unequipped for a career, even for earning his own living, or any semblance of a 'normal' life.

That obscure upbringing had produced a shy, inept, reclusive man disinclined to make friends outside the secure ramparts of his own class, further complicated by his confused sexuality, by his contorted view of women, his many artistic talents and his restlessly creative intellect. As a result, his closest friends, those with whom he felt most at ease, tended to be his male, aristocratic and landed sporting contemporaries. While the social connection to my family would and should not have mattered in any natural history context, I see now that it almost certainly did.

★   ★   ★

Setting otters aside, what strikes me now is that *Ring of Bright Water* is primarily the story of Gavin's escape from his complicated upbringing into the most extreme wildness Britain had to offer, brought unforgettably to life by his lyrical descriptive prose. The unidentified parallel that possibly enabled me to forge an immediate friendship with Gavin, thirty-two years older than me, when we finally met, was that from an early age I had also escaped into nature from the complications of my own family situation.

That meeting would happen by accident, brought about by one of his Camusfeàrna otter keepers, the boisterous and ebullient animal-obsessed fourteen-year-old London lad Terry Nutkins, whom Gavin had adopted as legal ward in 1960. A year later Terry had lost the greater part of two fingers on his left hand and half of one on his right to a savage attack by Edal, Gavin's second otter, injuries that resulted in gangrene and amputation. He was lucky not to lose his whole arm. It is testament to Terry's robust character that he recovered remarkably well from that near disaster, but he would eventually leave Sandaig under a spectacularly dark cloud.

By the sexually adventurous age of seventeen Terry had

matured into a tall and handsome youth who would lose no time in mobilising his virility. Sandaig was cut off from girls of his age and, entirely predictably, he told me he had begun to feel trapped – although I think the word he actually used was 'imprisoned'. When in January 1963 an attractive thirty-year-old American divorcee called Wendy came to stay as a friend of one of Gavin's guests, Terry plunged headlong into his first affair. Gavin was furious with both of them. An almighty row blew up and Terry, who had been restless for some time, eloped with Wendy to her remote cottage hideaway at Spinningdale in Sutherland, on the far northeast coast, 120 miles from Sandaig, a love nest where they holed up together for several weeks. A little while later he left Gavin's employ forever and debunked to Wendy's flat in London, in search of a job at the zoo.

Gavin always felt deeply guilty about the loss of Terry's fingers, so, in an attempt to repair the relationship, in 1964 he asked Terry to check out a small new wildlife park on the outskirts of Bristol as a potential final home for Teko, another of his otters that had turned vicious and savaged a visitor. Gavin was very particular about the conditions and facilities on offer. At the Westbury-upon-Trym site a pen and a pool would have to be built and Terry was asked to design it and broker the arrangements with the park's owners. In the end those plans would fall through, as had a previous attempt to house his otters at Woburn Safari Park, but long before they did, Terry had to find somewhere to live.

At that moment I was working in Bristol and had enjoyed some involvement with the formative park. I met Terry there and he ended up renting a room in my flat. It was not the cosiest of domestic arrangements. He arrived with a large, boisterous dog called Compass, half Labrador and half

English pointer. Compass was not only a bitch but she was also heavily pregnant. A week later she whelped eleven pups in the flat's only bath. Terry refused to move them, thereby denying all four other occupants anywhere to bathe for two weeks.

He was wild, a wildness certainly partly instilled by the freedom of the three unregimented years he had spent at Sandaig, but Terry was also impulsive, reckless and 'devil may care' by nature. If Gavin had taught him anything, it was to 'get out there and follow your dream', to which in Terry's case might have been appropriately added 'and to hell with the consequences'. He could be good company and fun in a laddish sort of way, and always lived life to the full, but he frequently left a messy trail of disruption behind him, almost always involving women and money. In later years when he had established a career as a television presenter of animal programmes, he would openly describe himself as 'a self-confessed sex maniac'.

In the autumn of 1965 and lacking a car of his own, he asked me if I would like to drive him up to Scotland on a brief visit to Sandaig. I didn't know it at the time but he was also unhappy at the way he had left Gavin's charge and sought to make amends. Still very much in awe of *Ring*, I leapt at the prospect of meeting the author and seeing the fabled Camusfeàrna.

*　　*　　*

Allhallows and its resplendent undercliffs would go on advancing and heightening my love of natural history for the full five years of my time. I rose to Tommy Wallace's effulgent tuition and excelled at biology, a synthesis of hard science with field knowledge and experience which seemed to click somewhere in the depths of my brain, suddenly firing my head with motivation and zeal.

I had come to love Allhallows. Not purely for the cliffs and my unceasing engagement with its wildlife, but also because I made good friends and, by any standards of normality, I had learned to conform and enjoyed moderate success. I played rugger for the 1st XV, ran a fleet 880 yards, won the silver bugle in the corps band, sung bass in the chapel choir, became a school prefect and eventually ascended to the crowning rank of Head of School. After five years I departed that blessed place with the Greek alphabet more or less intact but persistently in the wrong order; maths an impenetrable fortress; having played a drunken Trinculo in *The Tempest*, Bottom in *A Midsummer Night's Dream*, and Thomas Cromwell in Robert Bolt's *A Man for All Seasons*; able to recite, word perfect, a comprehensive suite of Shakespeare's most famous soliloquies and long chunks of *The Canterbury Tales* and *Paradise Lost*, and without the slightest clue as to what I would do next.

I also had a huge problem. Natural history had become a passion. In those days jobs in nature conservation were extremely rare and those there were required a science degree, something I was ill-equipped to achieve. But of far deeper concern, I also knew it was not what either of my parents wished for their son. My father had made it clear that nature was 'all very well as a hobby', but that he expected me to follow his example and pitch into industry or commerce. He saw no need for me to go to university. Perhaps understandably my mother had always hoped I would be a doctor, an aspiration I could never share. And anyway, neither of those bleakly conventional alternatives appealed to me in the least. I thought perhaps I could fall back on journalism.

Not long after leaving school I crash-landed unforgettably in *un moment délicat*. My parents were quietly enjoying afternoon tea. I walked in to find my father in his big wing chair invisible behind a copy of the *Daily Telegraph*, and my mother taking her mandatory afternoon rest with her feet up on a sofa quietly engaged in needlepoint embroidery. I sat down next to her and helped myself to a cup of tea from the trolley. After a few platitudinous exchanges she gently posed the question which, for all three of us, was as omnipresent as a tiger sitting on the rug at our feet. 'What are you thinking of doing next, Jay?' A long pause. No sign of interest from behind the newspaper, so I plucked up courage and replied softly, 'I'd really quite like to be a writer.'

The corner of the *Telegraph* collapsed inward and my father glared at me over his horn-rimmed spectacles before he spoke. 'Write *what*, exactly?' The words stung. His demand was accusative not inquisitive, entirely rhetorical and spiked with barely concealed contempt, from a face set in stony disdain. I knew only too well from previous exchanges that he considered writers and writing to be frivolous, not a proper job and certainly not a career. The corner of the newspaper rose again. He neither sought nor received an answer.

They were the wartime generation. They had witnessed real austerity and hardship and had lived through the colossal sacrifices of the war effort. Irreparably scarred by nationalisation of the family coal mines and what he saw as the double injustice of iniquitous death duties, my father had dedicated himself to restoring the fortunes of his family. He expected me to do the same. It had never impinged upon his tightly conventional perspective that his son might be hearing a different drummer.

Despite their relative prosperity, they would both have felt guilty about spending money on themselves for the rest of their lives. He had made his views entirely and immutably clear: a worthwhile career for me was 'getting out there and helping rebuild the national economy'. It was what he had always pursued for himself with absolute dedication – a successful businessman and head of an old and distinguished but rapidly failing family dynasty. It was the model he expected his only son to emulate. To 'knuckle down to a proper job and put the family back on the map'.

My mother's view was far more liberal, but blinkered by her health-imposed unworldliness. Her love of the Arts and the controlling Romantic in her nature sought to cast caution to the wind and to hell with convention, but the enforced invalid longed for her son to follow those she respected most, the medical professionals who had shored her up for so many years. Her own rudely truncated education had not included even the most fundamental principles of science or anatomy. I don't think she ever properly understood her own condition or the internal workings of her poor exhausted heart. She would listen, totally absorbed, when, as a keen biology student, I tried to explain to her some freshly acquired insight in human physiology. 'You really should be a doctor, Jay,' she would proclaim, her eyes shining with pride. Flattered by her belief in my ability, I would have loved to have made her prouder still, but I knew in my heart that I could never satisfy either of my parents' ambitions.

In the absence of any other immediately viable options, I gave in to inducements and did as my father wished. He had arranged for me to join an industrial stockholding company first in Bristol and then South Wales, servicing the heaviest sectors of all, the coal, oil and steel industries of Cardiff, Newport, Port Talbot and the Swansea Valley. I became what was euphemistically dubbed 'a management trainee'. My days became a drudgery burdened with a deep and simmering resentment, trapped by economic necessity while silently festering inside. I was desperate to escape but could see no possibility through the enveloping smog of those carbon-polluted, smoke-belching horizons of that tortured landscape. I could not have been more miserable in a dungeon.

22

'Future plans for this island'

Not long after I had started work in industry the opportunity to meet Gavin for the first time came as a sunburst of release. Just as *Ring of Bright Water* had spun its readers into a proto-nostalgic dreamland far removed from their everyday lives, so the chance to visit Camusfeàrna and stay with the creator of the idyll would have a similarly mesmeric effect on me, multiplied in intensity many times over.

After a twelve-hour drive we had arrived as a raging sun was crash-landing into the Cuillin mountains of Skye, the rims of their gabbro peaks kissed with fire, an ideal stage-set for high romantic drama. As the last rays struck the flat calm sea, it glowed like molten lava, crimson against the black rocks and islands in the shadow of the towering mass of Skye.

We left the car on the single-track public road and made the bracing, mile-and-a-half trek down to the house. The unpaved path snaked and veered steeply through tangled woodland and scrub. Terry was excited. He half ran, half stumbled down the hill until we arrived at the burn. The colour of brandy-wine, its water burbled merrily between gnarled alder trees sprouting from banks of mossy boulders, ringing round and past us to the little waterfall hidden from our view, the waterfall of which Gavin had written, '[it] always seemed to me to be the soul of Camusfeàrna, and if there is anywhere in the world to which some part of me may return when I am dead, it will be there'.

We stood catching our breath and gazing out over the tranquil scene spread in front of us: the lonely house, the bay, the gleaming sea and its dark rocky islets. I had been to Scotland before but never to anywhere as remote and indescribably beautiful as the ring of Sandaig Bay and its little archipelago beyond. It had halted Gavin in his tracks on his first encounter: 'The landscape and seascape that lay spread below me was of such beauty that I had no room for it all at once . . .'

Terry burst into the house with all the gusto of a Viking raider. Gavin and Jimmy Watt, Terry's companion during his four-year sojourn at Sandaig, were sitting in the kitchen-living room so evocatively decorated with the jetsam of years of beach-combing, lobster creels, baskets and netted glass floats hanging from the ceiling, Gavin with a cigarette and whisky glass in hand. A driftwood fire hissed and flapped brightly in the hearth with the famous and prophetically ironic inscription carved across its stone mantel, 'NON FATVVM HVC PERSECVTVS IGNEM' – It is no will-o'-the-wisp that I have followed here.

The room was largely unchanged in the six years since *Ring* had been published. It was precisely as the text described and the photographs illustrated, many of them taken long before, almost as if an idyllic past was being intentionally preserved, like stepping into the set of a much-loved film. I found myself distracted, gazing round all the time, recognising and identifying the component parts of the idyll.

Scallop shells and pebbles inscribed with the calcium hieroglyphics of the serpulid tubeworm, 'precise in every riotous ramification', crowded the mantel and a model yacht in full Bermuda rig precariously perched above them. A goat skull with long curving horns hung from the wall on one side, above shelves of books, contorted tangles of driftwood collected and arranged with the eye of an artist, alongside cans of food, bellows, a framed 'Spy' cartoon of Sir Herbert Maxwell, all mixed in with the general paraphernalia of daily living. Every item held a peculiar fascination of its own, demanding closer scrutiny, and while giving the appearance of being random, the whole came together like a carefully constructed still life in a distinctive assertion of its creator's multi-faceted artistic talents.

Gavin embraced Terry warmly, all signs of past animosity entirely dispelled. He was smaller than I had anticipated, less than six foot, lightly framed and wiry, looking fitter than he probably was. He smoked continuously, not like Mathey with a cigarette pendant from his lips but held between the fingers, each draw long and deeply inhaled so that smoke plumed from mouth and nostrils as he spoke. I learned that at times he had smoked up to eighty cigarettes a day. He was warmly welcoming and immediately handed me a large slug of whisky. Still palpably animated, Terry rushed me up the stairs to show me to my small bedroom with a steeply combed ceiling, typical of nineteenth-century Highland croft houses. It contained a single bed with a polar bear skin spread across it and the window in the gable a naval porthole salvaged from the great wartime battleship HMS *Vanguard*. I had never slept beneath a polar bear skin before.

My diary's selective scribblings don't record what we ate for supper that first night, but they do note that it was late – perhaps ten o'clock – and liberally diluted with more whisky, a universal West Highland habit it took me a while to adjust to. Afterwards I asked if I could go outside for a few minutes to imbibe the night air. 'Of course,' Gavin acceded with a broad smile, 'but please don't get lost, we don't go looking for people after dark.' He spoke in what used to be called 'the Queen's English', no hint of a Scottish accent or affectation, but with the precise enunciation of every syllable and graced by the prescribed politeness of an English public school education, which I knew very well from members of my own family of my parents' and grand-parents' generation. Terry came out with me; in a lowered voice he said he needed to talk privately to Gavin and when I came in would I mind going off to bed.

Slowly, I was settling back to earth. Gavin had greeted me so generously, had been so openly friendly and welcoming, well beyond expectation, that the aura of famous author had immediately begun to evaporate. I felt a heartening ease in his presence and his quick, bright conversation was cocooned in genuine warmth. Outside, the night was as dark as the sea, only the pale gleam of gently breaking waves rimming the beach below.

Terry had given me plenty of advance warning that the Camusfeàrna of the *Ring* had long since vanished and that the house had been haphazardly extended and fenced in. The otters, by then ageing, unreliable and dangerous, had been banished to their own jerry-built quarters at the back and the once unsullied site would be littered with the aban-doned junk and detritus of years of Gavin's chaotically alternative, idiosyncratic existence.

I walked only a few yards to a gated fence and thought better of going any further without a torch. As my eyes adjusted the sky emerged as a glowing rook's-wing purple, against which I could just make out the great bulk of the hills to the north and west, black and foreboding. The September air was chill on my cheeks and the only night sounds were the hushed gossip of water in the burn, the shrill piping of oystercatchers on the beach and the sibilant murmur of the sea breeze shimmying through the circle of alders. Camusfeàrna. Bay of the alders. *Blimey!* I thought. *I am here. Standing here in the dark.*

I stood for twenty minutes, waiting. Just waiting for it all to sink in, to settle around me like the closing night: the welcome, the famous house, the bay, the looming mountains, the whisky, the polar bear skin – the sheer splashdown jolt of being there at all. I felt myself emptying down. If there were parallels between Gavin's upbringing and my own, I had entirely failed to see them, swamped by the existential loading of the moment, and, of course, I had not the slightest inkling that this accidental collision of our lives might change mine forever.

All I knew was that something deep inside me was calling. I was overcome by a humbling, almost ethereal awe, as though waiting for the night sounds of that extraordinary place to claim me. There was no 'cry of the tiger-cat to its fellow', but I felt sure they were out there somewhere and one day – not then, perhaps not even very soon, but surely one day – I would locate them. Terry's loud voice and laughter coming from inside shattered the moment. A shiver passed through. I turned back to the house and tiptoed upstairs to bed. That night I dreamed sweet and long of the Manor House. I awoke to a steel dawn punching in through the round lens of the porthole, wondering where on earth I was.

We stayed for six days. By day we walked and beach-combed, the bay glistening with tidal newness; we fished for floppy silvery pollock (locally *saithe*) from a small dinghy with the resolute and dexterous Jimmy, who was clearly in charge of the whole Sandaig operation: boats, otters, household, catering, everything else. He marshalled us into dragging a storm-washed tree up above the high-tideline to dry out for firewood; I watched as together he and Terry fed fresh fish to the otters, Edal and Teko, in their respective houses and pens; and we saw nothing of Gavin. I never discovered what time he got up, but he had immediately shut himself away in his study to work. That first day he only emerged at five o'clock and appeared irritated that the fire in the sitting room hadn't been lit. He poured himself a large whisky and sat on a bench seat with a book he said he had to review. 'Please don't talk to me. I need to get this done.'

Again, it was nearly ten at night before we ate. My diary records fresh scallops sent across from the island of Canna by its Gaelic-scholar laird, Gavin's good friend John Lorne Campbell, followed at Terry's request by what was called 'a Maxwell bean feast', prepared jointly by Jimmy and Terry, consisting almost exclusively of Heinz baked beans and a tin of plum tomatoes stirred in with chopped up sausages and some indiscernible leftovers from a previous meal. It looked remarkably like tinned dog food but was surprisingly good and filling. We ate on our knees at the fireside.

After supper Gavin seemed to relax and we had a chance to talk. 'Wildcats?' I asked. 'Are they still around? I would love to see one.'

A snorted 'Hurrumph!' and an eruption of cigarette smoke was the eloquent retort. 'You'll be lucky. Your chances of seeing one are about the same as catching sight of Moby Dick.' Then he laughed. 'In twenty years I have only seen five or six out and about, despite their footprints, the one Jimmy rescued and got stuck in the chimney and the two kittens we tried to raise. They are *very* secretive, but they're here all right.'

When I returned to England, with my thank-you letter I sent Gavin a badger skull I had prepared for my own skull collection. A few days later I received a letter handwritten in fountain pen on his expensive, cream vellum Smythson writing paper printed in hand-engraved, die-stamped blood red, just as one might expect from the owner of a great country house, a distinctive hallmark of his aristocratic background. Like his speech, his handwriting was precise, perfectly spaced on the page, never a crossing-out or an altered punctuation, as fluent and elegant as a thoughtfully composed work of art:

That was a kind thought and a most magnificent gift – much appreciated. I should certainly be fascinated to know your secret process for cleaning skulls; I've never seen anything so perfect, even in the B.M. with their beetles. My own experiments – burying things and digging them up a year or two later – have been notably unsuccessful. I'm glad you enjoyed your brief visit here – so did we, and hope it won't be the last; you're always welcome, but you'll find the house is usually pretty thorough chaos.

* * *

Four years would drag by before we met again, although we corresponded regularly in a stimulating and for me often unsettling exchange of natural history anecdotes; four years of trying to come to terms with my own unhappy existence in the bewildering and deeply destructive world of heavy industry.

On 18 March 1967, the *Torrey Canyon* tanker, carrying 120,000 tons of crude oil from the Persian Gulf, ran aground on the Scilly Isles' notorious Seven Stones rocks – Britain's first major oil spill. The story ran for many weeks. It was also before we understood the full devastation oil spills always inflict on the marine environment.

Environmental journalists didn't exist in 1967. The press coverage focused exclusively on the economic damage to holiday resorts on the Cornish beaches where the oil slicks came ashore. I went to see for myself. What I found was profoundly disturbing, far more than had been reported in the papers. Frustrated and angered by what I discovered, I wrote an article for a national newspaper, outlining the horror of seeing so many dead and dying sea birds, seals and, yes, otters, as well as the beaches caked in thick, toxic oil. Gavin Maxwell's fame as 'the otter man' virtually guaranteed that someone would draw his attention to what I had written. Much later he told me that he had been impressed that someone who understood natural history had written about the impact on wildlife. I have often wondered whether that was what triggered the life-changing events that would follow.

Exactly a year after the *Torrey Canyon* ran aground, an envelope dropped through my Swansea apartment door. I immediately recognised the stylish, precise handwriting in distinctive blood-red ink. I ripped it open. On a small white card with his name and new address printed in red across the top, Gavin had written:

I wonder what you are doing now? I ask this not purely conventionally, but because I have future plans for this island that might be of interest to you. It is a little early to be definite yet, but I am keen to keep in touch as we might possibly co-operate on a small project.

★   ★   ★

During the intervening years Gavin's life had changed dramatically and catastrophically, because, he would later discover and come to believe, he had been cursed in what is perhaps the saddest and most contorted sub-plot to his literary success. In the early, halcyon days of Camusfeàrna (the 1950s), the celebrated poet and literary scholar Kathleen Raine had fallen helplessly and blindingly in love with him – an impossible love that was always destined to end in grief. She saw him as 'more than soul mate', above and beyond the romantic. She called him her 'man of light' and she would write, 'It was as though he had come from Eden itself.' It was an adulation he would never accept, reciprocate or be able to share.

In an extraordinary twist of insensitivity, even of fatal prescience, without her permission Gavin had taken the title for *Ring* from the first couplet of her poem 'The Marriage of Psyche, Year One' (1952): 'He has married me with a ring, a ring of bright water / Whose ripples spread from the heart of the sea . . .' Without her name, her poem, re-entitled *The Ring*, is printed in full as an epigraph to the book. He clearly intended his readers to view it as a lyrical eulogy to his beloved otter Mijbil, perhaps even to imagine it was his own work. In reality it was no such thing; it was a love poem, pure and simple, written by a woman utterly consumed by her love for Gavin. It is remarkable that it fits both causes so neatly – otter eulogy and requiem to an impossible love. It is only in the last two lines that a hint of the truth reveals itself: 'Or gathers cloud about an apex of gold, / Transcendent touch of love summons my world into being.'

It is also telling that in none of the hundreds of editions of the book, no authorial credit to Kathleen Raine appears on that page, nor any mention of her in the text of *Ring* or its sequels, despite the singular truth that she was central to the story of Mijbil and Gavin's early days at Camusfeàrna – so central, in fact, because she had been the cause of Mij's death by disobeying Gavin's instructions. She had allowed the otter to escape and swim out to sea while she was looking after him during Gavin's absence in London. A roadman had killed Mij with a pickaxe, crushing his head, although the full story of his demise took some days to emerge. She never forgave herself for this tragedy and it would condemn her relationship with Gavin to the dark chill of betrayal. It is probably the case that, despite ostensibly not blaming her, deep down he was never able to forgive her either. Her name only appears buried amongst others in the formal Acknowledgements page.

That their turbulent intellectual friendship recovered at all, and staggered uncomfortably on for several years, is a startling testament to both the depth of her devotion and Gavin's generosity of spirit and, perhaps, fatalism. Immediately after Mij's death he left Sandaig – 'I missed Mij desperately, so much so that it was a year before I could bring myself to go to Camusfeàrna again.' He departed the country altogether, immersing himself in his researches in Sicily. Yet their friendship did repair sufficiently for Kathleen to return to Sandaig many more times, almost always when Gavin was away – for him a house-minding convenience and for her a hopeless search for atonement.

Ultimately their relationship would almost inevitably founder completely when she made a devastating error of judgement. Some years later she asked him to read an early draft of the manuscript of what would be the last of her three volumes of autobiography, *The Lion's Mouth* (finally published after Gavin's death in 1977). She had sought his approval because so much of her story revolved around his own and she was desperate to achieve a reconciliation. It was a terrible mistake. An early passage related an incident from back in the early days before Mij's death. She revealed that she had roundly cursed him on the Camusfeàrna rowan tree when her love for him became oppressive and she refused to let go. Not only was he incapable of reciprocating her heterosexual adoration, but, never good at negotiating conflicts, Gavin had resented it angrily when her doting presence collided with his gay relationships.

In July 1956, only a month after Mijbil's arrival at Camusfeàrna, but time enough for Kathleen to have become utterly entranced by the otter, Gavin had asked her to look after Mij while he was away. She had been staying on her own at Sandaig, blissfully happy and loving every minute of bonding with the otter. She had come to view Mij as the living link that united her with Gavin, a bond both spiritual and temporal, and would write later in her autobiography: 'Such was my sense of kinship with him that I . . . imagined that in some former life we had been brother and sister.'

Gavin had written from London asking her to vacate Camusfeàrna in advance of his arrival and remove to Tormor, the house of mutual friends nearby. Clearly he didn't want to see her and wanted her out of the way, but had omitted to mention that he was coming with a boyfriend. Blinded by infatuation, Kathleen ignored him. Instead she filled the house with wild flowers, shells and stones from the shore, 'fairy gold for him to find' – the adoring woman's welcome at the door.

When late that evening Gavin and his friend arrived and found her still in residence, he was furious. After a blistering row he cruelly banished her from the house. On her way to cross the burn, through her tears she had placed her hands on the rowan tree and cried out into the darkness: 'Let Gavin suffer in this place as I am suffering now.'

Her extraordinary folly in revealing her curse to him, albeit years after the fact, became the final, tragic and catastrophic rupture of what had been a bountiful union of minds and spirits of two extremely gifted intellectuals, both deeply engaged with nature and literature, and one from which neither party would ever fully recover. Kathleen's deep-rooted bitterness would finally overflow into a long sequence of tragic poems entitled *On a Deserted Shore,* which she chose not to publish until 1973, four years after Gavin's death.

Looking back down the years of disasters, Gavin suddenly saw and readily chose to believe that Kathleen's curse had been the cause of everything that had gone wrong, as indeed did she, writing in her own autobiography: 'Such an invocation cannot be revoked . . . and awaken[s] forces beyond human control.' The significance of the rowan tree, a deeply symbolic tree in Highland folklore, was well known to both of them and had often featured in some of her finest poetry written at Sandaig: 'And yet I have . . . tasted the bitter berry red.' Gavin also chose to entitle the first chapter of *Ring*'s second sequel, *Raven Seek Thy Brother* (1968), 'The Rowan Tree' – 'the magic tree . . . round which is centered so much Gaelic superstition . . . infinitely malignant if harmed or disrespected' – and to make her curse and what he saw as its consequences the principal theme of that book.

Raven Seek Thy Brother and its prequel, *The Rocks Remain* (1963), are a sorry catalogue of accidents and disasters, finally shattering the idyll of *Ring*, following on from the murder of Mij: his Mercedes roadster stolen and crashed beyond repair; an expensive libel suit against him; Edal and Teko turning savage and severely injuring Terry Nutkins and another guest; hitting a rock and sinking his motor launch *Polar Star*; a crash in his Land-Rover from which he suffered a deep vein thrombosis in his foot; the gradually gathering storm clouds of financial collapse. Then, on 21 January 1968, the whole Camusfeàrna site went up in smoke in a devastating house fire, entirely gutting the building and its extensions, and destroying most of his possessions. It killed Edal, the second otter of *Ring* and certainly the most famous otter in the world. Gavin had been lucky to escape with his life, but even that luck was short-lived. Little more than a year later he would be diagnosed with terminal cancer. If it was a curse, it was possessed of a deep and acid vengeance. 'You are a destroyer, Kathleen,' he had told her at their final meeting. She would never forgive herself or recover peace of mind.

The fire had forced him to move to the lighthouse keeper's cottage on Eilean Bàn, the principal island in an archipelago of small islets and skerries lying midway between Kyle of Lochalsh on the mainland and Kyleakin on the Isle of Skye, and on which the Stevenson lighthouse stood guardian over the fast-flowing narrows. But, curse or no curse, he had also been busy, publishing the two sequels to *Ring*, as well as pursuing his career with a major work on Morocco, *Lords of the Atlas: The Rise and Fall of the Berber House of Glaoua* (1966), a classic of travel writing to this day. He had also published a commissioned book under the auspices of the World Wildlife Fund, entitled *Seals of the World* (1967), which had triggered the idea of a handbook of British mammals.

Despite the many personal difficulties so graphically documented in those sequels, to a young and unworldly outsider like me little had changed. I knew nothing of Kathleen Raine and no more of the curse than I had read in *Raven Seek Thy Brother*, dismissing it as fanciful at best and creative licence at worst. Not being superstitious by nature, and with no reason to believe it or not, I paid it no attention. Gavin was still a very famous author and his enthusiasm and productivity appeared undimmed. Now, with characteristic and Promethean zeal, it seemed that he was planning some new and exciting venture on Eilean Bàn and a new book on mammals.

* * *

That small white card had changed everything in an instant. My mind was whirling like a windmill, lifting off, levitating out of the mundane reality of my dreary job and the despondency – no, worse than that, depression – that had been dragging me down for months and was slowly eroding my soul. I read the card a hundred times. What? What 'small project'? What can he mean, 'be of interest'? Interest in what he's up to? Or interest in 'future plans for this island'? And why me? Me, a relative stranger half his age, an acquaintance of only a few years, living 600 miles away – and what plans might we 'possibly co-operate on'? What on earth could this famous author mean? This household name, this man of otters and islands and stags and wildcats in the far-flung wilds of Scotland – what could he possibly mean?

I have that card in front of me all these decades later. Holding it brings back to life those soaring emotions, the thumping heart, the sudden surge of hope, the sleepless nights and the turmoil I had been in for months, then so recently re-intensified by having travelled down to Coto Doñana and collecting my mother from the Palacio. Her words came winging back to me once again: 'Why don't you stay here for a few days and try to see some of the wildlife?' and 'I hope you can join expeditions like this one day.'

By 1968 I had managed to see most of such wildlife as the English countryside supported, but certainly no wildcats, and had definitely been no part of any expeditions to exciting places. *Ring of Bright Water* and its kaleidoscopic rainbow of red deer, golden eagles, otters, dolphins, killer whales and seals and, yes, wildcats too was still a pipe-dream a million miles away from the toxic smoke belching from the blast furnaces and hot mills of the South Wales steel industry – a trap I'd carelessly fallen into like a mouse in a bucket. The omnipresent pollution of industry nagged like toothache, adding to my expanding wreath of desolation. I longed for escape, existing in a cloying spiral of frustration, imprisoned within the slippery walls of economic necessity, dismally struggling to comply with family expectations, desperate to leap free but seeing no prospect of it, falling back over and over again. Suddenly, one small postcard had thrown me a lifeline.

23

Great hopes, dire straits

'Come and stay and we can talk it through. Come tomorrow.'
Gavin's response to my telephone call was characteristically
eager and typically unrealistic. I had a job. I couldn't just
drop it and vanish for a week. Not just like that. I had to
ask for leave, make sure my thirteen-year-old car was up to
a 1,200-mile round trip. I had other plans, engagements,
responsibilities. Could I even afford to? What about my
rugger club training sessions, my girlfriend, and my
Labrador puppy, Max, just acquired? I may have been miserable, but I did have a life. Yet that's exactly what I did. I
dropped everything, threw some things into a bag and left
that night. I drove north without stopping. Max came with
me in a cardboard box. By dawn I was in the mountains of
Glencoe.

March 1968 was memorable for a once-in-a-decade fling
of the Gulf Stream. For three weeks, it streamed balmy
sub-tropical heat from the Azores into the west coast of the
Highlands, T-shirt weather, sea-swimming weather, a false
spring more like Greece than a Scotland with snow still
pink-tinting its high corries. As I crossed to the Isle of Skye
on the morning ferry the seaway was Aegean, a shimmering
oily calm dotted with black guillemots and eiders bobbing
gently on the tide. Cormorants flapped past, bee-lining out
to sea, while high overhead in a squinting blue too hard and

bright to bear I could hear the rapid staccato calls of red-throated divers echoing from the hills.

Gavin had moved into the two freshly converted semi-detached light keepers' cottages on Eilean Bàn, now morphed into one very adequate bachelor house. I had just read *Raven Seek Thy Brother*, his latest and last sequel to *Ring*, in which he recounts the succession of disasters that had befallen him, apparently as a direct consequence of Kathleen Raine's curse. The book had catalogued them all and included a sketch of the burnt-out house, of the wording for the bronze memorial to Edal the otter 'Whatever joy she gave to you, give back to nature' – and photographs of Kyleakin Island. But the new house was still a surprise. Not what I expected.

In startling contradistinction to the fish-box furniture and beach-combed jumble of Camusfeàrna, his new abode was grandly appointed and furnished in the manner of the opulent country houses of his aristocratic background, a reversion to type perhaps, as an intentional escape from Kathleen Raine's curse and the trauma of the *Ring* years, but more likely a reaction to the dramatic change in his circumstances and a desperate clinging to familiarities while the fabric of his life unravelled.

The principal reception room, the Long Room, mirrored a formal drawing room, with antique furniture, chaises longues, winged armchairs, gilt mirrors, William Wordsworth's desk, gilt sconces and oil paintings on the walls, and Persian rugs on the floor. The two huge deer-hounds, Hazel and Dirk, lay sprawled in a Victorian Landseer-esque pose in front of a large open fire of logs and peat. Above the mantel hung a large, dramatic Michael Ayrton wax and bone bas-relief of Icarus falling from the sun, an irony Gavin cannot possibly have missed and which, if it was intentional, would have matched his impending awareness of mortality and sardonic sense of self.

The whole room was refined, elegant and stately, in many ways befitting a world famous author, artifacts from his travels and exploits such as shark harpoons, Berber daggers and carved soapstone ware prominently displayed, but all apparently in determined denial of the source of his fame and recent past – not an otter in sight. Teko, the sole survivor of the fire, was old and grumpy and housed in a fenced compound with a hut and a fibreglass pool. Gavin's only island helpers were Andrew Scot, the last of the Camusfeàrna otter keepers, and Kenny McInnes, a retired Skye crofter who came across each day to cut peats for the fire and maintain the boats.

I stayed for a week. He revealed the 'future plans for this island' that 'we might possibly co-operate on' as twofold: he needed a research student to do the legwork for the handbook of British mammals he had been encouraged to write by his publisher, Mark Longman, on the back of the successful seals book, and he wanted someone to live on the island to help him develop and be the 'curator' of the private zoo he was planning. Quite honestly, if he'd asked me to clean his shoes and sing sea shanties, I'd have leapt at both. Such was his reputation and the alluring milieu he had created around himself, and so great was the contrast from the toxic-fume-belching blast furnaces of Port Talbot that any hint of caution or uncertainty was strangled at birth. I was up for it, whatever it was, and whatever sacrifices it entailed. As we sat beside the fire drinking whisky and talking long into the night, without ever comprehending it properly at the time, I think we were two dreamers chasing entirely different dreams.

As if those enticements were not enough, in one brief

conversational exchange, and perhaps inadvertently, Gavin had loosed off another harpoon that found its willing target. It was late. We had been discussing poetry; there was a lull as I flicked through the pages of a favourite anthology he had given me. After a few minutes he broke the silence. 'What do you really want to do with your life, John?'

It caught me unawares. I stared into the fire before answering. My mind ricocheted back to the same question my mother had posed a few years before when my father had been so crushingly dismissive. I tried again. 'I'd really like to be a writer.'

Even as the words left my lips, I winced from the chill slap of folly. Gavin was a world famous author. I was a nobody, thirty-two years his junior. I'd only published a few articles. In front of the man whose writing I revered, my words suddenly seemed fatuous and, horrifyingly, even sycophantic. Remorse instantly overwhelmed me.

'Why aren't you, then?' His curt, penetrative inquisition was almost aggressive, demanding a response. It punched a hole through the smog of embarrassment that had immediately blanked me, not sure I'd heard right. Then, sensing my discomfort, his tone mellowed, 'You don't need any capital, you know. All you need is a piece of paper and a pencil.'

I laughed and think I must have muttered something like 'Perhaps one day.' The subject died, but not for long. It kept me awake all night. As I lay listening to the lap and swirl of the tide against the rocks and the gulls crying, it seemed to me that everything had changed. Doors I had never dreamed existed had suddenly opened, paths emerged and bright horizons beckoned. And for him? 'What, what, what, what?' he would say to himself about nothing in particular, running the 'whats' together in quick succession, as though it helped him think things through. I believe he had already begun to formulate a plan.

He was fifty-four and, although he made no direct mention of it, he was worried about his deteriorating health – he was smoking continuously and downing most of a bottle of whisky a day – and his dwindling income, which, unknown to me, had been a gradually darkening storm cloud for several years, was rapidly engulfing him. The heady years of *Ring*, when he openly confessed – boasted even – that he had never given money a thought, were long over. His extravagant taste for fast cars, and the large, powerful sea-going launch *Polar Star*, his hugely generous entertaining and largesse, and his habitual foreign travels essential for his writing, combined with an almost child-like unworldliness in all financial affairs, had consumed it all. Although he probably wasn't fully aware of its extent at the time, he was heavily in debt and, as had been a life-long trait, was still living well above his income. It would eventually become clear that he had wildly overspent on converting and furnishing the island house. Several years later one of his oldest friends, Eton housemaster Raef Payne, observed wistfully, 'Gavin was always either extremely well off or completely broke.'

There is a telling line in *House of Elrig*, where he writes of his family background, 'a timeless feeling of money not actively spent but just disregarded'. The give-away is 'disregarded'. If such things can be hereditary, such was unquestionably Gavin's approach to money, only in his case it was clearly and all too evidently 'actively spent'. This was certainly worsened by his habitual reliance on professionals, some of whom would later prove to have been incompetent or even exploitative. Their ineptitude and the saga of maladministration of his affairs over many years that would eventually be revealed to his stalwart friend and financial business manager, Richard Frere, raised many uncomfortable questions.

Many are the younger sons of landed families who have stepped onto the slippery slope of financial indifference in the belief that some well-heeled family member will bail them out. Gavin had inherited meaningful wealth three or four times, most notably from his mother, but, failing to acknowledge the difference between capital and income, he had immediately spent it, needing to be bailed out by his Percy relations and his eldest brother, Sir Aymer Maxwell, who had inherited the Monreith estates, on several occasions prior to the success of *Ring*. Yet disregard for his own long-term financial stability had remained a Gordian knot of his own devising, a character flaw he would never vanquish.

He had no investments or savings, no pension, no assets of any real value other than the island house. 'I am my own capital,' he insisted with highly persuasive confidence, which was true as long as he could keep writing and selling books, but what he omitted to comprehend – or chose not to – was that his literary capital was heavily mortgaged to Longman, his long-suffering publishers, always drawing heavily on the next book before writing it. By the time I knew him he was virtually penniless. After a whole sequence of expensive mishaps, he was desperately casting about trying to shore up his future in the only way his restlessly creative brain could work – by dreaming up new ventures.

And as for me? I had no real idea what I was letting myself in for – no game plan, no sense of direction or career, or even a future. I can now see clearly that I was escaping, clutching at straws to find a way of breaking free from what I had come to view as sordid industry, from overbearing family expectations, from outmoded convention, from a shackled existence I had come to despise. I was also worried.

* * *

My mother was ill again. Very ill. In truth she was worse than she had been back in 1953. Once again, without immediate heart surgery she would die. Her aortic valve, the one that feeds the body's principal artery with oxygenated blood, had finally collapsed, barely opening and closing at all. Her weary old heart was pumping like a steam engine and getting nowhere. Blood gurgled fruitlessly backwards and forwards within the chambers, starving her whole body of oxygen. She was blue and breathless; my father had to carry her upstairs. It was a decline we had all seen but had refused to acknowledge as the extremis it had become. Only one hope remained – back to the Brompton Hospital. But Paul Wood was dead. With an irony that now seems perverse, in 1962 he had died of heart failure, in his prime, aged just fifty-four. Russell Brock was sixty-five, now Lord Brock of Wimbledon, the grand old visionary of British cardiology, travelling and lecturing but no longer wielding a scalpel. Instead, at Brock's behest, Stuart Lennox, a very highly regarded young surgeon on the Brompton cardiac staff, was prepared to take my mother on.

On 11 August that year she underwent an aortic replacement with a pig valve, her second open-heart surgery and, including Paul Wood's catheterisation in 1957, her third experimental cardiac procedure. Had she not suffered a stroke in the recovery room, it would have been an outstanding success. It was a cruel twist. Her circulatory system was now working better than it had for years, but a clot had slipped away to her lungs and starved her brain of blood. It crippled her. She lost her speech, her handwriting and her mobility – her left arm and leg simply refused to work. Many months of rehabilitation and physiotherapy would follow. I have her letters scrawled in a tortured, childishly uncontrolled hand.

★   ★   ★

I told Gavin that while I would love to move north to the island and take on the full-time research for his mammal book, I could not desert my mother. To have moved 600 miles away at that moment could have been too much for her. Her whole determination to recover was built around her love for and dedication to her family. More than at any other time she needed us. Gavin's disappointment was all too evident. 'When do you think you could come?' his voice burdened with despondency. I didn't know what to say. I was in turmoil. I longed to say 'in a month, six weeks, two months', but I couldn't. I knew from past experience that strokes were glacially slow to repair, if ever.

'Can I aim for a year?' I asked tentatively.

He stared past me and out to sea.

I would discover soon enough that he was also very unwell, frustrated and deeply worried. Although the extent of his difficulties, both financial and medical, were yet to be fully diagnosed, I believe he sensed that the noose was fast closing; time was running out and he desperately needed help to shore things up. He was suffering unexplained migraines and an uncharacteristic loss of energy. Kathleen Raine's curse still played heavily on his mind – 'Oh Gawd! When's it all going to end?' had become a mantra. By making the curse public in *Raven Seek Thy Brother*, he had engraved it into his own subconscious like a malevolent subtext that refused to go away. He never mentioned any of this to me, but as I bade him farewell and headed back south at the end of that week, I knew he was a profoundly troubled man. A little while later he commented to Richard Frere that for the first time since the Camusfeàrna fire he had glimpsed a chance to build a team that could solve all his problems – the problems I knew virtually nothing about.

Had I known more I think I might have hurried, but I was beginning to enjoy myself. Gavin had handed me a cause and a sense of purpose. At long last I was working in natural history – still unpaid but loving it – and with a goal previously unimagined: that my name would appear alongside his as co-author of a handbook of British mammals. I attended meetings of the Mammal Society and its recently formed scion, the British Deer Society, to forge essential links. I corresponded with many experts in their own fields of mammalogy. Never once did it cross my mind that Gavin might be terminally ill.

In the event it would be nearer eighteen months, although throughout that time we corresponded and telephoned regularly about the mammal book at my end and the island animal collection at his. He was still urging me to come. Finally, in August 1969 I packed up and made the move. I had no real idea what I was going to and certainly no suspicion of what I would find when I arrived. Gavin was dying.

*   *   *

With all the sails of her lifelong fortitude fully unfurled, my mother was valiantly battling her stroke with the renewed vigour the replaced aortic valve had given her. I travelled to Frimley to see her and break the news that I was heading north. I had handed in my notice to my employers and my landlord. My bags were packed. 'Follow your dream,' she whispered. As she hugged me I felt a shiver of acceptance pass through her poor wrecked body like a breeze shimmers through corn.

24

Paradise lost and found

The sale of the Manor Farm, the disposal of the orchards beyond the moorhens' pond for a housing development and the sale of the Manor House itself were hard to bear. Until my mother's final surgery and then her death, the only time I ever saw my father evince heavy emotion was on the day of the house sale. Folk travelled from all over the country, antique dealers, local householders, villagers who had never seen inside the house, and nosy parkers on a spree with no intention to buy. The country lanes were jammed; a trail of vans and furniture lorries parked nose to tail all down the hill to the village green.

The auctioneers' men carried everything out onto the lawns. Huge oak dressers and chests that had been made for the house in the seventeenth and eighteenth centuries, the great dining-room table, the big wing chairs from the drawing room, tea chests full of pots and pans from the scullery, bookcases, grandfather clocks, marble wash stands, wardrobes, Victorian brass beds, scores of pictures and books, and the entire contents of the butler's pantry all vanished forever under the hammer. In stony-faced silence my father stood and watched it all.

At the end of the second day, after the last van and pantechnicon had pulled away down the lane, he closed the white gates on his home, his birthright, his own happy childhood and his family's past. I walked with him across the lane to the graveyard. It was March. Daffodils were bursting everywhere. We picked a dozen stems and placed them among the mass of floral tributes crowding my grandparents' grave. As rich as plum cake, a burst of pure notes rippled from a cock blackbird's syrinx. It was perched on the uppermost branch of a yew tree beside the lych-gate. He turned to look at it. 'Just listen to that. I hope Grandpa can hear it too.' We walked slowly back up the drive and entered the front door. The hall was hollow and empty. No solemn tick of the Bowler, no laughter from the kitchens. 'Come on, old boy, let's go.'

'What's happened to the rib?' I asked gently. I had been through to the old servants' hall earlier in the day and seen its empty nails.

'I have sent it to Warwick Museum,' he answered quietly.

'Oh,' I said. I didn't know what else to say.

When we got into the car, he slumped forward onto the steering wheel and buried his head in his arms. The car trembled. He was silently sobbing. Then he pulled himself together, blew his nose noisily and fired up the engine. 'It's been a long time coming,' he said without looking at me. 'But, my God, it's hard when it happens.'

My mother could never have lived at the Manor House. Neither of us knew it that day, but she was rapidly running out of time. It would only be a few years before she needed surgery yet again, but long enough for me to make the move to Scotland, to break free, to start a new life, and to try to reconcile the nagging losses of Nellie and the Manor House, where I still went in my head and my dreams almost every night of my life, and still do all these decades later.

My grandfather had left an estate cottage to Nellie rent-free for life. She was well into her sixties and accepted her retirement with grace and an assertive dignity as though it was promotion to a grander order befitting the erstwhile head of the lord of the manor's household. Her personality seemed to expand to meet the challenge, becoming the grand old maid of the village, in perpetual denial of the rapidly changing 1960s world around her. She heaped scorn on incomers and anyone who didn't properly belong to her past. 'Who does they think they are?' she would demand defiantly. 'They don't know nothin' about the village in the old days and never will.'

My father had given her his mother's fine Coalport tea service, which she had always admired. Whenever I called to see her, out it would come. 'Now, you sits there by the fire while I gets you a nice cuppa tea.' Then she would sweep in with a tray, the rosebud plates laden with scones and slices of her rich fruitcake. And when I got up to go her eyes would moisten and her voice quiver with more than a hint of emotional blackmail. 'When 'll I see you again, young Jack, cos I shan't be around forever, y'know?'

She did her best. Nellie West lived on in her cottage beside the village green for a further thirty-four years to the arboreal age of 101. Even long after I was married with a family of my own and both my parents were dead she had refused to concede my adulthood. I remained 'Young Jack' for the rest of her days. Then one day a neighbour phoned me. Before I heard the words I knew that it was the end.

As I drove the long road south for the funeral I felt the leaden cloud of a long-awaited grief descending like a bitter winter's night. A grief not just at the loss of my earliest *alter mater,* my beloved mother goddess, but also that the last silken thread to my childhood had broken. We buried her next to her parents, only a few yards from my grandparents, her headstone looking straight across the lane to the Manor House. As we lowered her into the land to which she had given so much, I knew that not just I but everyone gathered there that day would never forget Miss Nellie West, and that a small part of us all had departed with her into that grave.

*   *   *

When I arrived to take up my new job on Kyleakin Island, Gavin wasn't there. He had gone to hospital in Inverness for further check-ups, still struggling with headaches and what was thought to be another outbreak of the duodenal ulcers he had suffered for years, the cure for which, he had once written, was 'strong curry washed down with plenty of whisky'. The next day I travelled the eighty miles through the towering, craggy mountains of Glen Shiel to see him in the Royal Infirmary. It was everything you would not expect in a hospital. His small private room was full of cigarette smoke and a tray of drinks topped the locker beside him. He was sitting up in bed with a glass in hand. 'Come and have a dram. I'm on brandy and dry ginger, but there's plenty of whisky here.' He waved at the tray crowded with bottles.

He seemed brighter and spoke buoyantly of returning to the island very soon. We planned a visit to the nearby island of Pabay to shoot rabbits for the island freezers, food for the buzzard, tawny owl and foxes already there and for birds of prey he hoped to acquire. I showed him my work, sheaves of draft text and notes for the mammal book. He was pleased. The future looked bright. I drove back to the island convinced that everything would come right.

I could not have been more wrong. The following day came news of the shocking diagnosis – advanced generalised cancer. He already had well-developed secondaries in a heel, a kidney, his brain and his spine. The tiny primary tumour in his lungs, smaller than a pea, would not be discovered until the post-mortem. He would never leave that room alive.

The last time I saw him, three days before he died, he was calm and utterly fatalistic. I tried to persuade him there was still hope of a recovery, but he laughed it off, quickly changing the subject. He was worried that without him Longman might not honour the contract for the mammal book – something that had never occurred to me. I didn't know what to say. Suddenly my world seemed to be imploding, collapsing in on itself in an expanding heap of scuppered dreams. There was an awkward silence before he spoke again. 'You said you'd like to be a writer. Well, I need someone to finish my story. There are a lot of people out there who will want to know what happened to Teko, you know. How d' you feel about that?'

On the morning of 7 September 1969 the island phone rang. It was Richard Frere. 'The news is the very worst.' So died a man of many exceptional gifts. He was only fifty-five. He had been a racing driver, a portrait painter, a wartime intelligence officer and small-arms instructor for SOE, a basking shark hunter, a published poet, a celebrated travel writer, explorer and geographer, a naturalist, and a best-selling nature writer who would change the lives of a whole generation of naturalists. He was also hugely influential in conserving the British otter at a time when it was virtually extinct in England's polluted rivers and its wider future was in serious doubt.

In his comprehensive biography, *Gavin Maxwell – A Life*, Douglas Botting suggests that Gavin's death was a timely release – that perhaps he had 'shot his bolt'. I profoundly disagree. Given the dire circumstances of his health I accept that his quick and relatively painless death was a mercy, but his impending financial crisis notwithstanding, and knowing how he had wriggled out of debt many times before, had he not contracted cancer I believe that at fifty-five he could have had at least fifteen to twenty years of highly productive work ahead of him. Such was his restless and creative intellect, and his thirst for adventure and travel, that I am sure there were more books of the scholarly quality of *Lords of the Atlas* – in my opinion his finest work, published only three years before his death – well within his reach.

As for the island zoo, now with the benefit of knowing Skye well I am sure that the project would have quickly foundered upon its own rocks. It was a whim, a folly typical of the man: impulsive, impractical and badly thought through. Ferrying visitors back and forward to the island across treacherous tidal narrows in the seldom fair and often suddenly foul weather for which the Isle of Skye is renowned would always have been too great a risk and a perpetual hindrance.

On Thursday, 18 September, on a day bright with late summer warmth and high, sunlit clouds on a dry east wind, an intimate throng of Gavin's family, friends and associates led by Jimmy Watt and Terry Nutkins looked on as they buried his ashes on the bulldozed site of the Camusfeàrna house, around which the bright ring of the burn sparkled through its dark green curtain of alders. Last to appear, arriving by boat from Canna and walking up the beach to join us with her hair blowing in the sea breeze, came Kathleen Raine, whose title poem and perhaps whose curse had so changed Gavin's life.

There is no doubt that she had loved him with all the

passion a woman's love can muster, quite simply the unassailable love of her life. In a too-late valedictory letter that he would never read, she wrote:

> *you and I . . . have seen the beauty of Eternity, such beauty and such glimpses of joy. For me this earth is, simply, the place where you are, where we have met. Without you it will be the place where you are not, and we must enlarge our terms. The bidden world will then be the place where you are, and, please God, we shall meet again without all the burdens and tears.*
>
> *I have never been able to say how much I love you – but surely you know. And at any time, anywhere, you have only to think of me, and you will find me with you in thought and love.*
>
> *. . . I don't think it was ever as a 'lover' I desired your love. Something else – a more than brother. Something we are in Eternity, which has no name . . . in the practical terms of generation. Anyway, I am here now for whatever you may ask of me or need.*

For the following few weeks, life on the island was chaotic. The phone rang solidly for the first ten days and, as the news of his death slowly spread, so our mailbag expanded to up to sixty letters and cards a day. *Ring* had been translated into twenty languages. Millions of his readers around the world were shocked; in crazed and sometimes hysterical responses, reporters, magazine feature writers and other news media all craved special insight into what had happened, what would happen to the surviving otter, to the whole island project. Often brutally insensitive in their demands, ringing over and over again for the latest titbit of information, they demanded to know why he hadn't received proper medical attention, as though his illness and his death were somehow our fault.

Between us, Richard Frere and I answered every letter we received from his fans. We stencil-duplicated a thousand copies – a brief thanks and a short update on what was happening – and I dutifully mailed them off. I filed every letter by country, many from America, Australia, Canada, up and down the length of Europe as well as many hundreds from across Britain.

Initially, perhaps encouraged by the rush of public and media interest in Gavin, we clung to the hope that the island project could survive in his memory. I was left in charge and we continued to develop plans, building aviaries and fencing the paddocks. Although ageing, Teko the otter was alive and apparently well. We were all clinging to what I now realise was always an extremely slender hope that people would pay to come and see him; that he would be the star attraction.

It soon emerged that no one advising Gavin had properly understood the extent of his indebtedness or the simultaneous decline of his literary income. Nor had anyone succeeded in reigning in his extravagances. His books were still selling – seven titles in print – but principally in paperback, a far less lucrative format for the author. As the weeks passed the bills continued to pour in. Few records had been kept. We had no way of knowing whether they were genuine debts or cynical figments of avaricious opportunism. The island household's credit account with the local grocery store on Skye where Gavin bought all his whisky, cigarettes and most household supplies came as a shock. The vet's bills for the otters had apparently not been submitted for three years. The company in Kyle of Lochalsh that serviced the island boats submitted a startlingly huge invoice. Gavin's private company, Gavin Maxwell Enterprises Limited, was struggling with much more than a cash flow problem. It was insolvent.

As the financial crisis rapidly deepened, the project staggered on for only a few more weeks. I think all of us involved knew in our bones that it was a hopeless cause, but while Teko was alive we clung to a thread of hope. Then one crisp September morning, only two weeks after Gavin's death, Teko was missing. We searched his enclosure. No sign. The water in his pool was too murky until we drained it. There he was, dead on the bottom.

He could have died of many causes. At ten he was close to the end of his natural lifespan, perhaps an infection or a cancer, heart or vital organ failure – we would never know. I declined the idea of a post-mortem. He was the last of the Maxwell otters and I felt that his limp, wet body deserved the most dignified end we could manage. I buried him at the foot of a huge boulder a few yards from his pen. On the face of the hard metamorphic rock I chiselled his name and dates: Teko 1959–1969. It was the end of the otter saga that had gripped the public imagination for more than a decade.

I was summoned to Drumbuie on Loch Ness-side, Richard Frere's home. In 1966, before the Camusfeàrna fire, in a valiant attempt to turn Gavin's fortunes around, Richard had stepped in as managing director of GME Ltd. I drove the eighty miles through the mountains knowing very well that his forecast would be bleak. With Teko's death the few remaining sparks of hope had been summarily extinguished, but I still hadn't grasped how critical the situation really was.

The island project would have to close down immediately and the house sold as quickly as possible. I was out of a job. 'I'll do my best but I don't think we'll manage to pay you this month.' Richard looked embarrassed.

'That bad?' I asked, more as a resigned observation than a question. He nodded. I drove slowly back through the long winding glens to Kyle of Lochalsh in the dark. The winter sun was long gone behind the ragged skyline of Cuillin mountains and distant islands, and the narrows between Skye and the mainland gleamed black and sinister. I caught the last ferry to Kyleakin, where our dinghy was moored, and rowed myself slowly back through the darkness to Eilean Bàn. Only the lighthouse beam seemed welcoming. As I tied the dinghy to the island slipway with the salt tang fresh in my face, I thought that things couldn't get much worse. I was wrong.

The following day I received a letter from Gavin's literary agent, Peter Janson-Smith, informing me that Longman had withdrawn the contract for the mammal book because it was Gavin's name that would have sold it and he had not so much as put pen to paper. I hadn't received a penny in payment or expenses for the nineteen months' research work I had done.

A few weeks later, with no idea where I would go or what I would do, I packed my bags and departed that beautiful little island with a leaden heart. No job, no money, no prospects, no home. I had a car, a few possessions and my faithful Labrador, Max. That was it. Richard and Joan Frere generously offered me a roof over my head at Drumbuie, their nineteenth-century turreted home overlooking the sweep and mystery of Loch Ness, while I looked round for a cottage to rent. I was determined not to go back to England and to the career I had hated so much; besides, I needed a little time to gather my wits and recover from the sudden collapse of my world.

Christmas came and went. I found a tiny cottage for a few pounds a month – a 'but-'n'-ben' in Highland terminology – but more like an eyrie than a dwelling, perched high on a hillside overlooking Loch Ness and the Great Glen. Under a rickety corrugated iron roof it had just two rooms, a kitchen-living room and a bedroom with an outside chemical loo. An old-fashioned pot-bellied stove was the only source of cooking and heating, and I drew my water from a spring that trickled out of the ground a few yards away.

In a curious but uplifting sense of déjà vu, it was almost an accidental re-visitation of Camusfeàrna and the castaway lifestyle Gavin had so cherished in his early days at Sandaig. Long before the otters, he had his spaniel Johnnie for company; I had Max and, like Gavin, together we turned feral, surviving on shot rabbits, wood pigeons and the occasional roe deer. Birch logs I gathered from the surrounding woods and I baked potatoes in the ash of the stove. I washed and cleaned my teeth at the spring, tossing the soapy water into the bracken and the nettles, as Gavin had so succinctly quoted from Psalm 60: 'Moab is my washpot and over Edom do I cast out my shoes.'

For all its primitivism, I loved that little cottage. It was exactly the solitude and asceticism I needed, although I had no clue what the future might hold. In Gavin's own words from the closing lines of *Ring*, it was 'a fortress from which to essay raid and foray, an embattled position behind whose walls one may retire to lick new wounds and plan fresh journeys to farther horizons'.

Teko's death had closed the final door to the Maxwell otter saga and opened another for me – nothing for it but to sit down and begin the book Gavin had asked me to write. The time and the opportunity had landed squarely in my lap. It is a well-worn aphorism that 'hunger makes the best sauce', besides, hadn't I always wanted to be a writer? Later Richard Frere told me that in his last days Gavin had been deeply troubled by my looming predicament. 'He's given up a good job, abandoned his family, moved up here and now look what's happened. I can't deliver on the mammal book and the island zoo has a doubtful future.' I am sure that it was out of that concern that he generously gave me the chance to write my first book, *The White Island*, published by Longman in 1972.

But without ever knowing it, Gavin Maxwell had given me much, much more. He gave me self-belief. He showed me a lifestyle I had never dreamed could be possible. He had enticed me away from industry and up to the glorious, and in those days very remote, Highlands, where I have lived and worked ever since. But perhaps more than anything else he gave me a cause – to be what I had always dreamed of becoming: a naturalist and writer committed to nature conservation and environmental education. More than this, the unpaid research work I had done for the ill-fated mammal book would prove to have been an immensely worthwhile apprenticeship, providing me with many valuable contacts and friends in the conservation world.

There was one more gilt-edged bonus Gavin had inadvertently provided. All the many hundreds of letters and cards we had answered after his death were filed in cardboard boxes in Richard Frere's study at Drumbuie. Richard had become a close friend and I often dropped in to see him and to learn how the messy task of winding up Gavin's affairs was going. He, too, was facing the gloomy prospect of being out of a job. Ever cheerful and always comically given to the absurd, he made light of it. 'I suppose I could become a poodle clipper,' he quipped with an impish grin. Neither he nor I had ever seen a poodle in the Highlands.

One day soon after sending the *White Island* manuscript off to Longman, feeling lonely, bereft and project-less –

finishing a book is like abandoning a child – we were sitting together drowning our collective sorrows over a dram, the Highland remedy for all ills, when my eyes lit upon the row of letter-filled shoeboxes piled in a corner. 'What are you going to do with all those?' I asked.

'Dunno,' he replied, shaking his head and looking blank. 'I could light fires with them for the next ten years, or perhaps I could write a begging letter to everyone who contacted us asking for a pound to bail me out of penury.' We laughed together, lamely.

In my lonely cottage bed that night I was struck by a sudden spark of inspiration that jerked me instantly awake. If all those people had been sufficiently interested in Gavin's books to pick up pen and write to us, perhaps they would be interested in coming to see the places and perhaps even some of the wildlife he had so lyrically brought to life. I could scarcely wait for morning to put my idea to Richard. With an impulsiveness almost equal to Gavin's, by the time I arrived at Drumbuie it had grown tentacles in every direction. 'We could start a natural history guiding service. How about Highland Wildlife Enterprises for a name? It would occupy us both all summer and would give me time to write in the winter.'

Those cardboard boxes had handed me a brilliant marketing opportunity. Nowadays they would be called a mailing list or a database, but such things were virtually unheard of in the early 1970s. A month later we had printed a simple brochure and posted it off to the entire list. Our guests would stay in local guesthouses and hotels. We would collect them every morning and take them far into the hills and glens. I would concentrate on wildlife and Richard, who was a keen mountaineer, on walking in the glorious hills and glens that surrounded us. I drew a silhouette of a golden eagle as a logo. But I also wanted to dedicate the project to Gavin's memory. In the foreword to *Ring* he had written: 'I am convinced that man has suffered in his separation from the soil and the other creatures of the world; the evolution of his intellect has outrun his needs as an animal, and yet he must still, for security, look long at some portion of the earth as it was before he tampered with it.'

Those words and the compelling conservation philosophy they espoused would never leave my head. I quoted them in the very first Highland Wildlife Enterprises literature and have done so ever since. They would become the founding principle for the field studies centre Aigas would become a few years later – where I have now lived and worked for more than forty years.

The response to that first mailing was electric. Our little wildlife guiding service attracted press attention. It grew and grew. By 1976 it justified buying the crumbling remnants of the Aigas Estate on the River Beauly, which would become my home and my life's work. It is where I have raised a family and engaged deeply with the glorious wildlife, the otters, ospreys, golden eagles, pine martens and wildcats of the Highlands and the ever-challenging and absorbing world of nature conservation. And it is where we now work with the Scottish government's wildcat captive breeding programme, selectively breeding wild purity back in and domestic hybridisation out, in a last ditch bid to save the species, *Felis sylvestris grampia*, Britain's only native wild felid.

For me it has been a long journey, but one I have loved every step of the way. I know very well why 'the big foot-prints of the wildcats in the soft sand at the burn's edge' were so important to Gavin Maxwell, and many times I have listened, as Colquhoun did, 'in the calm twilight of summer to the cry of the tiger-cat to its fellow'. I now know, too,

what made me a naturalist and gave me the cause I have
pursued for so long.

★   ★   ★

Although my mother teetered on for a few years, she would
never know what we would make of the Aigas Field Centre
project. By 1976, when we first opened our doors to the
public, she was in dire straits once again. This time it was
a last resort. Under the leadership of Sir Keith Ross,
Southampton Hospital's cardiac unit had taken over from
the Brompton. With a view to making it their UK base for
their eventual retirement, my father had bought a cottage
in a picturesque hamlet on the Lymington River in the New
Forest so that they could be close to the hospital. Sir Keith
had pioneered and specialised in homograft – the miraculous
trick of grafting healthy valves from deceased patients into
living hearts. It was another breakthrough, an extremely
successful procedure on young, strong patients, giving them
many years of disease-free life. My mother's problem was
that she had been a guinea pig far too often. She urgently
needed a tri-valvular homograft: the aortic, the tricuspid and
the pulmonary all failing, all requiring to be replaced. Sir
Keith had told us that it would be touch and go, but that it
was her only hope – her last chance.

It took fourteen hours in theatre, during which there was
crisis after crisis of uncontrolled haemorrhage. More clots
leaked away. Twice Ross had to go back into her heart to
try to stem the bleeding. Afterwards he told me bleakly
that if he had known her heart's full condition he would
never have attempted the operation. 'There was so much
scar tissue, we couldn't find anything to stitch to,' he said
as she lay in post-op recovery. But she survived. Against all

the odds she pulled through. She was a poor, broken wreck of a woman, but she was alive and, incredibly, still determinedly smiling. In intensive care that night when she came round and first saw us she had asked in Arabic for fresh mangoes and dates. She was back in Cairo, an eleven-year-old, awe-struck, watching in fascination as the Bedouin tribesman unloaded their camel cargoes beside the whispering Nile.

Her recovery was slow and plagued with hideous complications, but her ceaseless encouragement for my new life seemed to give her strength. 'You must follow your dream,' she insisted. Over and over again I made the long trek south to see her. Every time I drove away I wondered if I would ever see her alive again. Although she was only in her fifties, there is a limit to what the human body can take. I knew she was losing her fight.

Not long after she was released from hospital, in a private moment my father asked me how much longer the operation would give her. I wanted to tell him the truth: that she was on borrowed time; that she could drop dead at any moment; that if she was extremely lucky she might last a few months. But I couldn't. I couldn't bring myself to say the words. I knew it would destroy him. 'Hopefully ten years,' I lied.

'Oh my God!' he said, the blood instantly draining from his face. 'Is that all?' I realised then that he didn't understand – didn't want to understand – and that the portcullis of denial was still firmly in place. He had never permitted the thought that they might not grow old together. He had closed his mind to the very possibility of losing her.

A few weeks later, sitting having afternoon tea together in their New Forest cottage, she with her feet up on a sofa quietly reading a Spanish novel, my father buried in his newspaper, he heard the book fall to the floor and saw a movement out of the corner of his eye. Her head had tipped back onto the arm of the sofa. Her poor, generous, endlessly loving, exhausted and battle-scarred heart had finally given up.

I knew my mother for thirty-five years. I have no proper recollection of her ever being well. We saw her through four experimental cardiac procedures, three of which were groundbreaking open-heart surgery. I watched her suffer cruel strokes and fight bravely back through many months of rehabilitation. I saw her in great pain and angry with frustration at her incapacitation. Yet in all those deeply troubled years never once did she evince the slightest shred of self-pity, nor did I ever hear her complain that life was unfair.

If I close my eyes I can immediately see her smile and hear her laugh, wide eyes flashing, throwing her head back with a little flick of her curls and that slightly startled look as if her mirth had caught her unawares. I know, too, that without understanding or recognising it at the time, it was her unexplained illness and her many absences that, from an early age, had made me seek solace by escaping into the wilds of the 1950s English countryside. I had buried myself in natural history because it surrounded me and it had irretrievably snared my boyhood imagination. More than that, she had become my only ally in the psychological struggle to defy convention and follow my own path. Her unflagging love and encouragement, even though she never properly understood what it was I sought, gave me the determination to break free.

Not long after she died I went to the museum in Warwick and withdrew the Dun Cow rib. Death had twice visited the family and I felt that my childhood fears had been laid to rest. It was bigger than I remembered it, and heavy, but not even remotely sinister. I felt its place was back at the heart of my family, here at Aigas, where it hangs on its old chain to this day.

Epilogue

After my mother's death my father took to visiting us at Aigas regularly. He became a lonely figure with a bewildered look that had taken charge of his face and never left him. Despite all its ghastly complications, theirs had been a marriage hallowed by the Gods of Absolute Devotion. He never had the words to express his love to his wife, but without her he had become lost, a fading echo of his former authoritative self. He needed his family to shore him up. I decided to teach him to fly fish.

He had never found time for the country sporting pursuits of his Manor House upbringing and had stubbornly refused to take up any hobby or activity my mother couldn't join in with. For those last years their principal pleasure was their home in Spain, sallying gently forth in their ageing car to explore little towns and villages in the mountains, chatting to the locals, returning to sit on their porch with a glass of amontillado to watch the Andalucian sun sink gently through the haze of crimson and purple bougainvillea that surrounded them. Without her, Spain was too painful for him. He couldn't bring himself to go back.

So he came to Aigas.

One bright June evening we took a rowing boat out onto the little hill loch, eight acres of sky that shimmers within a fold in our hills above the house. I took the oars. He'd been a good pupil. Over and over again his dry fly looped elegantly through the air to land well out on the glowing water. The loch was as still as a mirror. On gossamer wings and with long caudal filaments streaming out behind them, mayflies danced around us, touched the water with their dangling legs and lifted weightlessly off again, hovering tantalisingly over their own reflections. Trout rose in barely audible swirls, mouthed lazily at the flies and vanished again. 'You've got too much competition,' I teased. He smiled, pulled on his pipe and cast again. I was impressed. Fifteen yards or more, the line peeled itself out and gently dropped his fly in almost perfect emulation of those around us.

Unknown to either of us, deep below, a fine 2 lb brown trout saw that fly land. It fired into action, torpedoing towards the surface just as my father wiggled the line to give it life. High above the boat, emerging unseen from the gleaming white of the clouds, the burning binocular eyes of an osprey had also spotted that trout's move.

It happened so fast and so unexpectedly that it made us both jump. My father saw the trout curve to the fly; I glimpsed the shadow of the diving osprey. Delta-winged, blue feet thrust forward, talons spread wide, it crashed into the loch right beside the boat. Even as the trout saw the danger and swerved to dive, the osprey's black talons plunged into its olivine back. They crimped and held. For four seconds that exquisitely handsome fish hawk decked in mocha and cream lay with its wings outstretched across the swirling surface. Its amber eyes boiled with fire for a dazzling moment of triumph before its long wings rose on folded elbows to scoop bucketsful of sunlight and heave clear of the water.

The great bird seemed to lift in slow motion. Primaries like spread fingers, the wings pulsed and flailed in tight circles above the crested head, hooked bill thrust urgently forward.

The chocolate cream trousers emerged first, then came the pale blue legs and the black talons socketed deeply into the squirming trout. Droplets fell away like pearls. The wings grabbed air, levered and hauled. Ten feet off the water it halted in midair for a mighty shake, emerging from the primaries and travelling inward to the body and right down to the spread tail, enshrouding the whole bird and fish in a fine mist of loch. The wings powered forward again and its grip on the trout shifted. One foot grasped the fish's head, the other its back, so that it was slung missile-like beneath the bird's belly for minimum air resistance.

In less than forty seconds it was gone, rowing away into the bright evening sky, high above the birch trees that fringe that lovely little hollow. We watched in silence. Then my father slowly gathered up his rod and cast again, swinging back and forward three times before landing his fly well out on the other side of the boat. Satisfied with the cast he took the pipe from his mouth and, without looking at me, spoke quietly. 'I don't know why I've been fooling about in industry all my life.'

Almost exactly a year later he died suddenly and without warning, still in his sixties. It was three years and a month since my mother's death. A coronary thrombosis had felled him, the doctors said. I am sure they were right, but deep down I knew that he had died of a broken heart.

Acknowledgements

The events I have described are the memories of a schoolboy and took place many years ago. That is what they are: a childhood memoir. It goes without saying that while impressions remain firm, some details are hazy. After half a century the memory plays tricks, especially with dates and places that no longer exist. Wherever possible I have sought corroboration, often very successfully, sometimes not. This book could not have hatched without help from my sister, Mary Carrel, two years older than me, whose memories are clearer, and to whom I am extremely grateful. She kept me on track and provided the essential documentary evidence of my mother's letters from hospital. That we were sent away to different boarding schools at an early age inevitably meant that our lives began to diverge. So it is both pleasing and gratifying that she now lives only a few miles away and we are regularly able to reflect upon and share our memories. With her invaluable assistance I have reconstructed these events and personalities to the best and most faithful recollections I can achieve.

I have changed the names of schools that still exist, and, of course, many of the personalities. While the memories and opinions of one pupil from sixty years ago can have no bearing upon the present-day performance of those schools, I would not wish to impugn anyone's reputation. Where my references are glowing, as in Martock's Dr John Parker of blessed memory, the schoolmaster George Barron and his mischievous and delightful daughter Susan, I have stuck with their real names, as, of course, I have with Lord Brock and Dr Paul Wood and the other medical and surgical professionals whose astounding skills kept my mother alive for so long. When I came to research Martock and its village school, the happy chance of discovering that Susan Barron, now Stevens, still lived in the village, was a huge leap forward. Without her spirited and generous encouragement I would have had real difficulty piecing together what the village and the school were like in the 1950s. Her unstinting friendship throughout the writing of this book was a great support.

Allhallows College closed down in 1998, and I left the school thirty-five years before that, but I have disguised the names of some fellow pupils where I felt that my words might cause offence. Certainly none was intended and I apologise in advance if anyone feels I have been unfair or incorrect.

It is probably true that if I hadn't gone to Coto Doñana, I might never have written this book. It was the boundless enthusiasm of Dr Antonio Rivas and his team at the Iberian lynx captive breeding centre at El Acebuche which, entirely incidentally, spun me back to such a vivid vision of my mother at the Palacio Doñana. So I am doubly grateful to Antonio for both spurring our wildcat project on and providing the accidental setting for that haunting reminiscence.

I am most grateful to the authors of *British Cardiology in the 20th Century* (2000), Malcolm Towers and Simon Davies, and Emeritus Professor of Clinical Cardiology at Imperial College, Celia Oakley, for references, biographical sketches and opinions on the extraordinary careers of Russell Brock and Paul Wood. My thanks, too, to the estate staff of the Royal Brompton Hospital for allowing me to revisit the tunnel under the Fulham Road, now disused and closed off. To James and Katie Baillie for accommodation and hospitality in Fulham, my gratitude and love. For assistance with research and access to archives and my mother's medical records, I am extremely grateful to Angela Redmayne and Dorothy Watkins, and archivist Chris Newbold from the British Library and the Department of Health.

I am also grateful to Chris Newman, Peter Isaacs and Roger Potter for insights into the prep school, Hill Brow, also closed down, and particularly Chris Newman's collation of reminiscences of old boys and the history of the school.

To my friend and reviewing colleague David Robinson, former literary editor of *The Scotsman*, my most sincere thanks for reading an early draft and making extremely helpful suggestions.

My thanks are also due to Jimmy Watt of Gavin Maxwell Enterprises Ltd and to Random House for permission to quote from *Ring of Bright Water*, *The House of Elrig* and *Raven Seek Thy Brother*, and especially to Gavin Maxwell's biographer, Douglas Botting, for generous help. To Virginia McKenna, who starred with her husband Bill Travers in the film of *Ring of Bright Water*, I extend my heartfelt thanks for all the work she did to perpetuate Gavin's memory with the Maxwell museum on Eilean Bàn, and for being such a supportive friend at Aigas.

Several good friends who are no longer with us also deserve recognition and my wholehearted gratitude: the late Lovell and Lilian Foot, who so kindly lent me their cottage in which to write *The White Island*, and the late Richard Frere, who provided so much support, company and fun in the early days of Highland Wildlife Enterprises and Aigas

Field Centre. Kathleen Raine died in 2003 aged ninety-five. In the early years of Aigas Field Centre she became a friend and often came to stay. She valued and supported the positive influence Gavin had given otter conservation in particular and nature conservation in general. For her help and encouragement I will always be extremely grateful. Also the late Professor Russell Coope and his son Rob, both of whom enabled us to begin our wildcat captive breeding project. Without their contribution of solid advice and the gift of our first live wildcats, we would never have got it off the ground. I cannot thank them enough.

My agent, Catherine Clarke of the Felicity Bryan Agency, always shores me up and has been delivering wisdom and encouragement for many years. Her friendship and help are invaluable. Simon Thorogood of Canongate has been my editor and friend throughout the production of this book and my thanks go to Jamie Byng and his staff for wanting to keep me in the Canongate fold.

My son, Warwick, and my loyal secretary, Sheila Kerr, have generously afforded me the time to write, and have put up with my absences from Aigas at times when I should have been more attentive to other work. Others who have helped and encouraged me along the way, and to whom I am very grateful, are our daughters, Hermione, Amelia, Melanie and Emma, our son Hamish and *ma belle fille litéraire*, Christelle Baillie; good friends Leslie Cranna, Jonathan Willet, David Dixon, Paul and Louise Ramsay, and Peter and Fran Tilbrook; invaluable help with the wildcats from Alicia Leow-Dyke and Louise Hughes; inspirational fellow writers Helen Macdonald, Mark Cocker, Brian Jackman, Jay Griffiths and Jim Crumley, and my dear friend and long-term literary sage, Martha Crewe.

But as always, my wife, Lucy, has put up with my almost

constant distraction throughout the several years and the historical assault course through which the book has picked its way. Research can be a lonely and sometimes depressing task when brightly remembered places are found to no longer exist, or to have been ravaged by crude and vulgar development. As well as lovingly tolerating my many cerebral and physical absences – she calls herself a literary widow when I'm writing – Lucy often came with me, and propped me up with loyal and nourishing moral support on many of those essential expeditions.

John Lister-Kaye
House of Aigas, 2017

'Generous, poetic and wise, John Lister-Kaye
is a national treasure '
PATRICK BARKHAM, author of *Badgerlands*

CANON▌GATE